A REAL AMERICAN CHARACTER

HOLLYWOOD LEGENDS SERIES
CARL ROLLYSON, GENERAL EDITOR

A REAL AMERICAN CHARACTER

THE LIFE OF

WALTER BRENNAN

Carl Rollyson

University Press of Mississippi • *Jackson*

www.upress.state.ms.us

Designed by Peter D. Halverson

The University Press of Mississippi is a member of the Association of American University Presses.

First printing 2015

∞

Library of Congress Cataloging-in-Publication Data

Rollyson, Carl E. (Carl Edmund)
A real American character : the life of Walter Brennan / Carl Rollyson.
pages cm. — (Hollywood legends series)
Includes bibliographical references and index.
ISBN 978-1-62846-047-6 (cloth : alk. paper) — ISBN 978-1-62846-048-3
(ebook) 1. Brennan, Walter, 1894–1974. 2. Motion picture actors and actresses—United States—Biography. I. Title.
PN2287.B684R65 2015
791.4302′8092—dc23
[B]
2015005906

British Library Cataloging-in-Publication Data available

CONTENTS

ACKNOWLEDGMENTS

ALTHOUGH THIS BOOK IS, OF COURSE, ABOUT THE WALTER BRENNAN who made so many great movies, it is also about a man who believed in a certain way of life, and in certain principles he was determined to enforce just as firmly—and even fiercely—as did any of the western characters he played. I did not know when I began this book if I would be able to re-create the home and family life that meant so much to Brennan, and without which he could not have sustained a career that endured for fifty years. As a biographer, I wanted to know him both as the man who created so many memorable roles, and as a father and grandfather, a rancher, and a man who cared deeply about the fate of his country and its people. Knowing this man—in detail, in situ—would not have been possible without the generous contributions of his two sons, Mike and Andy, of their children— as well as their sister Ruthie's children—and of many of the Brennan neighbors and business associates in California and in Joseph, Oregon. Ruthie died in 2004, and the consequences of her loss are significant—not only for her family, but also for Walter Brennan's biography. Perhaps only she could have answered many of the questions I pondered about her father.

How I was able to secure the cooperation of the Brennan family is a story in itself, one involving a concatenation of events I could not have imagined. During a talk about my Amy Lowell biography at the Philadelphia Athenaeum in the fall of 2013 I mentioned I was working on a biography of Walter Brennan. David Brewster happened to be in the audience, and after my talk he told me about his connections in Joseph, Oregon, where Walter Brennan owned a twelve-thousand-acre ranch, and where several members of Brennan's family still live. David put me in touch with Anthony Robinson, who seconded David's advice that I contact Rich Wandschneider of the Josephy Center in Joseph, and that connection made all the difference. Previously, I had written to several members of the Brennan family and had received no reply. But Rich ran into one of Walter Brennan's granddaughters, Tammy Crawford, and began to tell her about my work. Tammy, for her part, remembered my unanswered letter. Through Rich and Tammy, I was able to organize a trip to Joseph, where I met with Walter Brennan's son Mike, and where I took a tour of the ranch—made especially enjoyable by the camaraderie of Mike Crawford, Tammy's husband, who once worked on the ranch and generously shared his memories with me. At an event Rich organized at the Josephy Center, many of Walter Brennan's friends turned up to hear about my book and to reminisce. I was very pleased to meet them and then to meet Mike's son Dennis and daughter Caroline, and correspond with another of Mike's daughters, Patricia.

Carol Jean Smetana provided invaluable assistance in sorting out the dating of events from Walter Brennan's early years—including his marriage in California in 1921, which was a puzzle owing to the different dates in different documents recording the event. I wish to thank fellow biographers for answering my queries and offering suggestions and encouragement. These biographers include: Chip Bishop, James Curtis, Charles DeFanti, Marion Meade, and Steve Taravella. Carol Easton deserves special thanks for putting me up during several of my trips to Los Angeles.

In Lynn, Massachusetts, Abby Battis, assistant director of the Lynn Museum and Historical Society, helped me locate important documents. Joe Coffill, in the reference department of the Lynn Public Library, retrieved several articles for me and was a great source of cheerful encouragement.

In Swampscott, Massachusetts, I had the good fortune to happen upon Mrs. Dorothy Gregory, the owner of 29 Franklin Avenue, who took me on an impromptu tour of the house where Walter Brennan grew up. Lois Longin, principal of the Clarke School, suggested I contact local historian Louis Gallo. Maureen Shultz gave me Lou's phone number, and I had the benefit of a conversation with him about Walter's years in Swampscott. Lou supplied me with some photographs of young Walter and his friends, and provided other materials about the early years of my subject's life.

In Hollywood, Valerie Yaros, historian of the Screen Actors Guild, kindly arranged an interview with Kathleen Nolan, who related vivid and important memories about her work on *The Real McCoys*. Ms. Nolan was gracious with her time and her support of my project. With Alan K. Rode's help, I was able to get in touch with Angie Dickinson and hear about her experiences with Walter Brennan on the set of *Rio Bravo*. And with the kind assistance of James Garner's daughter, Gigi, I received from him a comment about his work with Brennan in *Support Your Local Sheriff!*

In Joseph, I had delightful and informative discussions with Vivian Strickland, Judy Lamy, Darlene Turner, and Louise Kunz. Many others who attended the Walter Brennan event at the Josephy Center spoke to me about their memories, and I'm grateful to the many people who attended my talk. I'd also like to thank Genene Kingsford of the Joseph Public Library for making available a recording of a Walter Brennan interview.

My research began in the summer of 2012 with an exhilarating week at the National Cowboy & Western Heritage Museum in Oklahoma City. Melissa Gonzalez, Karen Spilman, Laura Heller, and Gerianne Schaad provided excellent guidance for my work in the Walter Brennan collection. I owe a tremendous debt to the archivists and librarians who discovered and made available both primary and secondary sources. Heading the list is Ned Comstock at the Cinema Arts Library at the University of Southern California. Not only did Ned send me many items for this biography, he went out of his way to make my work in the archives a productive and efficient process. Jonathan Auxier, Ned's colleague at USC, provided me both with access and assistance in going through the Warner Bros. archive. At the Academy of Motion Pictures Arts and Sciences, I am grateful to Gregory Walsh, and especially to Stacey Behlmer, who helped me navigate the Academy archives. At UCLA, I relied on Mark Quigley to help locate certain rare Walter Brennan films. Julie Graham, helpful as ever, handled my query about UCLA's RKO files. Charis Emily Shafer, of the Columbia University Library, kindly sent me a copy of Walter Brennan's oral history. I thank Melinda McIntosh at the University of Massachusetts for assisting in the search for public records of Walter Brennan's marriage and other family records. At Simmons College, Justin Snow provided me with several documents about Ruth Brennan's secretarial studies.

I am grateful to the Brennan family for providing many of the photographs in this book. Jeff Mandor of the Larry Edmunds Bookshop in Hollywood also made available his large selection of Walter Brennan film stills.

I deeply appreciate the encouragement I have received from my friends, online and off: Kendra Bean, Felicia Campbell, Rosemary Clark, Gayle Feldman, Lorna Gibb, Elena Gonzalvo, Beverly Gray, Laura Grieve,

Tara Hanks, Adele Kenny, Michelle Morgan, Christy Putnam, Will Swift, Mike Yawn.

My wife, Lisa Paddock, was with me as I wrote every word. She does not need to read this book because she has been a faithful editor of all my work.

A REAL AMERICAN CHARACTER

Introduction

I think Walter Brennan was the greatest example of a personality that
I've ever used. . . . When I was in trouble, I called on Brennan. He al-
ways came through.
—HOWARD HAWKS IN CONVERSATION WITH JOSEPH MCBRIDE

The real acting parts go to the character actors.
—DANA ANDREWS

WHERE IS THAT GREAT BOOK ABOUT THE HOLLYWOOD CHARACTER
actor we are all waiting to read? Turn to typical tomes on the subject—
such as Alfred Twomey's *The Versatiles* (1969) and James Robert Parrish's
Hollywood Character Actors (1978)—and all you get is one-paragraph biographies, photographs, and filmographies. The most insightful study
of the character actor consists of two pages written by the renowned
film critic Rudolf Arnheim, and even he manages only one truly arresting sentence: "The character actors' acting surrounds that of the heroes
like a baroque frame surrounds a Renaissance painting." Otherwise, he
states the obvious: "They lend spice to a film." And then he mentions the
wrinkles, warts (actually I'm adding the warts), and scruffy appearance
that are such a relief to witness after too much of a good thing: the star's
shapely form, which never loses its "charming symmetry even in intense
pain." About all that can be added to this anatomy of the character actor
is the glancing notice of esteemed film historian David Thomson, who
remarks that character actors are the "system's conciliatory gesture to the
unlovely masses; they are meant to be like us."

In Parrish's gallery of character actors, Walter Brennan is clearly the
standout. He is what Arnheim has in mind when he mentions the character actor's missing teeth. Brennan's toothlessness is part of the decrepit

appearance and intractable demeanor that epitomize the disparate collection of human curiosities Brennan portrayed—beginning in the silent era and concluding in the television age, when he starred in *The Real McCoys* (1957–63) as a cantankerous grandpa with a hitch in his gait and a barb in his tongue. Brennan, who appeared in more than two hundred films and countless television productions over a fifty-year career, *is* Hollywood. He arose out of the ranks of extras and stuntmen to become an indispensable foil to Gary Cooper, Humphrey Bogart, Jimmy Stewart, and John Wayne. No other supporting player won three Academy Awards, and you would be hard-pressed to name another character actor whose performances frequently overwhelmed those of ostensible leads like Joel McCrea and Barbara Stanwyck in *Banjo on My Knee*. "We're supporting you. Be nice to us," McCrea and Stanwyck joked with Brennan. Those stars had the fights of their lives trying to stay on equal terms with old Walter. Sure, other character actors have had their star turns—especially in television, which gave Ward Bond in *Wagon Train*, Raymond Burr in *Perry Mason*, and Harry Morgan in *M.A.S.H.* their respective moments of fame—but no character actor other than Brennan dominated the Hollywood century of popular entertainment, or attained the iconic status he achieved. To follow Brennan—beginning with his career as a seven-dollar-a-day extra—is to learn all you need to know about Hollywood and its mythologizing of the American dream. Walter Brennan became an archetype, not a stereotype. He was the frame that Rudolf Arnheim described—and also the picture itself.

Walter Brennan (1894–1974) is considered one of the finest character actors in motion picture history. His three supporting actor Oscars were awarded for his roles in *Come and Get It* (1936), *Kentucky* (1938), and *The Westerner* (1940). He was nominated a fourth time for *Sergeant York* (1941). In *The New Biographical Dictionary of Film*, David Thomson argues that Brennan should have won awards for even better performances in *To Have and Have Not* (1944), *My Darling Clementine* (1946), *Red River* (1948), *The Far Country* (1955), and *Rio Bravo* (1959). Thomson counts no less than twenty-eight high caliber Brennan performances in still more films, including *These Three* (1936), *Fury* (1936), *Meet John Doe* (1941), and *Bad Day At Black Rock* (1955). Brennan worked with Hollywood's greatest directors—John Ford, Howard Hawks, William Wyler, King Vidor, and Fritz Lang—while also starring in Jean Renoir's Hollywood directorial debut, *Swamp Water* (1941). To discuss Brennan's greatest performances is also to comment on the work of Gary Cooper, Henry Fonda, Dana Andrews, Spencer Tracy, John Wayne, Humphrey Bogart,

Lauren Bacall, Anne Baxter, Barbara Stanwyck, Lana Turner, Linda Darnell, Ginger Rogers, Loretta Young, and many other stars.

Although I grew up watching Brennan's folksy performance on the television series *The Real McCoys*, I first became aware of his brilliance while watching him perform opposite Gary Cooper in *The Westerner*. I was interested in this film because it features Dana Andrews's first screen appearance, which I needed to describe for my biography, *Hollywood Enigma: Dana Andrews*, part of the Hollywood Legends series published by the University Press of Mississippi. Several commentators on the film laud Brennan's acting, and some go so far as to say he stole the picture from Cooper. And it is true that Cooper was initially reluctant to star in *The Westerner* because he thought Brennan's role, as Judge Roy Bean, superior. But owing to their astute timing and shrewd responses to one another's performances, Brennan and Cooper both excel in their scenes together. As Bean, Brennan is excitable and extravagant, while Cooper as Cole Harden is droll and low-key. Each actor perfectly set the scene up for the other, and while their reciprocity remained paramount, much credit has to be accorded Brennan's off-screen preparation and concern for his fellow actors. Brennan was known for his generosity and mentoring of other performers, as I learned when investigating his relationship with Dana Andrews on the set of *Swamp Water*. Brennan took the meaning of "supporting actor" to heart and welcomed talent, new and old, to the cinema community.

Brennan was as wily as many of the characters he played, which meant he finessed the constraints of the studio system, mocked studio bosses—even playing tricks on them—and took possession of his roles with an aplomb and shrewdness that made his appearance on movie sets a welcome relief to fellow actors worried about their own positions in the highly stratified Hollywood system. To study Brennan's life and career is to learn much about the way some of the greatest performances were put together—not only by Brennan, but also by his co-stars and fellow character actors such as Brian Donlevy, Andy Devine, Donald Meek, Ward Bond, John Carradine, Joe Sawyer, Harry Morgan, Margaret Hamilton, John Ireland, and Jack Elam. To study Brennan is also to understand what it took to remain at the very top of a precarious profession for more than thirty years. Through Brennan and his pictures, we see Hollywood in the early stages of the sound era, its ascent to a golden age in the late 1930s and early 1940s, and then its decline owing to the advent of television—a technological innovation as formidable and threatening as sound had been to silent film in the late 1920s.

Brennan's performances signify something more than individual achievement in film after film. Not only is his work an integral part of Hollywood history, his roles have become embedded in the national consciousness. His centrality did not occur to me until I read Manny Pacheco's recent book, *Forgotten Hollywood, Forgotten History*, which takes an unusual approach to character actors, examining them in terms of the historical epics in which they appeared. In a chapter devoted to Brennan, Pacheco evokes the persona of a man seemingly destined to play archetypal characters. Brennan, Pacheco writes, "embodies any individual that may have been born around and west of the Mississippi. Looking far older than his years, Brennan could be called upon to play roles that were based in fact or fiction. He seemingly lived throughout the nineteenth century and the fight for this country's quest to reach 'from sea to shining sea' . . . at least on celluloid." The ellipsis is Pacheco's and seems to suggest that he paused when he realized just how much movies and history become conflated in our imaginations. They became so for Brennan, who joked about playing so many old man roles (beginning in his mid-thirties) that he was older than any man alive. In effect, he expressed the continuity of American history, as well as that of Hollywood itself. This was an actor who was never out of work and who never suffered a decline in talent or popularity.

How did Brennan achieve this mythic status, this power over not just audiences but also his fellow actors? Today, the question remains unanswered, and this figure key to understanding the power of Hollywood remains largely undiscovered. Of course, his work is mentioned in books about important directors and movie stars, but surprisingly, no biography of Brennan has been published. He sometimes gets at least brief mention in histories of Hollywood, but his key film roles are slighted or merely referenced in comments that cry out for further investigation. A case in point is a passage in Ronald L. Davis's *The Glamour Factory: Inside Hollywood's Big Studio System* (1993). Davis notes that like many performers, Brennan arrived in Hollywood with a background in the entertainment business—in Brennan's case, vaudeville—but no experience acting before the camera. "Few directors devoted much attention to their character people, spending most of their time with the stars. Supporting players were expected to know their craft, and aside from grouping actors before the camera, directors allowed lesser performers to find their own interpretations. The focus in lighting and camera placement was consistently on stars."

So what did Brennan do when he was called onto a set to perform what was, in effect, piece work? He fitted himself seamlessly into a scene. Unlike a star, whose longevity depends upon a certain unvarying look, a style that producers, directors, and screenwriters support as much as they shape, the character actor conforms to whatever the role demands, often showing the director or producer what he or she wants. As Howard Hawks explained in John Kobal's *People Will Talk* (1986):

> The unit manager said, "I heard you telling the kind of character you want in the picture [*Barbary Coast* (1935)]. There's a guy that just fits that. He hasn't done much, he's really an extra man. But I'd like to have you see him." I said, "Okay, but look—instead of going through a lot of . . . ritual, meeting him and all that, can you give him the lines and I'll tell you how to get him dressed. Bring him up here and just let me hear him read." So he brought in Walter Brennan. Well, I laughed when I looked at him . . . the way he was dressed. I said, "Walter, we haven't got too much time. How about you and I reading that scene?" "Fine. Without or without." I said, "With or without what?" "Teeth," he said. I said, "Without *teeth*?" And he turned around and took out his teeth and put them in his pocket. And he was supposed to do four days' work. I kept him for six weeks, and he got mentioned for an Academy Award.

You can be sure that Brennan had a good talk with the unit manager before the actor appeared before Hawks as the character the director sought. Even the with or without teeth question is a simplification of what Brennan had in his inventory. He had something like a dozen sets of dentures—all different—that he could wear, depending upon what he thought the part called for.

The collaboration between unit manager, director, and actor in such situations is subtle and seldom remarked. The character actor has to work fast, figuring out how to make a scene work and how to deliver lines before opening his mouth—all while seeming only to satisfy what, as in this case, the director believes he has found. But that is not all there is to the story. Brennan almost never accepted the clothes that studios designed for his parts. He called himself a "dirty actor," by which he meant that the grungy duds he wore on-screen were his own. Brennan had to smell his own dirt and would not wash his getups, which became so soiled that his wife insisted he keep them in the garage. During his legendary performance as the reprobate Old Atrocity in *Barbary Coast*, his co-stars, Edward G. Robinson and Miriam Hopkins, suggested he might want to launder his rags, but the only concession odiferous Brennan would make to their sensibilities was to lay his clothes out in the sun to dry after a day of performing. (He also, for more than a decade, showed up on set wearing the same pair of shoes.) Only the easygoing Joel Mc-Crea, who played Hopkins's love interest, seemed not to notice Walter's odor. In Brennan's files at the National Cowboy & Western Heritage Museum, an inscribed photograph of McCrea testifies to his admiration for Brennan: "To Walter, I think you are a swell guy even if you do steal the picture."

Brennan, who never took an acting lesson, attributed his success to acute observation. He watched everything and everyone. You can see as much in his movies, in how he studies John Wayne's every move, every gesture the laconic Jimmy Stewart makes, and the calculating way Gary Cooper leans against a bar. Brennan's acting drew strength from the actors performing opposite him. Although he was sometimes accused of scene stealing, in truth he used other actors as launching pads for his own performances. His technique would not have worked had he not absorbed the moves of other actors sharing a given scene with him. As a result, both on and off the set Walter Brennan was much loved. His acting was reciprocal, a kind of response to the call of his contemporaries.

Brennan was equally adept at reading his bosses. He loved to mimic them, going so far as to telephone other actors while pretending to be Sam Goldwyn, for instance. A superb raconteur, Brennan put his fellow actors at their ease and flattered directors with his seemingly ingenuous behavior. During the *Red River* shoot, Hawks explained to Brennan that his character, a cook named Groot, had only one line. But the actor would lose his teeth to an Indian in a poker game, and "every time you want to have dinner, you're going to have to get them back from this fellow and he's not going to be too happy about it." Professing disbelief, Brennan responded, "We can't do that." "Yes, we can," the director insisted. "Oh, God can we really do it?" Brennan asked again. Well, they did it and, Hawks notes, Brennan "got mentioned for another Academy Award . . . And he didn't even have any part. I just called him to do scenes."

As Farley Granger noted in his autobiography, it just felt good to work with Walter Brennan, who served as a mentor to the young actor. Marsha Hunt felt the same way about appearing with Brennan in *Joe and Ethel Turp Call on the President* (1939). Brennan had already won his first Academy Award and was now playing a character who had to age significantly alongside Hunt, who later recalled: "On the first day, Walter came to me and said, 'I've played so many codgers. Please help me. When I play the young man, tell me if my tummy is sticking out or if my shoulders are slouching, if I'm doing anything inappropriate.' This distinguished actor was asking this much less experienced actress, me, for help. He put me completely at ease and I said to myself, 'What a thoughtful man.'"

Hunt, a Hollywood liberal, would later learn that Brennan was a committed conservative, as were many others in his Hollywood generation, including Howard Hawks, Joel McCrea, Ward Bond, and John Wayne. But when it came to his work, Walter Brennan put politics aside. The ideology of the western hero appealed to Brennan, who was brought up in the conservative atmosphere of Calvin Coolidge's New England. Brennan became a scholar of the Old West, and it is not surprising that his papers are housed in the National Cowboy & Western Heritage Museum. He disliked movies and television shows that sanitized the gritty history of the frontier and cowboy life. Robert Mitchum biographer Lee Server describes Brennan on the set of *Blood on the Moon* (1948), watching Mitchum appear for a scene not in the customary star's pristine duds, but in a soiled Stetson, with greasy hair and a beard, and sporting an attitude that complemented the raunchy getup. Pointing at Mitchum, Brennan exclaimed to his pals, "That is the *goddamndest realest* cowboy I've ever seen."

Mitchum was clearly testing the production code. Hollywood's self-censorship forbade not only sexually explicit language, gestures, and scenes, but also graphic depictions of violence and immoral behavior that went unpunished. These prohibitions resulted in the softening of characters like Brennan's Tom Keefer in *Swamp Water*, who is a much darker figure in the novel than he is in the movie. Exploring the production code's affect on the realism of Brennan's performances will be another important aspect of this biography.

Like the best character actors, Brennan brought a badly needed realism to the screen, where it served as an antidote to the soft-focus lighting and toupee-topped stars that romanticized movies. Watch Walter Brennan's performance in *The North Star* as Karp, the wizened old Russian peasant, a man old enough to remember pre-revolutionary Russia. He is a survivor and mentor to the younger generation bent on inventing a new world, even as they march into the first bombing run of the German invasion. He has some sad wisdom to impart, but he is also in charge of the wagon, leading this shell-shocked company toward safety so as to fight another day. The image is sentimental and yet grounded by Brennan's quiet, drawling voice, the sound of a man who will not be hurried by history and whose spirit cannot be crushed. His own experience in World War I prepared Brennan to drive a wagon in the midst of shell-fire—or at least to make us believe he could do so.

By the time Walter Brennan began his star turn on *The Real McCoys*, he had come to embody a quintessential American character he called "the old codger." Eccentric, ornery, avuncular, comic—and sometimes seemingly just an ordinary person—Brennan brought to this contradictory set of characteristics a chastened cheerfulness that epitomized the hopes and disappointments of a country still young and often under siege. As Allison Graham notes in *Framing the South: Hollywood, Television, and Race During the Civil Rights Struggle* (2003), Brennan remained in character playing Grandpa McCoy, photographed in his denims dispensing common sense advice about how to remain active in old age and respond to the younger generation.

Walter Brennan spent virtually his entire life making motion pictures, perfecting a persona, and embodying a range of characters that he began to observe and imitate during his earliest days on the docks in Swampscott, Massachusetts, where he got his start, and where this biography properly commences.

- CHAPTER 1 -

The Beginning

(1894–1927)

Heaven is not reached at a single bound
But we build the ladder by which we rise
—JOSIAH GILBERT HOLLAND

NO NEW ENGLAND BOY BORN AT THE TURN OF THE CENTURY COULD grow up without knowing the meaning of thrift. It was a word that meant much more than economizing. It also meant thriving by saving, which involved not spending, and using the resources at hand, and hard work, in order to reap future reward. Charles Forbes, founder in 1894 of the new granite and sandstone Forbes Library in Northampton, Massachusetts, never bothered to purchase a raincoat because he could carry the same gingham umbrella for decades. Such behavior not only saved pennies, it was also an expression of perseverance and fidelity to principle. At the same time, elevating thrift as a summum bonum meant moving to wherever the prospects of reward for hard work were greatest. For every New Englander like Forbes who made his fortune in Massachusetts, there were as many or more who migrated to the Midwest and even to California. So it was that Walter Brennan never felt that he had to end up where he began.

Walter was born in Lynn, Massachusetts. He used to joke that his father took one look at his big-eared son and commented, "Is he going to walk or fly?" Judging by a photograph, Walter entered the world possessed of a performer's personality. As an infant he already seems to be posing for the camera, his mouth arranged in an incipient smile, his eyes looking out observantly, looking for all the world like an only child. In fact, he had an older brother, William Irvin Brennan, born on

11

September 6, 1891. The publicly available biography of Walter Brennan reveals about as much about William as is known about Jesus's brother James, even though William died on March 19, 1969, and lived much of his adult life in Pasadena and Los Angeles. When Walter was asked about his brother during an interview for a television documentary, he curtly acknowledged William's existence, then gave the interviewer such a stony look that nothing else about this sibling was asked or revealed. And it's worth noting that Walter never mentioned to his family his parents' sorrow over the death of their only daughter, Helen Margaret, who died on August 24, 1897, just two days after her birth.

If Irvin was a sort point with Walter, this is because Walter's mother favored the older brother,, believing he would distinguish himself. Walter, apparently, seemed destined for failure. "My grandmother thought more of Irvin than she thought of my dad," Mike Brennan reported. Irvin was going to work in a bank, and "she thought that was the greatest thing in the world." Her younger, independent-minded son was restless, had trouble paying attention in school, and did not seem to take himself or others seriously. William Irvin will appear but fleetingly in this biography. He disappeared from Walter Brennan's life like a quick dissolve.

Today Lynn is a rather run-down community tied by a long stretch of road to Swampscott, one of those shore communities that by virtue of geography become, for some, a means of docking with a larger world. But on July 25, 1894, the day of Walter Andrew Brennan's birth, his parents lived inland, in West Lynn, in the new parish of the Sacred Heart, where his family joined a growing population of Catholics who regularly attended mass. The church still stands, with its barrel vaulted ceiling, and at the rear, its impressive organ, elevated and enclosed in a second story coffered alcove above two confessionals. The communicant, having been absolved of sin, proceeds toward the altar, set in an alcove before five vertical stained glass windows that anoint the redeemed in beautiful filtered light. The overall impression is of symmetry and balance, of the perfection sought in the observance of faith. Walter, a devout Roman Catholic, would often attribute his success to his religious belief. But although he considered his fate ultimately to be God's, he recognized he would be held responsible for his own actions.

In the early part of the twentieth century, Lynn, a town of about ninety thousand souls accustomed to burning coal, gaslights, and dirt sidewalks and roads, was just entering the incandescent age. A boy like Walter would be entertained by torchlight parades that proceeded past the Common, a grassy area dating back to the late seventeenth century that had been enclosed as a park. "I wish they'd have them again," Walter reminisced. "They were truly a part of the American scene." This was an era of band concerts, when Walter came to the Common to hear his favorite musical composition, John Philip Sousa's "Thunderer March."

Lynn factory workers boxed up light bulbs that were shipped all over the country. "The Lights," as the General Electric plant was called, loomed large in the consciousness of Sacred Heart parishioners, as a church history puts it. Lynn had once been known for its shoe manufacturing, and many church members were still employed boxing up shoes and making all manner of leather goods advertised in the Lynn directory: boots, shoes, shoe trimmings, fancy leathers, cut soles, hand sewed slippers, lifts, shanks, taps, stiffenings, heels, rands, cut top lifts, belts, taps, gloves, French Glazed Kid, Morocco "in all their varieties," sheep leather, skivers, dull and bright dongola (sheepskin, calfskin, goatskin) and shoe stitching. But now General Electric was lighting up the neighborhood on Mace Street, where Walter lived with his mother, the Boston born Mary Elizabeth Flanagan (1869–1955), and his father, William John Brennan (1868–1936), a native of Malden, Massachusetts, and the son of an Irish immigrant. William was a draughtsman (the British spelling, then preferred over "draftsman") working for General Electric, which had become one of the chief sources of income for Lynn residents. Walter later described his father as an eighteen-dollar-a-week employee—and not a success. William had secured more than twenty patents while working for the United Shoe and Machinery Company, but he owned none of them. "He was one of the most wonderful men in the world, but he didn't know how to make money," Walter said.

By the time he was six, Walter was luring tramps and other unsavory characters home with the promise of a meal. He loved to hear their tall tales. A year later, imitating an Irish neighbor, he began collecting dialects, a lifelong pursuit that helped him, by listening carefully, play characters by ear, getting their "voice tone" and phrasing right. He had an unusual sympathy for old people, a fondness for underdogs, and a "fine scorn for stuffed shirts" that would later make him a good choice to play "the Colonel," Gary Cooper's anarchist sidekick in *Meet John Doe*. This precocious identification with the down-and-out, and with others society marginalizes, complemented young Walter's profound lack of interest in schooling. "I wasn't very bright," he said equally to Ralph Edwards, host of the popular television program *This Is Your Life*. Edwards prompted, "You often talk about the three happiest years you spent in your childhood." "3B," the actor replied, provoking much laughter from the audience. Could it be true that Walter spent three years in the third grade? I asked his son Mike. "Oh, yea," Mike said. "He told me, 'I thought I was going to have to marry the third grade teacher to get out of school.'" The education Walter valued occurred during deliveries he began making by horse drawn carriage by the time he was eleven. All his life, Walter Brennan enjoyed delivering the goods, meeting people and drawing them out, learning about their jobs and asking them what they thought about their work. Sarah Hills (Walter's wife's younger sister) told Edwards that Walter first wanted to be a fireman, but he thought driving a grocery wagon "would be an ultimate achievement." Margaret Brennan wanted her son to aim higher. "But I don't want to be Abraham Lincoln, I want to be Walter Brennan," he told her.

By 1905, Walter had realized some of his ambitions by driving an express wagon for three dollars a week in Lynn. He'd move a trunk a mile or two for fifty cents or a quarter. A good meal consisted of liver and onions, two slices of bread with butter, and a big piece of pie—all for twenty cents. This entrepreneurial experience built character, he would later tell interviewers: "Those were the days kids of today will never have a chance to experience." This wasn't merely an expression of nostalgia; it reflects how Walter Brennan always thought things should be. You scrounged and scrapped for a living; nothing was handed to you. You learned what it cost to live; you made your luck. In a *TV Guide* interview he insisted, "I never cost them [his parents] a penny." To another reporter's question about his early years, Walter responded, "What do you mean upbringing? I've been on my own since I was 11."

In 1906, the family moved to Swampscott, settling into a home his father had built at 29 Franklin Avenue. The two-story, four bedroom home has had only three owners, including the Brennans. A coal-fired furnace provided heat through cast iron radiators that remain operational, according to Mrs. Dorothy Gregory, the current owner. The home had gas lighting. On a wood stove in the basement the family would cook their Saturday night beans. The kitchen had a gas stove, an icebox, and a good-sized walk-in pantry. Upstairs were bedrooms, an attic for storage, a linen closet, another closet under the eaves, and a laundry chute in the floor to send clothes down to the basement. The bathroom had a freestanding claw foot tub, made of cast iron with a porcelain liner and considered a luxury at the turn of the century.

"I think he was a little cheap," said Mrs. Gregory, referring to Walter's father. "All the windows are a little off," she noted, suggesting that the irregular measurements (a problem when she had to order shades) probably resulted from installing seconds. William Brennan may indeed have been trying to economize; it was always Walter's impression that his father's income was insufficient for the family's needs. And yet, on a stairway landing, William installed a beautiful stained glass window with a top pane featuring a stylized arrangement of three flowers, and the lower pane displaying Tiffany-style depiction of a fairy in a flower.

The move from Lynn to Swampscott—a matter of a few miles—was nevertheless momentous. The narrow neighborhood streets of Lynn give way to a seaside panorama in Swampscott. Suddenly the world opens up, seeming larger and less confining. Walter liked to hang around Fisherman's Beach in Swampscott, studying the old salts as they brought in their catch. He watched them mend nets and paint boats. Already, the world was presenting itself as a casting call for characters, none of whom Walter ever forgot. He later claimed that every one of his roles was based on some person he had carefully observed.

Twelve-year-old Walter went to Swampscott's Clarke Elementary School, attended mass at the new St. John the Evangelist church, where he sang in the choir, and worked in his uncle's bakery at the corner of Summer and Commercial Streets, making $1.75 a day "from 5 a.m. to unconscious." In 1910, in high school, Walter earned money doing chores for twenty-five cents an hour. He swept the school's hallways for the same pay, and he worked in the summer for the highway department as a "fancy shoveler." Paul Curtis, a childhood friend, mentioned playing instruments, with Walter on the drums. Walter also played fullback and guard in the days when players did double duty on offense and defense. He played rough and was known as a "scrapper," having lost a tooth during one game. Schooling itself was of no interest to him.

Local newspapers reported Walter's three-mile swim from Swampscott to Egg Rock, an island visible from Lynn Shore Drive that since 1931 has served as the site for long-distance swim competitions. Walter and his steady girlfriend accomplished their round-trip swim in one afternoon. Like the brother who never got a mention in articles about Walter Brennan, this girlfriend is lost to history, replaced by the woman he would marry who would become, in his own version of his life, the singular object of his affection.

Paul Curtis mentioned childhood scrapes, the time he and Walter put leaves in the ventilator, and the whole school closed down. Reminiscing later about his youth, Walter said, "As a boy I'd get into trouble now and then—break a window or something—but we kids would always go back and offer to replace it." In April 1914, just two months before graduation,

Walter was asked to leave Swampscott High. Ralph Edwards reported this fact as Brennan and the *This Is Your Life* audience laughed. But when Curtis mentioned other "scrapes," Walter said, genially enough, "Let's not talk about that." Never a very good student, he scored in the 70s and earned a few 80s at the beginning of his senior year. But then in his last marking period (March and April), his teachers called his conduct "disorderly" and gave him several zeroes and no grades above 30. Walter was not paying attention, they reported, and tended to mumble asides. His whispering became disruptive. In fact, one teacher noted, because of his "idleness," he was downright annoying. In all likelihood, he affronted teachers because he did not take them seriously.

Perhaps this eventuality explains why Walter's father decided to enroll him in a more disciplined school. Walter spent his senior year at the Rindge Manual Training School in Cambridge, Massachusetts. Established in 1888 with a donation from Frederick H. Rindge, the Cambridge Manual Training School (as it was called at the time) was a place where students of "average talents" were taught the "plain arts of industry" in order to "learn how their arms and hands can earn food, clothing, and shelter." Walter passed his classes in woodworking, drafting, and various other technical trades, but he preferred playing football and acting in school plays. He smiled and bowed his head—almost hiding a smirk—when Ralph Edwards said Walter's parents would not have "looked with any favor on any theatrical aspirations Walter might have had." In his class picture Walter appears to be disaffected, as if saying to himself, "What am I doing here?" He decided, as he told an interviewer, that he liked spouting lines better than plotting stress curves, adding "[I] just didn't know how to tell my father."

Walter was a good football player, playing guard and tackle as befitted a future character actor who did not have starring roles, but who performed as part of a group practicing intricate teamwork. Two of his teammates, Ralph Hamilton and Mel Carver, remembered Walter as the spark plug of the team. When Brennan heard their voices on *This Is Your Life*, he mimicked their Massachusetts accents, saying "spak plug." Ralph said, "Walter actually saved our Thanksgiving game in 1914 by making a spectacular last second tackle as our opponents were approaching the goal line. We won that game, by the way, 15 to 14." A musing Walter Brennan said, "I think I remember that." He never forgot to honor his beginnings. He returned to Rindge when his coach celebrated his fiftieth year of teaching and coaching. Even if the school did not perform the transformation in Walter that William Brennan had wanted, the school's ethic was etched in Walter's character. The inscription above the front entrance— where Frederick Rindge wished it placed—read, "Work is one of our greatest blessings. Everyone should have an honest occupation." It would always be a point of pride with Walter Brennan that he was never without employment in his chosen profession.

After Rindge, Walter worked for six months in Maine as a logging camp bookkeeper. "It is cold, exacting work," he told a reporter. "My chief fun was watching the table manners. The cook gave the men forks only when they had meat to cut. Everything else from beans to pie was accomplished with a knife. You never saw such dexterity. I learned a lot about voices and dialects which has come in handily since I've become an actor. French Canadians, Squareheads, Yankees. . . Squareheads often referred to Germans and Scandinavians." Later, he would put his Maine experience to good use playing a Swede in a logging camp in *Come and Get It* (1936).

Walter then tried a fifteen-dollar-a-week pick-and-shovel job, but his family frowned upon this work, so he became a bank clerk at eight dollars a week. Then he worked briefly as business reporter for a Boston newspaper before embarking on what would be a short, desultory career in Vaudeville, performing in small-town comedies and what he called "turkey shows." Photographs of him during this period reveal a wiry and spirited personality. He was already a mimic who blackened his face for minstrel shows and specialized in portraying old men. Without makeup, without a character costume, Walter was nondescript.

In a letter dated May 30, 1937, Arthur McNamara, a friend from Brennan's youth, recalled what a versatile and agile artist Walter already was in his early twenties, "where [Brennan] did a quick change from black face to that English dialect part." Those were happy days, spent performing in the St. John's Temperance Minstrels when he was not cavorting on the beach. Walter appears, tall and thin, as the centerpiece in a photograph taken in 1916 on the "Fishies" beach, with five pals forming a human chain by their hands on one another's shoulders. They all have their left feet thrust out, with their toes sticking up in a chorus line of youth. Walter continued playing "oldsters" on stage. It was the kind of employment he enjoyed, but he wanted to make it pay. "I was never really stage-struck," he later insisted. "Acting has always been a business with me, something to make a living by." But in another mood, he admitted that doing comedy and vaudeville "awakened the ham in me."

By 1917, to please his mother, Walter Brennan was working for a second time in a Boston bank, a fact memorialized on his draft registration form, which he signed on June 5. It was the same day his older brother William, listing his occupation as commercial artist, declared he was unfit to serve because of a physical disability. Walter hated his job, and on April 6, the day war was declared, he enlisted in the army, later admitting, "[I]t was a good chance to get away." When he signed his draft registration in June, he already knew he would be serving as a private in the artillery. Later, to journalist Joe Hyams, Walter laughed while he admitted that given a second chance, he would not have volunteered for military service.

For more than a year, all the talk had been about "preparedness." When the Harvard Regiment paraded before forty-five thousand people in May 1916, the event was front-page news in the *Boston Globe*. Going off to war was a kind of show. On July 27, 1917, close to twenty thousand people cheered and cried, as the young men of Lynn and surrounding communities marched off to battle. People lined the railroad tracks, crowded onto sidewalks, and sat on rooftops to enjoy the spectacle. Lynn's mayor and other public officials were there for the sendoff. Church bells rang at 6:30 a.m. for this "half-holiday."

On *This Is Your Life* Ralph Lindsey recalled, "Walter and I enlisted a week apart, went through training together." Walter smiled, closed his eyes, and seemed to hunch over with glee upon hearing his old friend's voice and perhaps remembering the excitement of those days. "I went to Europe in 1917 with sixty-five lbs. on my back," he told Hedda Hopper in a May 17, 1960, radio interview. To another interviewer, he quipped, "I learned to run the 100-yard dash in eight seconds flat, carrying a full pack." He served for nineteen months as a private in the 101st Field Artillery Regiment in France. He never said much about what combat was like, except to confess that he was "severely frightened 500 times." He made it through the war intact, even after driving an ammunition supply wagon with a team of four under shellfire. Every caliber shell had a distinctive sound; and Walter knew them all and later would imitate them during his work on Hollywood studio lots.

Walter was among the American expeditionary forces gassed with high explosive projectiles northwest of Toul, on April 3, 1918, in the course of intense shelling that lasted through the night. How much damage he sustained is hard to say. By 1918, after more than three years of chemical warfare, troops were equipped with gas masks with charcoal filters, and there were relatively few casualties. In some accounts, Walter attributed the loss of his lower front teeth to the gassing, which also altered his voice, giving it a wizened, reedy quality that he would exploit so well for comic effect and adapt when he had to play characters older than himself. On *This Is Your Life*, when Ralph Lindsey mentioned they took "a little shot of mustard gas," Walter cut him off: "We're not going to talk about that." The two men fought together in four major campaigns in 1918: Aisne (May 27–June 16), Champagne-Marne line (July 15–18), Saint-Mihiel (September 12–15), and Meuse-Argonne (September 26–November 11). At Aisne, the Germans bombarded the Allied line with four thousand artillery pieces, and seemed to be winning until the American expeditionary forces arrived and counterattacked. Similarly, at Champagne-Marne the Germans were driven back, with American, British, and Italian divisions supporting four French armies. At Saint-Mihiel, the first solo American offensive demonstrated the effectiveness of artillery but was stopped short of victory, although the campaign demonstrated the crucial United States contribution to the Allied cause. Meuse-Argonne involved more than one million American soldiers and was the largest battle in American history. It resulted in twenty-six thousand casualties. According to some historians this campaign finally convinced the Germans they could not win the war. Over one hundred thousand Americans died in the war, and twelve thousand of them were from the "Yankee Division" Walter Brennan had joined.

Mike Brennan believes that the gassing cost his father his teeth. What cannot be disputed is the kind of terror the very idea of gassing instilled in soldiers. Judy Lamy, whose father worked closely with Walter in Joseph, Oregon, remembered Walter mentioned many times how he buried his face in the mud hoping to mitigate his exposure to the gas. That's how he survived.

Altogether Walter experienced about nine months at the front, and spent just about as much time entertaining troops in company shows directed by Osgood Perkins (1892–1937), the father of actor Tony Perkins. "I probably knew Tony's father better than the kid knew him," Walter told a studio publicist, although he did not say what he picked up from Perkins. According to actress Louise Brooks, who appeared in a film with Perkins in 1925, he had exquisite timing. "Osgood Perkins would give you a line so that you would react perfectly. It was timing—because emotion means nothing." She likened her work with Perkins to "dancing with the perfect partner. You don't have to feel anything." Walter later said the company shows helped him gauge audience expectations: "They defied you to be good." But show business as a career still seemed farfetched to a young man whose family members were of the practical sort.

Brennan credited his time in the army with shaping his deep suspicion of government. While he was fighting at the front, his draft board sent a letter to his home stating he would be fined and imprisoned if he did not turn up for his physical. "Just goes to show how much the government knows about what's going on," he said.

On April 4, 1919, Walter Brennan was one of six thousand returning troops that Governor Calvin Coolidge saluted as their ship docked. Six days later, while the demobbed Brennan was marching in a Swampscott parade, he spotted Ruth Wells, the daughter Lynn's local sheriff, crossing the street. Walter's and Ruth's families knew one another, but Walter, three years older than Ruth, had not paid that much attention to her until he went away to war and began writing letters to her. When Ruth was six, she broke a bottle belonging to Walter's mother, and nine-year-old Walter teased her to tears by telling her, "she'd get it when they got home." During the war, she attended Simmons College, graduating in 1919 from a three-year program in secretarial studies, having taken courses not only in shorthand, typing, business practices, commercial law, and economics, but also in English, History, French, and German. Her yearbook entry in *The Microcosm* gives the impression of a lively and sociable personality with interests in the theater, parties, and dances. She was not one to sulk or spend much time worrying. "He kind of discovered you," Ralph Edwards said to Ruth. "Oh, I did that," she explained. "We were invited by Walter's mother to dinner, my mother and my two sisters . . . Walter opened the door and that was for me," she said delightedly, as Walter smiled.

Walter liked to say that when he proposed to Ruth, he asked how much money she had. She had one hundred dollars, only twenty-five dollars less than he had in savings. He suggested they pool their resources—which meant, among other things, they would go fifty-fifty on the wedding ring. But Ruth had no need to be romanced. She was sold on Walter Brennan and never doubted he would make a success of himself.

Walter thought he had come out of the war remarkably unscathed. His buddies, as he later recalled, "landed in the hospital with nervous collapses. When I'd run into fellows from my old outfit, the first question was always, 'Well, have you folded yet?'" And Walter always answered, "No, thank God." That would change, but in the meantime he secured a job at the bank for twenty-five dollars a week. He managed to stick it out a year, but then, as he later put it, he "decided to take Greeley's advice." With Ruth's backing, he informed both their families of his plans. He did not have much more than the ten-dollar gold piece his parents had given him when he first went out on his own. Ruth's father was especially displeased and refused to give the couple his blessing. And another obstacle stood in the way, Walter later admitted: "My wife is a convert, and her [Baptist] parents were madder than wet hens when we got married. But neither of us were ever sorry." In the 1920s, when Roman Catholics were often called Papists and suspected of putting their fealty to the Pope ahead of their country, a Baptist's conversion to Catholicism was indeed a shocking choice, one that could estrange the convert from family and community. Al Smith's Catholicism was a factor in his defeat in the presidential election of 1928, and as late as 1960 John Kennedy had to give a speech declaring his belief in the separation of church and state, and his loyalty to his oath to defend the Constitution above all. So Ruth Wells showed strength of character and even courage in becoming a Catholic. Her commitment was surely one reason Walter felt he could rely on her, *always*.

The hostile reaction of the Brennan and Wells families meant, at the outset, that Walter and Ruth were very much on their own—especially since Walter had no solid plan, let alone a job in California. The prospect of an unmarried couple setting off on a cross-country trip could not have pleased either family, although given the couple's religious convictions, it is difficult to believe they actually did anything immoral. According to Walter, they drove west in an old touring car. Once, caught in a downpour, they put the top up and drew the side curtains. But the curtains, missing several buttons, flapped in the wind. Then a strong gust tore part of the car's top loose, and the drenched Brennans stopped to buy a cheap umbrella. Walter stuck it through the hole in the car top so that Ruth could hold the swaying umbrella over them as they sailed into Los Angeles. On June 4, 1921, they were married by a Catholic priest at the Cathedral Chapel of St. Virbrana.

Walter Brennan was part of a wave of World War I veterans hoping to make a killing in the golden West. He worked for a developer, Charles B. Hopper, who packed people into buses, gave them lunch, and took them out to tour properties that some of them would buy. Walter later told a *New York Times* reporter, "I made $69 the first week, $79 the second and $89 the third. And then for four weeks I didn't make a dime. Later on, in 1921 and 1922, I made a lot of money, until I decided in 1923 that I could make it a lot faster and lost my last nickel. For the next 10 years I was on my uppers. I sold stapling machines, insurance, anything. Now and then I'd make a try at the studios, but I hadn't thought of pictures as a career. No class or respectability." The land bust of 1926, which put an end to housing bubbles in California and in Florida, foreclosed hope of returning to selling real estate. Andy, while still quite young, heard his father talking about this hard up period. "We lived in a little shack in Pasadena," Andy recalled, "and my father was unable to make a payment on the house." Walter went to Irvin and asked for a loan of three hundred dollars. Walter knew his brother had the money, because Irvin was doing well as a sales manager. But Irvin refused to give his brother the money. As Walter was leaving, he said, "Irvin, someday the tables will turn." Irvin slammed his fist down on the table and said, "I won't let 'em turn."

Walter might seek help, but he never shirked responsibility for his plight. Coming home from work one day he saw Ruth on her hands and knees, washing the floor. He walked over to her, helped her get up, and said he did not want to see her washing the floor. If he couldn't provide someone to wash her floors, then he should do it. And then he got on his hands and knees and finished the floors for her.

Walter's fortunes fluctuated wildly, but the Brennans did not wait to have a family. Arthur, "Mike," was born on January 6, 1922, Walter Jr., "Andy," on July 21, 1923, and baby Ruth "Ruthie" on September 22, 1924. By 1924, Walter's mother and father had also moved to California, settling in Pasadena. With three children to feed, Ruth supplemented the family's meager budget by growing her own vegetables and raising chickens. All three children would quickly learn two fundamental facts about their father: He worked almost all the time, and he expected them to carry their own weight. No Brennan child would be out on the road in a delivery wagon at the age of eleven, but every Brennan child would—certainly by the age of eleven—know what it cost to obtain the things he or she wanted.

Then one day, Walter looked Ruth in the eye and abruptly announced that he was going to become an actor. He joined a generation of World War I veterans who, failing to make a killing in real estate, ended up working as extras in the film industry. Indeed, they arrived by the bus-load and trainload, according to Anthony Slide in *Hollywood Unknowns: A History of Extras, "Bit" Players, and Stand-Ins*. It was a hard life for most extras, who were lucky to get a day's employment in a crowd scene and suffered the embittering experience of serving as observers of the lavish wealth that surrounded them. They were rather like indentured servants, their prospects of emerging as even bit players—let alone as character actors or stars—seemed exceedingly doubtful. But a few, including Walter Brennan, loved the speculative and sporting atmosphere of Los Angeles in the 1920s, and endured the boom-and-bust cycles that broke the spirit of many men and women. A lifelong conservative, Brennan never questioned the nature of such an economy. He seemed to thrive on risk and to enjoy the company of other risk takers.

Asked about how he got into pictures, Brennan replied to a Columbia University interviewer, "I got in purely from hunger. I went over the back fence. Nobody took me by the hand. I worked in this atmosphere and from there on, which many others did. Cooper did, too, the same thing, you know, and Gable, and several of them worked that way." Walter became a tramp, drifting from one studio to another, with casting directors pointing out the exit as Walter wondered what to do next. But then, on an outdoor set, he watched a donkey braying at all the wrong moments, angering the sound technicians, who could not get the animal to perform on cue. (Walter loved to tell this story, and of course it got better every time he told it.) "I can bray," said Brennan, buttonholing the director. So he brayed, and both the director and the donkey were delighted. "How much?" Walter asked the director. "Ten bucks," came the reply. "Not enough," the actor responded. But that was the pay scale, the director said. "Then I don't bray," Walter rejoined. "Tell you what," the desperate director offered, "you bray for the ten-spot, and tomorrow come around and I'll give you a bit part. You can collect twenty-five on that." So it was that Walter Brennan brayed himself into motion pictures. Or as he liked to put it, "I got into pictures by making a jackass of myself." True story? True enough, I suspect, because it was often said of Walter that he knew the value of a dollar and knew how to make himself useful. He also saved money by having his one pair of pants pressed every day by a friendly wardrobe man. Ruth liked to reminisce about washing Walter's one shirt, putting it out on the line to dry, and then getting up at 4:00 am to iron it.

Walter got his first job as an extra with the help of Tenny Wright, then an assistant director at Universal Pictures. Walter got wet in *Lorraine of the Lions* (October 11, 1925), a girl and gorilla story. He was part of a crowd scene in which he was soaked with a hose. "For this we got $10. A big gorilla [escaping from a circus] was climbing up the side of a building, coming out from a dance, and there was this crowd in white tie and tails," the actor recalled. "I was glad to get the dough." In *Webs of Steel* (October 24, 1925), he is one of several railroad workers indistinguishable in a long shot.

In *The Calgary Stampede* (November 1, 1925), a Hoot Gibson western, Brennan can be glimpsed as a spectator in the rodeo crowd. In *The Ice Flood* (October 2, 1926), a timber camp melodrama, he appears as a lumberjack in a story about a young Oxford graduate who has to overcome a bully and the rigors of the outdoors, although the main feature of the film, a Universal Pictures production, is the ice flood, memorably described in a review (October 19, 1926) by *New York Times* critic Mordaunt Hall:

> After a series of shooting scenes the ice flood has its turn. It is announced in anything but subdued language. The ice is first described as a "resistless, mighty monster straining at its wintry leash."
>
> Then come the following captions:
>
> "Cracking, stirring, tearing—Winter's last artillery before the mighty assault."
>
> "Helpless Marie—in her ears the thunder of the avalanche let loose upon her. Now the mighty roar fills her ears—terror clutches her heart."

Much of Brennan's early work was on the Universal Pictures lot, including *Spangles* (November 7, 1926), in which he plays a lunch counterman. More importantly, he was able to watch, for the first time, the great Cecil B. DeMille in action. A decade later the director would award Brennan one of his best roles in *The Buccaneer*. Although Universal made high quality films using important filmmakers like DeMille, it was better known as a producer of "programmers," cheap action films with lots of thrills. Established in 1912, Universal was the oldest studio, and, as film historian Thomas Schatz puts it, "a world unto itself, a self-contained municipality devoted exclusively to making motion pictures. There were restaurants and shops and even a police force." Universal had factory-size production facilities, including a shooting stage sixty-five feet by three hundred feet. There was no better place for Walter Brennan to get work and learn his trade in every kind of genre film.

According to biographer Larry Swindell, Brennan and Cooper met on the set of *Watch Your Wife* (April 4, 1926). Both had uncredited bit parts. Brennan later remembered that quiet, unassuming Cooper was the first actor he met on the Universal lot.

> I said, "What's your name?"
> He said, "Frank Cooper."
> I said, "What?"
> He said, "Frank Cooper."
> I said, "I can't hear you."
> He's shy, you know.

By the time Cooper arrived from Montana and before Gary became the actor's new first name, Brennan had been canvassing the studios for two years and was still doing crowd scenes. The two aspiring actors became friends and sometimes socialized together and shared their meager earnings. Walter remembered a day in 1926 when he and Cooper were driving to work in a 1919 Buick when the brakes gave out. "Those were the days when the brake bands were on the outside of the wheels," Walter explained. "We'd heard somewhere that if you put castor oil on the bands, it would make them swell. Well, we tried it and it worked, and Gary and I came down over that steep pass praising God for castor oil."

Cooper caught a break with a featured role as a doomed aviator in *Wings* (1927), but Walter remained on the periphery, observing the unwritten rule that extras did not consort with stars, yet taking pride in work that reinforced the function of character actors. As character actress Beulah Bondi said, "We are the mortar between the bricks." For Walter Brennan, it was enough to know that a chosen few—Joan Crawford, Norma Shearer, Gary Cooper, Clark Gable—began as extras and ended as stars. For a television documentary, the actor Richard Arlen, one of the stars of *Wings*, was asked what Walter Brennan was like in these early days as an extra. "He was not too unlike Gary Cooper in his mannerisms in those days. A slow way of talking—very much like Will Rogers," said Arlen. "Walter sounded very much like he does today. Very dry and one of the nicest men I've known."

Andy Devine, who began as an extra in 1926 and befriended Brennan, remembered many days when they showed up for jobs and Walter would go through a routine. Anything for Walter Brennan? If the answer was no, then Walter Brennan would not get his ten dollars a day. Anything for Walter Andrew? If not, then Walter would not earn his $7.50. Well how about for Philip Space? If so, Walter would earn three dollars that day. "Philip Space" was a joke Devine and Brennan shared. They knew there always seemed to be some sort of work for the three dollar extra who would fill the space on the casting director's worksheet.

Much time on movie sets is spent simply standing around, but in those periods an alert and keen extra like Walter Brennan watched the featured players hit their marks, position themselves for close-ups, gauge camera range, and adjust their actions to what camera speeds could capture. Since thrifty producers used extras to perform more than one role in the same picture—so long as the extra did not become conspicuous—Walter learned to take direction that helped to perfect his versatility. Cecil B. DeMille, the consummate director of crowd scenes, noted, "[M]ost audiences never notice it, but some of my finest actors are extras." Anthony Slide explains that veteran extras became adept at understanding exactly what individual directors wanted and catered to "these men's whims, their fancies, and their weaknesses." This is exactly what Walter Brennan did nearly a decade later when he showed up on the set of *Barbary Coast* (1935), already knowing what Howard Hawks wanted before Hawks had cast him in the picture. Brennan had been working in pictures as long as Howard Hawks himself. And Brennan had seen everything from the ground up.

Brennan also observed that certain extras built up a repertoire of gimmicks that won them employment in picture after picture. There was, for example, "Old Pop" Purdy, who was called on to play judges and talkative old coots. Depending on the role, he wore his false teeth or he took them out. Brennan would eventually do Purdy one better, playing young and old, toothsome and toothless after he lost more teeth in a fight scene during his stint as a stunt man in one of his early pictures. Working could be dangerous, especially since Walter was still in the expendable category of "extra." During a radio interview in 1960, Hedda Hopper reminded him of their work together on a picture. The director, Brennan recalled, gave them "quite a time. Now he's dead I say a prayer for the repose of his soul." A surprised Hopper blurted out, "You wouldn't say a prayer for him!" But Brennan was insistent: "[N]ot just for him—but for everybody I don't like." When Hopper said, "He made you very unhappy," Brennan corrected her: "No—he hurt me. And I said to him, '[Y]ou don't have enough money to hire me again.'"

The unnamed director was not the only one who injured Walter Brennan. In reminiscing about his early days, he used to tell Kathleen Nolan, his co-star on *The Real McCoys*, that the extras and bit players were not treated any better than the horses. For all his conservatism, Brennan went out of his way to honor every request Nolan made of him while she served as president of the Screen Actors Guild from 1975 to 1979. In June 1929, Actors Equity, then representing film actors, engaged in a dispute about working conditions and living standards for actors. The producers retaliated by claiming to have signed non-Equity contracts with 164 Equity actors, including Walter Brennan, although Equity president Frank Gilmore called the list "patently exaggerated, and false in many instances." Whether or not Walter Brennan signed a non-Equity contract, his deep feelings about his mistreatment never subsided, and he regarded the Screen Actors Guild as essential to protecting actors' working conditions.

A favorite on movie sets, Walter Brennan enjoyed the company of his fellow extras, bit players, and stunt men. They had their favorite hangouts in 1920s Hollywood: Dad Kelly's Corned Beef Parlor, Al Marsh's Poolroom, and Raphael's Drug Store. Extras organized baseball games and other sporting events, as well as dances and other social gatherings. In the mid-1920s, nearly forty thousand extras sought employment from the forty producers active in Hollywood. Out of that forty thousand, about four thousand could count on steady employment. And out of that four thousand, only a handful would go on to careers as major character actors or stars. Only one of them achieved the distinction and acclaim that lasted to the end of his life. How did Walter Brennan do it? To an unusual degree, he kept his own ego out of his business. As he told a reporter, "I don't go out nights. I get through with one picture, start on another, and with a wife and children and a nice home I don't need anything else. Besides, the man who saves his money out there doesn't have to worry about slipping back. I watch these fellows make a few dollars, get all puffed up and first thing they know they're out in the cold. I work for it, save it, and, I tell them, that's why I've got it. I could stick a pin in some of these stuffed shirts."

- CHAPTER 2 -

The Racket

(1928–35)

BY 1928, WALTER BRENNAN HAD APPEARED IN DOZENS OF UNCRED-
ited roles as a customer in a store, a lunch counterman, a lumberjack, a
yacht crewman, a cashier, a gangster, a pool hall shark, a ranch foreman,
a train conductor, a clown, and a musician. If you watch any of these
films, don't blink—you may miss him. At this point, we are talking about
a career that can be telescoped into a few minutes or so of film. And yet,
as DeMille emphasized, this was acting—and in an impressive variety of
roles. And Brennan was making a living, gradually working his way up
to between twenty-five and one hundred dollars a day, although during
his best week he made $150. Of course, there were layoffs and times
when the family really had to stretch its budget, but no one went hungry. Walter emphasized, "I never missed any meals, but I sure postponed
a lot of them." Short of funds during a period in 1928, Brennan agreed to
do a stunt: driving off a pier in San Diego into forty feet of water. "I had
to be doing 45 miles an hour," he later told an interviewer, "and there
was another dummy in the car with me, but he had his hat nailed on.
And when I hit the end of the pier, I tell you, the first thing I thought
of was my insurance." It took him three years to fully recover from the
back injury he sustained. Some actors would think themselves lucky to
escape injury, if not death, but Walter thanked God—and he meant it.

Ralph Edwards asked Mike, the Brennans' oldest son, if he was aware
that his father was struggling. Mike said no, "but the roof leaked and we
would see who could get the most pans out and the one who got the
most pans out for the leak . . . ." Walter interrupted and said, laughing,
"He's telling things that shouldn't be told." Andy remembered asking his
father about the man in the house. Later Andy learned the stranger was

there to shut off the water. But Walter got a job the next day and paid the water bill. Walter was very moved when his daughter, appearing with him in *This Is Your Life*, looked at him and said, "For years you'd bring home two pages of script and say, 'someday they will bring me the whole script.'"

The Racket, a 1928 gangster picture directed by Lewis Milestone, puts Brennan center screen for perhaps the first time (some of his early films appear to be lost). He is dressed in a suit and bowler hat, standing in front of a barbershop talking to a few men. He appears for just a moment in the hurly burly of a gang warfare scene—an urban type, you might say, but no more. He is merely a face in the crowd. Brennan doesn't even try to come up with some sort of "business," gestures that extras notoriously tried to bootleg into scenes in order to get themselves noticed. Walter Brennan was never flashy, never an obvious scene-stealer, but he inhabited his roles so naturally and effortlessly that he often appeared to dominate the screen.

Brennan had learned how to thrive in the motion picture racket. I use the word "racket" because movie magazines so often used that term of art. Film producers and moguls have always had more than a little of the gangster about them, and the stars have often been the subjects of scandal. *Modern Screen* praised Dana Andrews for his genuine, un-Hollywood demeanor and family life, which reporters contrasted with the "racket" that employed him. Ruth, Walter's rock, was just as practical and shrewd as her husband. She shared his respect for a dollar, and she raised her children the Walter Brennan way. "My wife Ruth and I have always had chickens around our place," Walter said. "And a long time ago I learned something important about them. If you help the chick out of its shell when it's hatching, it's going to be too weak to survive. It's the struggle that develops its muscles. Ruth fed our family of three children on a dollar a day, plus what those chickens and our backyard garden contributed." Mike remembered that his mother had "every kind of vegetable around the house. And I had to go out and clean the chicken roost. She'd have me spread fertilizer on the garden. After school she'd give me a bucket and say, 'Fill that up with weeds.'" He earned a dime for every filled bucket, carefully marked on a calendar, and then she would pay him at the end of the week. Mike never resented doing chores or the other tasks required of him as a young boy, he said. "We never spoke back to our folks. There were never any beatings. We were always polite and said thank you and please. We always told [our father] where we were."

During a 1960 radio interview, Hedda Hopper asked Walter about his childrearing method. He joked, "[W]hy I belted them around until they got too big I had to put up my hands in self defense. My kids never gave me any trouble." In a memoir about his father, Andy Brennan describes a firm but fair parent, and one who never stopped praising his wife. He was "not embarrassed to talk of his love and respect for our mother."

Early on, the Brennan children learn the value of working for what they wanted. There were no allowances. If a child asked for something, Walter set him or her a task, a job that would be paid for upon completion. Ruth sometimes thought he was hard on the kids, but Andy could not remember any arguments between his parents. Ruth never opposed Walter's regime and never contradicted him, and he reciprocated by publicly acknowledging her unstinting loyalty to him. Theirs was a marriage based on a shared worldview. Ruth was as Republican as Walter, and later, when he became a national celebrity, she became involved in Republican Party politics. But in their early days together, she seemed content in the conventional housewife's role, raising their three children. In this case, photographs do not lie. Pictures of her reflect what she was: utterly content and happy to be Walter Brennan's wife. The couple had no interest in the Hollywood social scene, and when Walter was not working he was at home with her sharing family responsibilities. Their relationship did not change as he grew more successful. Ruth realized that aside from maintaining his happy home, Walter most wanted to work in pictures. This need would be with Brennan until the day he died.

Movie making itself was the racket Brennan relished, but it took a few years for him to learn how to make the camera bring out his distinctive features and perfect his timing. In 1929, he appeared in three Hoot Gibson pictures. The Nebraska-born Gibson grew up with horses and became a horse wrangler and rodeo performer. He was at the height of his popularity in the 1920s. His easy manner and boyish looks appealed to audiences, who liked the way the actor spoofed himself. In *Smilin' Guns* (March 31) and *The Lariat Kid* (May 12), silent films that seem to be lost, Brennan had bit parts, but in *The Long, Long Trail* (1929), a talkie, Brennan emerges as a supporting player, Gibson's sidekick. Watching Brennan in this early programmer, you would be hard put to recognize signs of greatness. He is not bad. He is just not given much to do—in part because he is there to prop up Gibson after he is drugged by others betting he will lose a high stakes horse race. Lanky and loose-limbed Brennan is hampered by a huge hat. You almost expect him to pitch forward at every tilt of his headgear—although the pedestrian director (Arthur

Rosson) does not take advantage of what might have been a welcome bit of comic relief.

Between 1929 and 1932, Brennan appeared in twenty-six pictures in exceedingly minor and usually uncredited roles, including a bit as Paul Revere in a costume ball scene in *One Hysterical Night* (released October 6, 1929). An exception is his credited performance in *King of Jazz* (April 20, 1930), the first color film produced by Universal and starring, among other acts, Bing Crosby and the Rhythm Boys before Bing became a solo crooner. This lavishly produced musical revue, featuring Paul Whiteman, then at the peak of his fame as the "king of jazz," comes closest to revealing the Walter Brennan who honed his stage skills in vaudeville, a form of theater that consists essentially of musical numbers with comedy acts, acrobats, fancy dancers, impersonators—and virtually any eccentric or exotic performer who entertained across the country between the 1880s and the early 1930s. Brennan appears in four brief bits as a desk sergeant taking in a report of a stolen car (a couple enters with a car seat). Then he is one of several returning World War I soldiers who all ask the same sweetheart if she has been "true to me." When an officer shows up and prepares to take her away, Brennan is the first of several soldiers to pop out from behind closed doors and ask, "Is there room for me?" His next bit is as an expressionless waiter asked by a drunk to serve him "most anything." When the drunk nearly convulses after taking the drink, he asks the waiter what it is, and the waiter says, "Most anything." The drunk then goes on to describe the sad story of what happened to his favorite two goldfish. As he tells the story he puckers his lips like a fish. At the end of the sad story, when the goldfish are no more, the waiter is overcome with grief and exits inquiring "No more?" as he makes fish lips. Then Brennan appears briefly in a horse suit, taking off the front end and saying, "I feel like a horse's neck," while the performer in the rear peeks out and says, "How do you think I feel?" In his final bit he is part of a quartet singing about Nellie, "just a child, a little wild" who may have been led astray, "heaven forbid!" The chorus ends with the plea to send her back to Shamokin, Pa. If there is little to do in these fractional scenes, at least they show off Brennan's sharp timing.

In *Grief Street* (released October 1, 1931), Brennan has six scenes, strategically placed in the picture—enough to make any bit player pleased. He gets to play a drunken, stuttering newspaperman in the first scene. When a fellow journalist says Jim Ryan (John Holland), the reporter-hero who helps the police solve cases, should be on the police payroll, Brennan says no, Ryan should get—and never gets past the first syllable, "re" — when Ryan supplies the word, "remuneration," as a grateful Brennan says thanks, patting Ryan's hand. Brennan is sitting before an egg upended on top of a bottle. When Ryan asks what the egg is doing there, Brennan has trouble saying "when," dragging the word out before answering, "When it's crossways I know I've had enough." As the egg becomes horizontal, Brennan abruptly gets up—although Ryan grabs him and sits him down. Brennan's stutter becomes a genial invitation to his pals to help him out. Variations of this routine occur throughout the film. When Ryan, still seated at the table with Brennan and his buddies, learns of another murder and gets up to cover the story, Brennan cracks the egg and drinks it, punctuating the end of the scene. Already, alert directors—in this case Richard Thorpe—knew that Brennan could offer expert comic relief, never simply repeating himself, but making a slight shift in delivery of a line or in body language so that the audience could anticipate with pleasure the next variation in scenes that become a kind of refrain and comment on the action.

At about this time Walter was doing so well that the Brennans were able to afford a secondhand car, black with red wheels. "[N]othing they have had since has given them so much pride and pleasure," they told a *Baltimore Sun* reporter in 1940. But even stretched out performances like the one in *Grief Street* did not mean Brennan could count on getting better roles. His appearances as a street musician with no lines in *A House Divided* (December 5, 1931) and as a silent plainclothes detective in *Curtain at Eight* (October 1, 1933) are apparitional, although his thirty-second performance, as a stuttering mechanic in *Strange Justice* (October 7, 1932), is arresting. He has only half a line, "Wally, the handle is is is . . . ," but Wally walks away from the car before Brennan finishes. Such moments contribute virtually nothing to plot or character development, but Brennan brightened otherwise dull segues from one scene to the next, providing viewers with a delightful, if momentary, reprieve from business as usual. None of his stutters, by the way, is the same as the others. Sometimes he seems to gulp on his words; other times his delivery is staccato. In still other variations, his words are elongated as he trips over syllables or gasps out a sentence. This body of work, so minor in the scheme of Hollywood film history, would probably never have been noticed if Brennan had not broken through to bigger roles.

It is curious that Walter Brennan should make a specialty of a human frailty that he played not for pathos, but for laughs. Yet what his stutterers have in common is persistence. They will not let go of words, even when those words elude and subvert them. As the main characters go about their business, Brennan's role remains that of the sidelined attendant, plugging along, resolute in his infirmity. If such scenes now seem insensitive, we laugh anyway, in spite of our discomfort about someone else's disability. But remember, Brennan's plucky stutterers do not invite our sympathy. They are there to play the game, so to speak, and they never exhibit the slightest shame or chagrin about their predicament and their minor contributions to the action. However slight their achievement, they are part of the scene and participants in the ongoing show.

Walter Brennan never doubted he would secure more articulate parts. It was just a matter of doggedness and timing. He has more strategically placed bits in *Manhattan Tower* (December 1, 1932) as a stuttering mechanic and in *Women Won't Tell* (January 1, 1933). At the beginning of *Manhattan Tower*, Brennan, in overalls, just manages to express his sarcastic view of marriage to his foreman, the leading man who loses, then wins back his girl. In the final scene, as the couple embrace on the way to be married, Brennan reappears, suggesting they hire a room (a line that would never be permitted in the Production Code era). Already he was playing characters who provided comic relief, or a sense of irony, in otherwise bland and conventional B pictures. He is the common man, the groundling never permitted near the main stage of the action, as in *Women Won't Tell*, where he appears raking refuse in a dump. He is a Depression-era worker, happy to have even this lowly employment. He proves as much by singing cheerfully, "*Oh*, you got to be happy, and keep on the job, and have a strong stomach when you work in the dump."

One of Brennan's early and more complex performances is in *Law and Order* (March 1, 1932), starring Walter Huston and based on a script by W. R. Burnett, a great screenwriter and novelist best known for *Little Caesar* (1929), a novel he adapted for film in 1931. Brennan often said his performances were only as good as the writing, and when the roles were poorly conceived, his acting suffered. Burnett, a consummate craftsman, is able to meld character development and action, while maintaining the melodrama that audiences craved. The inimitable Walter Huston (his son John worked on the dialogue for this picture) brings to his role a quiet depth of moral seriousness that is foreign to the sunnier Hoot Gibson and Tim McCoy westerns that Walter Brennan was also making at the time.

Law and Order seems to be the first western to depict the gunfight at the O.K. Corral. John Ford would memorably restage it in *My Darling Clementine* (1946), in which Walter Brennan would reach one of the high points of his career playing Old Man Clanton, the patriarch of an evil clan. *Law and Order* captures some of the grittiness of the Old West that Brennan felt was lost when westerns became star vehicles. He first appears for a few seconds working in a saloon as Lanky Smith, seen descending some stairs. He hesitates when he is called to show Frame Johnson (Walter Huston) and his pals their beds. He responds with just the hint of a stutter as he speaks one word, "Yeah." In another brief scene, Brennan ushers Huston into the room and says, "Them beds ain't buggy, Mister." He appears in a third scene polishing a cuspidor. He is part of the local color, like one of the rustics in a Thomas Hardy novel— only here he is defined by the crude western milieu. In a fourth scene, during a hanging, Brennan holds on to a post above the gallows and puts his hands to his neck, as if in anticipation of the condemned man's ordeal. Brennan's dismay is reflected in the faces of the men and women who are also apprehensively awaiting the execution. Burnett and the film's director, Edward L. Cahn, crafted a film that makes maximum use of Brennan's bits.

With John Wayne, Brennan appeared in two Tim McCoy westerns, *Texas Cyclone* (February 24, 1932) and *Two-Fisted Law* (June 8, 1932). McCoy was already a huge star of silent films and early talkies when Wayne and Brennan were just getting started. Although McCoy had real experience in the West as a cowboy (he was an expert rider and roper), his rudimentary acting skills—especially the way he telegraphed his reactions—passable in the silents, rendered him stiff and implausible in talkies. In contrast Wayne, a USC football player, and New England-bred Brennan appear more authentic simply because they do not mug for the camera and are able to deliver their dialogue naturally. As Brennan, playing Sheriff Lew Collins in *Texas Cyclone*, approaches "Texas" Grant (McCoy), mistaking him for an old friend, Jim Rawlins, Brennan demonstrates that he has already mastered the folksy sidekick slang that would be one of the signature voices he would modulate from one role to another over four decades. Brennan strides in and takes control of his first scene, pressing his hands against McCoy. When a cutaway shot shows Utah Becker (Wheeler Oakman) emerging from a saloon, the bartender standing next to McCoy points out Becker, and Brennan turns his head to look pointedly at Becker before turning back to McCoy and telling him that Becker is "still out to get you." Although "Texas" Grant knows he is not the man the town supposes, Brennan's character galvanizes Grant into action, so that he takes it upon himself to break up the Becker gang of rustlers terrorizing the town of Stampede. All you need to know about John Wayne, playing Steve Pickett, a cowhand, is that he stands apart from the others in his crew, who are cowed by the Becker gang. When

McCoy asks Pickett if Becker has him "buffaloed too," the handsome bareheaded Pickett gets up from his bunk, stands taller than McCoy, who wears a ludicrously large Stetson, and announces, "Ain't nobody got me buffaloed." From this point on, with the stalwart backing of Steve Pickett, Brennan's Sheriff Collins becomes McCoy's confidant and revels in watching the McCoy-Wayne duo go about thwarting, rounding up, and roping the Becker gang. In two scenes the sheriff shakes with joy, wryly amused at the turn of events, but also anticipating and advancing the story that, of course, requires the heroes to restore order to a lawless community.

Brennan's character plays his part by requiring town attendance at a lecture about crime and law enforcement. As he enters the lecture hall someone says, "Here comes Father Time." And so Walter Brennan advances his career as the bent over but resilient and reliable old timer fulfilling his function as rectifying moral compass. He proceeds up the aisle—inquiring about the health of his townsmen, saluting and complimenting the ladies—then takes a seat and scrutinizes the faces of several rugged cowboys. The cowboys seem to realize they are headed for a trap, as they call on the sheriff to get on with his lecture, which he tells them will start in two minutes, at precisely three o'clock. The rowdy audience members begin to hoot and stamp their feet when he addresses them as "ladies and gentlemen." He has been stalling while awaiting the hero's arrival, which is signaled by cuts to McCoy and Wayne, who appear just in time, locking the doors as they enter. The sheriff holds up a list of men who have no visible means of employment and yet have money. "The people of Stampede are asking you to leave town pronto," he declares. When Becker's men get up to leave, Grant and his posse draw their guns and tell the rustlers to sit down. Each gang member is forced to relinquish his gun when the sheriff calls his name. The eleven criminals are escorted at gunpoint out of Stampede and forced to walk twenty miles to the next town. Becker returns and announces his discovery that "Texas" Grant has been masquerading as Jim Rawlins. Becker actually says, "This town ain't big enough for the two of us," and challenges Grant-cum-Rawlins to a showdown. Of course the hero prevails—and then learns that he has been suffering from amnesia for five years, and that he actually is Jim Rawlins!

In *Two-Fisted Law*, Brennan's role is more integral to the action than Wayne's. Brennan plays a corrupt deputy sheriff, Bendix, in cahoots with the villain, Bob Russell, performed once again by Wheeler Oakman. Russell has swindled Tim Clark (Tim McCoy) out of his ranch. Bendix is also in on a Russell-led robbery. When Clark, accused of the crime, comes close to discovering the true criminals, Russell pressures Bendix into arresting Clark for an earlier shootout, telling the deputy that he can then kill Clark and claim he was resisting arrest. But Clark is too fast for Bendix, who is then shot by the eavesdropping Russell, who, in turn, is killed by Clark. A dying Bendix confesses, not only putting Clark in the clear, but also establishing that Clark is the rightful owner of the ranch that Russell falsely obtained. All along, Brennan plays his character as a dupe and a wary malefactor, intently watching Clark's every move so that he can report back to Russell. When directly interrogated himself, Bendix's impassive expression conveys the banality of evil.

In another Tim McCoy western, *Man of Action* (January 20, 1933), Brennan plays Summers, a timid bank cashier implicated in a bank hold-up. Nervously twitching his fingers, he lies to the sheriff about not seeing the robbers. In a later scene, just as Summers is about to confess his part in the robbery, his twitching fingers relax just as he is shot before revealing what he knows. In *Fighting for Justice* (August 28, 1932), Brennan plays a small role as Fletcher, a cowhand, in Tim McCoy's successful efforts to reclaim his ranch. In *The Prescott Kid* (November 8, 1934), his role is smaller still. As Zeke, he is a stagecoach driver who punctuates every high-pitched sentence with a spit.

At home, Walter Brennan converted the scenarios of his Westerns into family lore. After dinner, he'd gather the kids together in the living room and begin: "There we were . . . our Wells Fargo wagon surrounded by Lobo and his gang. But Andy, sitting on the chest of gold, drew and winged the first robber. Ruthie tossed the Winchester to Mike who, with deadly aim, swept three of them out of their saddles. Lobo's horse reared and, before he could settle him down, Lobo got it through his sweatband from Ruthie's derringer. So once again the Brennans brought Wells Fargo in on time!" Who would not love such a father, bringing work home with him in such a delightful and inviting way? He gave his children much better roles than he could win. He had just a bit part as a court bailiff in another Tim McCoy vehicle, *Cornered* (August 5, 1932) and a bit as a toothless town drunk in a Tom Mix western, *The Fourth Horseman* (September 25, 1932).

Like the westerns that Brennan appeared in, the ones he made up for his children were all about action, not character development. That's what he liked about Tim McCoy westerns, he told an interviewer in 1971, "[T]hey looked like the West." In other westerns, "You see when a guy steps on a horse and he's got no spurs on, you wonder where he's going, or he's been out two or three days and he's smooth-shaved. This is a lot of baloney." Walter liked to watch the way actors like Tim Mc-Coy and Hoot Gibson mounted a horse: "I'm not a roper but I watched little things that I would know if I had to do this, that I could do it." He was careful about horses, holding on to the cheek strap and the pommel before putting a foot in the stirrup.

Brennan's roles in other genre films tended to be slight, if remarkably effective. In a twelve-chapter serial, *Phantom of the Air* (May 22, 1933), he plays Skid, a mechanic-cum-driver-cum-henchman for Mort Crom, the villain who is the nemesis of Bob Raymond, pilot for Thomas Edmunds, inventor of the super plane, Phantom, and of an anti-gravity device. In every episode Skid has the opportunity to eliminate the hero: sabotaging Raymond's plane, causing a crash, and shooting at Raymond in aerial duels. Skid relishes the part he performs in evil plots and, as critic Jerry Blake observes, Brennan "shows signs of his great character-acting talent even in this early and largely nondescript role, particularly in his shrilly indignant reaction to his head-to-head aerial crash with Tyler ('That Raymond guy must be crazy—rammin' his plane into me!')"

In *Sing Sinner Sing* (August 17, 1933), Brennan is one of three gangsters boarding a floating casino for a holdup. This time, dressed in a sporty bowler hat and dark clothes and standing tall, he is a credible criminal. He keeps his hands in his pockets, the calmest of the three henchmen, declaring one of his crew is as "nervous as a June bride." Later, speaking out of the side of his mouth, he suggests to one of his fellows in crime that they split the take two ways instead of three. But then, his character just drops out of the plot after some gunfire, his fate unknown.

In the first scene of *One Year Later* (August 25, 1933), Brennan makes an offbeat entrance onto a train platform wearing a straw hat and suit. He is looking left while a railroad employee loading cages of chickens asks, "What's all the excitement about? Looks like this train is going to take on another young chicken and a rooster." Brennan says, "Yep," raising his left arm to gesture toward the employee. "They're going to the city on their honeymoon." The employee says, "They sure got a swell day for it." Brennan retorts, "Gosh, it ain't the *day*," a word he emphasizes by thrusting his fingers upward twice. "It's the night." He cackles as he gives the employee a leering look and then turns, continuing to laugh as the camera tracks his movement toward a couple boarding the train. This neat opening, which takes only twenty seconds, capitalizes on Brennan's acting economy to get the picture started, delighting in Brennan's ribaldry, a cameo of titillation that just a year or so later would have been censored.

When director Victor Schertzinger told Brennan he needed someone who could do a radio announcer audition in the "worst possible fashion" so that the film's lead, Victor Jory, playing a program director, could throw the character out of the studio, the actor devised the role of a stuttering animal imitator. Walter was especially proud of his ability to imitate the sound of almost any animal, and was given an opportunity to demonstrate his prowess in *My Woman* (October 5, 1933). Halfway through his repertoire of South American fauna, he is cut short by a stagehand. "Nerts to you," Brennan stutters. One IMDb reviewer found Brennan's bit the best thing in the film: "He's the only character I wanted more of." In *The Invisible Man* (November 13, 1933), Brennan delivers a few lines in an impeccable English accent, complaining because the invisible man has stolen his bicycle. He does so again as a gossiping townsmen (a fifty dollar bit part) in *The Mystery of Edwin Drood* (February 4, 1935).

In *You Can't Buy Everything* (January 26, 1934), Brennan is a train vendor selling papers. When he fails to make sale to a penny-pinching Mrs. Hannah Bell (May Robson), he leans toward her and brays, "All the New York papers. Latest edition." He looks sour in his four-second scene. As he brushes past Robson, he continues to yell about all the New York papers and wakes up the passenger whose paper Bell is coveting. Brennan brays again, "Candy, chocolate, chewing gum, peppermint, fruit, bananas." When he asks Bell if she wants something, she says, "I wish you were in Halifax." He turns and starts his spiel, but begins with "Nice fresh Halifax," then corrects himself, smiling slightly, "I mean peppermint, chocolate, chewing gum." What makes the scene just a little more than ordinary is the vendor's assertiveness, which verges on rudeness and yet is restrained enough to obviate complaint.

In *Riptide* (March 30, 1934), Brennan is a chauffeur picking up Herbert Marshall and Norma Shearer for a costume party. For most of his minute on-screen he functions as an audience stand-in, watching Shearer fuss with her "Lady Sky Bug" outfit. *Sensation Hunters* (January 3, 1934), features Brennan as a stuttering waiter in a nightclub, whose scenes usually end before he can finish a sentence. Dressed in a short cutaway jacket with a lock of hair curled in the middle of his forehead, he is ridiculously slow on the uptake when he is addressed ironically by his employer— "Hey, Handsome," "Hey, Honey"—as she brushes past him. Before he can say much, she is gone, leaving him to stare dumbly at the tray in his hands. This a typical example of the comic relief he brought to otherwise ordinary scenes, but in this case he also serves as a foil to the fast-paced world of showgirls, con artists, and pickpockets. In a way, Brennan became a specialist, employed to get scenes off to a fast start, or to make a snappy transition with just a little bit of the actor's business—in this case straining for words that his impatient employer cannot bother to take in. His one moment of joy comes when several showgirls jostle him on their way to the stage, his one brush with stardom. And then he vanishes from the film, no longer of use to the plot.

Brennan's bit in *Radio Dough* (February 5, 1934) is a tour de force, in a class with the agile antics of the greatest silent comedians. The situation—a drunk being fitted for a suit—is inherently comic, but Brennan's supple performance is extraordinary. "Here, slip your arm in this," the haberdasher says to the swaying Brennan, who lurches left, putting his arm into a sleeve, and then lurches right, slipping his arm out of the left sleeve as the haberdasher is helping to guide Brennan's right arm into a sleeve. As expected, the routine is repeated with the right sleeve, so that Brennan comes out of the fitting half-dressed. Before the procedure can be repeated, he pitches forward, and the haberdasher has to grab his left arm and haul him back to vertical as if reeling in a big fish. Taking no chances, the haberdasher grips Brennan's left arm and shoulder in a half nelson, while tucking the right arm into a suit sleeve. But he makes the mistake of backing up to admire his achievement, and a seemingly boneless Brennan rocks backward, only to be caught just before he falls to the floor. With his hands at the ready to steady the swaying Brennan, the haberdasher is nonplussed when he hears Brennan slur, "Swell, but I don't like it." The suit has too many buttons, Brennan declares, as he rips two of them off and throws them on the floor. "Issh too tight," Brennan blurts out, as he flaps the suit coat open, then closes it with enough force to split the back. He then complains that the suit doesn't fit at all, "Take it, I don't want it," and wrestles his way out of his apparel and throws it on the floor. Instead of punching Brennan, the haberdasher lightly taps Brennan's left cheek in mock affection, then grabs his nose, coming down on it with a slap. He grabs Brennan's bowler hat by the brim and brings it down on his ears, and finishes up by kicking Brennan in the ass and driving him off-screen. In so many of his roles, the six-foot-one Brennan is shown stooping, bent over, or otherwise engaged in actions that minimize his height, but in this two-minute scene he is a tall column using his slender build in an imposing manner that makes his drunken assertion of authority all the more amusing.

Brennan's build is also a perfect foil for the Three Stooges in *Woman Haters* (May 4, 1934), where he plays a train conductor who becomes interested in their woman haters club. He is initiated in a typical Stooges routine culminating, of course, in some eye gouging. Later, he encounters Larry and Moe fighting, and in rhyme (all the characters do) tells them:

> *Say, what's the idea of this rough stuff*
> *I've stood enough guff from you two.*
> *Now you two behave.*

Brennan appeared in another Saturday afternoon serial, *Tailspin Tommy* (October 29, 1934), a Universal Pictures production based on a popular comic strip featuring the heroic exploits of Tommy Tompkins (Maurice Murphy), an airplane mechanic turned pilot, ably assisted by his redoubtable sidekick, Skeeter (played with innocent bravado by Noah Beery Jr., who would later appear with Brennan in *Red River*). In chapter eight of the serial, Brennan appears in whites as a hospital orderly Skeeter slugs so that he can take the orderly's clothes to Tommy, who has been confined to a hospital bed and is just rousing himself (after the interference of villains) to compete in an aerial race. The bit calls for Brennan to be unassuming, easy prey for a sucker punch. In such roles, he could seem the quintessence of the ordinary, a prop for the plot, so that the idea that such a character (or actor) could do much more seems inconceivable.

In yet another variation on a stuttering character—this time in *Northern Frontier* (February 2, 1935)—Brennan, playing a cook, recognizes that Mack Mackenzie (Kermit Maynard) is a Mountie working undercover to expose a gang of counterfeiters. The cook, working for the gang boss, Stone (LeRoy Mason), begins to reveal the truth, sputtering "I-I-I, well I'm sure I-I-I know." But he cannot "spit it out" fast enough for Stone, who raises his right hand and knocks Brennan to the floor. Given his bent over, obsequious manner, Brennan hardly seems like someone Stone can take seriously. Even when Brennan writes the vital intelligence out on a piece of paper for Stone to read, the boss cuffs him and says, "Well ain't that interestin'." Playing such thankless roles after a decade of working in Hollywood strained Walter's nerves, he later admitted. In fact, he was on the verge of a nervous breakdown, but somehow he kept going, picking up yet another bit part in Tim McCoy's *Law Beyond the Range* (February 15, 1935).

A perkier bit at the beginning of a Three Stooges comedy, *Restless Knights* (February 20, 1935), has Brennan playing their father, decked out in a large night cap and a fake white beard, lying on his deathbed calling for his sons. He confesses in tremolo that they are of royal blood: "Years ago I was the royal chamberlain of the Kingdom of Anesthesia." Now, he urges them to offer their swords in service of their imperiled queen. The quality of the writing is best exemplified in Brennan's telling Curly that his title is "Baron of Grey Matter." Brennan then says, "Come close my sons so that I may bless you," and rises enough to give them a sweeping triple slap, as the light fades on his 120-second part in this sixteen minute short.

Brennan's contribution to *The Wedding Night* (March 8, 1935), starring Gary Cooper and Anna Sten—the Russian beauty Samuel Goldwyn was promoting as the next European import to rival Greta Garbo and Marlene Dietrich—was of a different order. The anxious producer, worried about Sten's accent (even though she was playing a Polish American), began to take notice of Brennan in a seemingly forgettable role he nevertheless freshened with his rapid-fire delivery. Brennan is Bill Jenkins, a cackling Connecticut cab driver, spitting tobacco juice (actually licorice) and showing the tobacco fields to Tony Barrett (Gary Cooper), an alcoholic writer modeled on F. Scott Fitzgerald and trying to dry out in a country hideaway. Goldwyn had been much impressed with the velocity of dialogue in *It Happened One Night* (February 23, 1934) and wanted his actors to perform at the same screwball speed. Brennan manages this feat more deftly than the picture's ostensible stars, although Cooper perks up when doing scenes with Brennan. Unfortunately Sten did not the have the same opportunity. "I never even met Anna Sten," Brennan told biographer Carol Easton. When Jenkins drives up to deliver a telegram to Barrett, walking along the road, neither the writer nor Jenkins has a pencil to use to reply to Barrett's wife, who wants him to return to the city. So Barrett simply gives a verbal response: "My work won't let me. Love Tony." Jenkins repeats the message twice to fix it in his mind, but as soon as he drives off the message gets garbled: "My love won't work me." He tries again: "My work won't love me." Not satisfied, he begins again: "My work won't love me." In frustration, he spits, and says, "Gosh, I'm losin' my memory." His role is inconsequential, and yet so necessary to the local color that director King Vidor works Brennan into a scene whenever he can. Brennan would have made his character even more authentic if Goldwyn had not complied with a request from the Breen Office, the enforcers of the Production Code, that Brennan's use of "damn" and "hell" be cut from the film.

Howard Hawks often took credit for discovering Walter Brennan and touting him to Goldwyn, but Goldwyn's interest in Brennan—according to the actor—had been stimulated by Ralph Bellamy, who appeared in both *Surrender* and *The Wedding Night* with Brennan. It was Bellamy who encouraged the producer to select Brennan for key roles. The attention of Samuel Goldwyn notwithstanding, Walter Brennan was still several months away from securing a breakthrough role, and was still doing bits: In *Gold Diggers of 1935* (March 15), a Busby Berkeley musical, he is a bellboy/porter; in *Bride of Frankenstein* (April 22), a neighbor; in *Party Wire* (April 27), a railroad telegrapher; in *Spring Tonic* (June 27), a bum; in *West Point of the Air* (August 18), a soldier. In *Lady Tubbs* (July 2), his small role as a relative of a camp cook who by inheritance becomes a lady, earned Brennan a notice in *Daily Variety* for giving one of the film's "sound characterizations." He was paid three hundred dollars for two days work, a rather good return compared to bit players and extras who received anywhere from $7.50 to $50.00 a day.

In *Man on the Flying Trapeze* (August 3), one of W. C. Fields's finest films, Brennan plays Legs Garnett, a burglar in the basement getting drunk on Fields's applejack, which he calls "Joisey Lightening." In a sweet, high-pitched, and softly caressing voice, Brennan tunes up with the opening line of "On the Banks of the Wabash." Fields's frightened wife finally rouses her husband from sleep. He has already imbibed some of his own brew in the bathroom while pretending to brush his teeth. Hardly disturbed by the intruders, he wonders why they are singing in the basement. After Fields drunkenly puts both of his socks on his right foot, he finally stands up, telling his wife he wishes the burglars had at least waited until later in the morning (it is five a.m.). He leans over to hear their songs coming out of a grating. "Oh, what rotten voices," he remarks. The burglars are so far gone by now that when Fields accidentally fires his gun in the bedroom, they pause for a just a moment, calmly noting that it sounds like a pistol shot. After more delay as Fields organizes himself to confront the burglars, a cop arrives to handcuff Brennan and his pal, but stops to ask "What's that you're drinkin' there?" The next shot shows the cop has joined the singing act, now a trio. Fields takes a tumble down the cellar stairs before noticing the cop and the two burglars and accepting the cop's invitation to share a drink with them. As Fields belts out the song, his family hears a quartet. The cop takes a jug as evidence, and all four walk down to the police station. Brennan sways through most of the extended gag, a silent counterpoint to the increasingly raucous Fields. The upshot is that a judge imposes a sentence on Fields—a fine or a jail term, whichever Fields prefers—for making applejack without a permit, and the burglars are uncuffed and released.

"Tammany Young and Walter Brennan were standouts in their antics of letting apple jack get the better of them," was the representative verdict of *Daily Variety* (June 26, 1935).

Between *The Long, Long Trail* and his big break in *Barbary Coast* (December 27, 1935), Brennan worked in over one hundred films, usually appearing uncredited and speaking a few lines. He portrayed, variously: a side show barker, a peasant, a desk sergeant, a singer in a quartet, a milkman, a bodyguard, a driver, a musician, a sheriff (twice), a cigar stand proprietor, a Texas ranger, a police dispatcher, a cowhand, a farmer, a toothless town drunk, a lighting technician, a mechanic (twice), a worker in a dump, a protestor, a cashier, a counterman in a diner, a stuttering waiter, a garage attendant, a ticket taker, a radio repairman, a farmhand, a stuttering thief, a reporter, a detective, a stuttering animal imitator, a bicycle owner, a soda jerk, a bus driver, a Niagara Falls boatman, a stuttering boarder, a train vendor, a coroner, a ship's officer, a chauffeur, a bicycle repairman, a train conductor, a radio announcer, a switchman, a hot dog vendor, a prisoner on a ship, a reporter on a ship, a stagecoach driver, a hospital orderly, the proprietor of a diner, a stuttering cook, a bellboy, a porter, a soldier, a bum, a gangster, and a stonecutter. Small wonder Brennan was well prepared when at last he auditioned for a great director, Howard Hawks.

CHAPTER 3

Acclaim and Awards

Samuel Goldwyn, Howard Hawks, Fritz Lang, and How Walter Brennan Became a Real Character
(1934–39)

WALTER BRENNAN HAD ALWAYS BEEN A FIDGETY MAN, HIGHLY ATTUNED to his environment. He picked up and imitated the sounds of everything—a baby crying (recorded for *Little Accident*, August 3, 1930), a mule braying, different birds, cows, dogs, cats, bees, and musical instruments (he does a little trumpet solo in *Grief Street*). And then there were those artillery shells that he continued to imitate long after his service in World War I. He put his twitching hands and feet to work in several bits, and his nimbleness is on display in *Radio Dough*. Brennan himself called his set of behaviors adolescent. He did "screwy" and "goofy" things.

This restlessness served him well as an actor—or to put it another way, all the work kept him going, steadily plugging along. And yet by 1934, Walter Brennan was in a state of near collapse. "What my grandma said," Walter's granddaughter Claudia Gonzales remembered, "[was that] he was eating his dinner, and he put down his fork. He looked at her, and he said, 'I don't know what to eat next.'" He had made it through World War I in reasonably good shape. Indeed, he had scoffed at the idea of shell shock. But then, as he told Goldwyn biographer Carol Easton, "Boy, I cracked up." There were nights when he just wanted to sink into his bed. Then he would wake up at 2 am with a "nameless numbing fear." As he also told Easton, "If it hadn't been for my wife, I'd have jumped off the Pasadena Bridge. I fell away to nothin'. I weighed about 140 pounds. Gee, when I got a job in *Barbary Coast*, I was carryin' my ground-up vegetables in a mason jar. They had to build muscles into my clothes." Brennan's son Walter Jr. ("Andy") recalled that as a young boy he had not understood what his father was going through, but he knew that his father was in trouble.

Then he landed the part of Old Atrocity. For the first time, Brennan brought home a whole script, just as he had promised his family he would do one day. He cried, and as his daughter remembered on *This Is Your Life*, the family cried with him. Brennan looked down as his daughter spoke on the program, trying to close his lips and control his emotions.

Did Brennan know that his big break came in a film that almost did not get made, which in its first draft did not even include the character he played? In the pre-Production Code era, the film's setting in a brothel in San Francisco, itself presided over by a corrupt mayor, would not have been problem. But to get the film made after July 1934, when the code was in full force meant that Goldwyn would have to meet with the Breen office and provide assurances that his film would not be deemed morally offensive. At first all went well, with Goldwyn giving an anodyne description of the project so as to allay Joseph Breen's suspicions. More was at stake than just this particular film, as one of Breen's associates noted: "There has never been a time within my experience when this office has been called upon for so much advice on proposed stories. It all indicates that studios are at present more keenly conscious of the wave of public criticism against the industry, and appear to be more sincerely desirous of full cooperation with this office." Indeed, the Breen office would have rejected some of the films Brennan had already appeared in: *A House Divided* (1931), in which a new wife falls in love with her husband's son, and *Scandal for Sale* (1932), which shows a woman beating her rival to death with a hammer.

On July 3, Will Hays, the prime instigator of the Production Code, reported to the Breen Office, "We had a conference with Mr. Goldwyn at which he asked us our frank opinion as to the advisability of attempting to make this script at this particular time. We gave it as our advice, that it would be well not to attempt it, and he thereupon decided to shelve the story." But on July 25, the *Christian Century* editorialized:

> If there are any who have believed that the moving picture industry is as good as cleaned up, just because of the formation of the Catholic Legion of Decency and the spreading of that movement to Protestant and Jewish circles, events of the past few days should prove enlightening. This battle has not been won; it has no more than started. Hollywood is just beginning to wheel its forces

into line. Its counterattack is just opening. Such apparent retreat as there has been is disclosed by Mr. Samuel Goldwyn to have been nothing but a trick to deceive the public. Mr. Goldwyn states that after the present storm has died down he will go back to making pictures like the "full-blooded, strongly flavored" but now suspended "Barbary Coast."

On August 27, Breen wrote to Goldwyn that the script outline was

> *definitely in violation of our Code*, chiefly because of the illicit sex . . . . The ruling of the code on this point is quite clear—"Sexual immorality . . . should never be introduced as subject matter unless *absolutely essential* to the plot. . . . It must not be presented as attractive and beautiful . . . and it must not be made to seem right and permissible" . . . . We suggest that you do *not* characterize *all* the women who come as prostitutes; and that you do not definitely characterize *any* of them as such. The whole flavor of the story is one of sordidness, and low-tone morality. . . . We recommend you *tone down* the several phases of the story which may suggest extreme brutality, or cruelty.

These exchanges between Goldwyn, Hays, and Breen are central to the understanding that from now, on no matter what old reprobates Brennan would be called upon to play, scripts would have to demonstrate his characters' redeeming qualities. The actor would have to tread an exceedingly fine line between the realism he wanted to bring to his roles, and the moralistic sentimentality that the Production Code prescribed. The outspoken Goldwyn showed more independence than most producers and wanted to push his film right to the edge of respectability, making it possible for Brennan to maintain much of Old Atrocity's raunchy behavior.

By October, Goldwyn was working on a way to obviate the Breen office objections, even while, according to a Breen office staffer, insisting that, "in order to put 'punch' in the story, he must include some questionable elements, which we advised him that if they could be portrayed at all, they would have to be handled with great care. I have an idea that Mr. Hawks would handle them successfully if Mr. Goldwyn will allow him to do it." Goldwyn had trouble leaving writers and directors alone, so Hawks would have to employ all his finesse to satisfy the contending judges of his work.

From November 1935 to March 1936, Breen sent Goldwyn articles that protested the making of the film, and Hays put pressure on the producer to shut it down, arguing that *Barbary Coast* was ruining Goldwyn's reputation. But as Breen informed Hays several months later, Goldwyn would not relent: "[A]t one stage of the discussion, Goldwyn was in favor of moving into Chicago, hiring a battery of lawyers, and suing the censor board, the Legion of Decency, and everybody else in striking distance. This notion, however, has been tossed aside." By May, Goldwyn had coaxed and cajoled the Breen office into approving the Charles McArthur and Ben Hecht script. Now it became a war of attrition, as the Breen office tried to chip away at language and scenes it deemed offensive. Here is a Breen's May 3, 1936 censorship list:

Omit God-forsaken
Don't show actual operation of gambling machinery
Make sure the violence against Old Atrocity is not excessive
No effeminacy about the architect
Be careful on use of sexual innuendo in the line "You know what
    I want."
The business of Swan [Miriam Hopkins] pressing her knee against
    the table and stopping the roulette wheel should not be shown.
Don't be too realistic in showing Swan on a couch the "worse for
    drink."
Don't let Louis Chamalis [Edward G. Robinson] spend so much
    time in Swan's bedroom.
Eliminate "Oh my God"
Eliminate "to hell"

On June 11, Breen requested the following nips: "omit Chinks," "omit Greasers," and questionable lines such as, "It's hard making love on one drink. Wait until I have another." At this point, in other words, the Breen office was requesting a trim—with just a little off the top. Walter was in the habit of using ethnic epithets, and Hawks encouraged his actors to use their words so as to shape the characters to the actor's sensibility, but Brennan was not so different from Breen in deploring sexual innuendo on the screen.

Goldwyn, Hawks, and other Hollywood adepts understood that they could evade some of the worst aspects of Code censorship by complying with Breen's requests for changes in wording, while preserving a good deal of their original scenarios. The point was to keep negotiating, giving in a little but sliding as much past Torquemada as they dared, making him own, so to speak, the final production. So it came to pass that Joseph Breen sent Edward G. Robinson a telegram on August 30: "Barbary Coast is the finest and most intelligent motion picture I have seen in many months. Stop. Your characterization is one of the finest it has ever been my good fortune to witness on a screen and I congratulate you most heartily." Samuel Goldwyn and Howard Hawks received similar messages. Even so, the film was banned in Australia, India, and Estonia, and New York, Ohio, Maryland, Virginia, Kansas, and the Canadian provinces of Ontario and Quebec requested deletions.

Brennan's Old Atrocity is a wily, ingratiating character who is rather proud of his skullduggery, overcharging passengers as he ferries them from ship to shore during the California Gold Rush. He is a thief and confidence man who surprises himself by going straight, helping out the befuddled Jim Carmichael (Joel McCrea), who opposes Luis Chamalis (Edward G. Robinson), a nefarious casino owner who rules over San Francisco. Brennan's character becomes the conduit through which the plot is resolved by uniting Mary Rutledge (Miriam Hopkins) with Carmichael, in defiance of Chamalis's diktat to Rutledge that she become his mistress. Old Atrocity also becomes the foil to Chamalis's henchman, Knuckles Jacoby, played with polished villainy by Brian Donlevy (an actor who, like Brennan, sometimes served as a character lead). Next to the dour Donlevy, Old Atrocity is positively radiant, seeming to reflect Brennan's joy in finally finding the role that would establish a persona. Brennan was also fortunate to have as a counterpart to his exuberant criminality Donald Meek, playing a love crazed sore loser, Sawbuck McTavish, whom Donlevy guns down. Meek, a fixture in films of the 1930s and 1940s, made notable appearances in *Stagecoach*, *You Can't Take It With You*, and *State Fair*. Usually playing characters with a docility that mirrored his last name, he breaks out in *Barbary Coast* with a creaky exuberance that rivals Brennan's conniving energy.

Barbary Coast was rather a mess when Howard Hawks took over direction of a film initially assigned by Sam Goldwyn to William Wyler. Hawks was famous—and sometimes notorious—for rewriting scripts on the set, inviting his actors to contribute lines. At the same time, he was loath to cede his authority, or to allow actors to take over a production. Meta Carpenter, Hawks's secretary and sometime script supervisor, vividly recalled how curt—even insulting—the director could be. "Shut up, Walter," Hawks barked after Brennan apparently offered one too many suggestions. Carpenter never forgot the sight of the deflated actor, who took a day to recover from this rebuff. But Walter was resilient and adaptable. He later told his granddaughter Claudia that he survived the exhausting work of filmmaking by taking catnaps during breaks. He could sleep anywhere on anything—even a coil of rope.

Brennan had signed on initially for about three days, but Hawks kept plugging him into scenes to liven up the action—which otherwise featured the tepid triangle of Edward G. Robinson, Miriam Hopkins, and Joel McCrea (who often got parts that Gary Cooper rejected). Hawks had another problem to deal with: Edward G. Robinson and screenwriters Ben Hecht and Charles McArthur were liberals lined up against conservatives Hawks, Hopkins, and McCrea. "The arguments on the set were appalling," Robinson wrote in his autobiography. "There was little socializing among us. There was a good deal of political freezing and occasional bursts of rage."

> Look at the time: F.D.R. was still in his first term, and anti-administration forces were calling the New Deal un-American, bolshevik, communist, and socialist. These inflammatory points of view were constantly being aired on the set, as indeed they were being aired all over Hollywood and all over the country.
>
> There was a desperate fear of innovation, of change. The definition of a Communist supplied to me over and over by members of the cast was: "What's yours is mine; what's mine is my own."
>
> The wealthy, the celebrated, the successful (and, realize, I could now count myself among them), saw F.D.R. as an enemy trying to change the fundamental fabric of the Republic. On the other hand, we saw him as a man trying to save capitalism by dealing with fundamental inequities in the nation.

Robinson does not mention Brennan's reaction to these fights. At this stage in his career Walter likely held his tongue, wanting to take advantage of the opportunities Hawks was in a position to offer him and which producer Sam Goldwyn supported. Brennan enjoyed imitating Goldwyn: "Valter, you are the greatest actor in the vorld." As Alvin Marill concludes in *Samuel Goldwyn Presents*, "the treacherous barfly easily walked off with the film and, in all likelihood, would have won an Academy Award had they been giving them out in 1935 for supporting roles." The *Hollywood Reporter*'s reaction is representative of the contemporary reviews: "The fellow who practically steals the picture is Walter Brennan. . . . He's worth the price of admission he's so exactly right in this comedy and characterization of the alley rat."

Howard Hawks later admitted that he was "quite worried" about Walter, "whether he was going to be funny," but he never worried after the first public screening, when the audience roared with laughter. *Film Daily* reported on September 12, 1935: "The enthusiasm of California preview audiences for the performance of Walter Brennan . . . has won a long-term contract for the actor from the producer." Brennan was under a Goldwyn contract for the next ten years and worked on forty films, many of them loan-outs to other studios. Like other actors who worked for Goldwyn, Brennan was fond of repeating famous Goldwynisms, such as, "in two words: im-possible," and "include me out." Then there was the time Goldwyn called studio head Darryl Zanuck. "Darryl," said Goldwyn, "we're both in trouble." "Both," replied Zanuck. "Why?" "Because you got an actor," said Goldwyn, "and I want him." Actors often questioned Brennan about why he worked for Goldwyn so long. "If he makes money on me, that's his business," Walter declared. "I get paid for what I do."

In "Minor Actor Steals Show in New Film," Rosalind Shaffer in the *Chicago Daily Tribune* (October 27, 1935) gave Brennan the star treatment, supplying a potted biography and listing several of his film credits, including his role as an "annoying old fellow" fixing the phone in *I'll Tell the World* (April 21, 1934), and as a snooper appearing in just one effective scene in *The Life of Vergie Winters* (June 22, 1934).

But if *Barbary Coast* was a triumph for Walter Brennan, it was less so for Howard Hawks. Although the film received several good reviews, subsequent critics have not considered it one of the director's best. As Peter John Dyer notes, for the first time Hawks was attacked for turning rawly authentic material inside out and producing an innocuous formula picture. No wonder the director kept augmenting the Old Atrocity part, realizing that Walter Brennan's performance practically saved the picture from becoming completely formulaic and bland.

In effect, Brennan had built a bit part into a starring role. Rather than being discovered as a star and given the studio publicity treatment, he had emerged organically from the dozens of roles, the seconds and minutes of film, that he had patiently and resourcefully put together as his resume. And he would continue to integrate himself into the filmic consciousness of millions by taking lesser parts, no matter how small—a bellboy/porter in *Gold Diggers of 1935* (March 15, 1935), a grandpa in

Metropolitan (November 8, 1935), a station agent in *Seven Keys to Baldpate* (December 13, 1935)—that made him a fixture in the public mind.

And then he was offered a film that he often called his favorite, a work that gave him the most intense gratification he had ever had on a movie set. It was rare for Walter Brennan to express more than satisfaction at work well done. But *Three Godfathers* (March 6, 1936) was something special. With its combination of an unusual director, Richard Boleslawski, and an ensemble of actors—Chester Morris, Lewis Stone, and Brennan— inspired by what has to be called a spiritual western, *Three Godfathers* told the story of how three outlaws come to care for and save the infant of a dying mother they find in the desert.

Much of the credit for the picture's religious intensity goes to Richard Boleslawski (1889–1937). Born in Poland, he studied with Stanislavsky at the Moscow Art Theater and appeared in some early Russian films. In 1918 he returned to Poland where, as an anti-Bolshevik, he served as a cavalry officer during Marshal Pilsudski's triumph over the Red army outside of Warsaw on the banks of the Vistula on August 21, 1920. Boleslawski filmed part of the battle for *The Miracle of the Vistula* (1920), using a semi-documentary approach he would later perfect in Hollywood. After working in Germany with important directors such as Carl Dreyer, Boleslawski made his way to New York and worked as an acting coach before settling in 1929 in Hollywood, where he became the foremost exponent of the Stanislavsky method long before other practitioner-teachers like Lee Strasberg and Stella Adler appeared on the scene. Indeed, Boleslawski's *Acting: The First Six Lessons* is one of the founding texts of what has become known as "the Method." Boleslawski had several notable successes in Hollywood, including *Storm at Daybreak* (1933), featuring a remarkable reconstruction of Franz Ferdinand's assassination, which precipitated World War I, and *Men in White* (1934), an exposé of deplorable conditions in modern hospitals. He made slighter films, comedies and melodramas, but as critic C. A. Lejeune noted, Boleslawski was especially adept at "emotional mechanics," the interplay between characters that is the hallmark of *Three Godfathers*.

Brennan had already appeared in three Boleslawski pictures: in 1934, *Fugitive Lovers* and *The Painted Veil* (Brennan's scenes were cut), and in 1935, *Metropolitan*. Although Brennan was not a Method actor—and indeed often said his work was based simply on observation and experience—he had the habits of a Stanislavskian, staying in character all day on the set and even remaining in character when he went home. Acting may have been a business he never cared to comment about—his advice to young actors was "Don't let them catch you acting"—but it was nonetheless a morally and esthetically serious business for him. His belief in naturalism, in playing characters as true to life as possible, would certainly have given him an honored chair at Lee Strasberg's Actors Studio and in Boleslawski's heart. Of Boleslawski, Brennan later said, "that man's death affected me as much as the death of my father."

Like Fritz Lang, a refugee from fascism who would soon see in Brennan an intriguing emotional depth and sensitivity, Boleslawski gave the actor a role that transcended the mannerisms and the tricks of the trade that character actors typically employed. Brennan's first close-up occurs at the beginning of *Three Godfathers*, when three horsemen appear against a dry, bleak, landscape and ride in to the distant sound of a male voice singing a soulful song. Brennan is reacting to Chester Morris's bitter dismissal of the "sanctimonious" town, New Jerusalem, where he ("Bob") grew up. Compared to the grudge-bearing Morris, Brennan ("Gus") seems dull witted—just a jolly criminal. "What do we care, so long as they got a bank," the nearly toothless Brennan laughs, "and they got money in it." Lewis Stone ("Doc"), the most thoughtful of the three, smiles with satisfaction while saying it is "almost a sacrilege" to rob the peaceful, unsuspecting town. As the robbers ride toward the town in a two-shot with Brennan and Stone (one of Walter's best Hollywood friends), Stone begins to cough, the first indication of the lung cancer that is killing him. Gus leans close to his friend Doc—who, we later learn, is not a medical doctor, but a doctor of philosophy who reads Schopenhauer. Gus says that maybe with the money they get in the robbery they can go to some place where Doc can take care of his cough. Gus expresses compassion and empathy—emotions not usually associated with criminals. Walking into a saloon, Gus canvasses a poker table and signals to the player who has been losing that he should bet against the man holding the weaker cards. When the loser becomes a winner, the loser asks Gus, "Why did you do it?" Gus walks away saying, "I guess I'm just a no good rat." In fact, his action represents some impulse to even the score. It is true he helps a man cheat at cards, but he also wants there to be more than one winner. But then this sentimental view of Gus is undercut when the cheater offers Gus a cut of the winnings before the rest goes in the bank. "Oh, I don't want any of your money," Gus smiles. "Put it all in the bank." Criminals capitalize on opportunity.

Gus and Doc—who form a kind of comedy team, with Doc as straight man—are invited to a Christmas social, during which Gus has a hard time wrenching off a chicken leg from the carcass on his plate, as he is obliged to pass several platters of food down the table. But as many viewers have noted, the highlight of this repast is Gus's confrontation with a platter of asparagus. He cuts the tops off every single spear on the plate, and then solemnly passes it along. Then he picks up each truncated spear and sucks it into his mouth the way a baby would consume spaghetti.

When Doc is shot in an otherwise successful bank robbery, he tells Gus there isn't time to dress his wounds, since they have to get to the next water hole (this part was shot in the Mojave Desert). Doc quotes *Macbeth*, "Blow wind come rack / I'll die with harness on my back," substituting "I'll" for "we'll." The illiterate Gus laughs and says, "Took the words right out of my mouth." By now, this unlikely trinity of desperadoes has begun to take on a symbolic significance—in effect, representing an inversion of the three wise men who attend to the baby Jesus. Only Bob, at this point, lacks fellow feeling for Doc, and for the town he has wreaked his revenge upon for rejecting him many years earlier. "I'll help you up, Doc," Gus says as the men mount their horses after resting from their escape from New Jerusalem. When they find a dead man (a suicide) in the desert, Bob just laughs at the tenderfoot with his fancy clothes and gun, while Gus insists that he tend to Doc's arm. "Should we bury him?" Gus asks. "What's the use?" Bob answers, observing that the buzzards are doing a good enough job. "Robert the perfect realist as usual," says Doc, shaking his head. It is a comment about a view of life that favors the strong, dispenses with the weak, and predicates everything on self-interest in this Depression-era western made during the rise of fascism. When they find what looks like a deserted covered wagon, Bob says maybe something was left behind that they can use. "Nice fellow Bob. Such a strict utilitarian," Doc observes wryly. "Sure, ain't he, though," Gus chortles, now taking on the classic role of the Shakespearean fool, following his king's lead. Bob takes one look in the wagon, says the woman inside "looks dead," and walks away. Doc examines her and says she is alive. "Get your canteen," he says to Gus. When the dying woman calls for her baby, the gentle Gus gives her the infant, saying politely, "Here she is, ma'am." She dies shortly afterwards. While Bob grouses about this turn of events, "Mother Gus" and Doc take care of the baby, diapering and feeding it. Bob would just as soon put the infant "out of its misery." It doesn't help Bob's case that the baby seems quite happy. "Water's short," Bob points out, and he announces he is pulling out alone in the morning because the baby will just delay them. Gus seems ready to fight over the child, but Doc calms them down, noting they have gotten along quite well so far. Then, over the campfire, as Doc reads his Schopenhauer, he makes explicit the parallel. "A long time ago," he says stretching out the words, "just about Christmas time too, three men sat around with a baby like this." "That so," Gus says. "Anybody I know?" Doc answers, "Nobody you knew Gus." Gus says, "Friends of yours, huh?" Doc responds, "No, not friends of mine either." These men are alone, more alone than they realize, in their separation from civilization and moral values. Stone, perhaps best known as Judge Hardy in the Andy Hardy pictures, gives an extraordinary performance that is Shakespearean in its grandeur and pathos.

The scene darkens, as night falls on this unlikely savior story. Then Bob discovers the horses are dead after drinking poisoned water, and he has to rejoin his gang on their return to New Jerusalem, their only source of water. "But I'll have nothin' to do with that kid," Bob hollers in his best Jimmy Cagney imitation. Reaction shots show Gus sending an almost imploring look at Bob, even though he tells Bob, "[N]obody asked you to."

The quality of this film is revealed in Chester Morris's line to Lewis Stone about getting rid of his books because they are "dead weight." Stone takes the books out of his saddlebag, looks at one of them, and says, "The only complaint I ever heard about your poetry, John Milton: 'too heavy.'" Not until *My Darling Clementine* will Brennan appear in another film that is so Shakespearean and biblical. When Gus gives his last drink of water to the dying Doc and asks for one of his books to remember him by, Gus says that someday he is going to get him some of that education, which must be a mighty fine thing. Doc answers where you start has nothing to do with where you end up or how. He recites Macbeth's "Tomorrow and tomorrow and tomorrow" speech, ending with the words about life being a tale told by an idiot signifying nothing. As Bob and Gus walk away in the distance, a shot is heard, telling them Doc has taken his own life. This bleak moment is mitigated only by the gradual awakening of Bob's humanity. Even though Gus will die before they get to New Jerusalem, he keeps Bob going, refusing to relinquish the link with life he has made holding the infant in his arms. In spite of himself, Bob, who has been prepared to leave the baby behind, shoots a rattlesnake that endangers the infant, and, like Saul on the road to Damascus, finally has his conversion experience and accepts his mission to save the baby— which he does.

Hollywood could not seem to let this story alone. William Wyler filmed it first as *Hell's Heroes* (1929), and then John Ford released his own version, *Three Godfathers*, in 1948. Neither Wyler nor Ford captures the same mixture of crudity and erudition, of immoral and moral, that is the distinguishing feature of Boleslawski's film. In Wyler's adaptation, the overbearing Charles Bickford diminishes the interplay between his character and the other two criminals, and thus destroys the ensemble Boleslawski so carefully constructed. In Ford's rendition not only does Wayne dominate the story, his character's rough edges are so softened and sentimentalized that his care for the baby is hardly a dramatic development. Brennan, a man of deep religious conviction, believed in the power of redemption, so it is not surprising that he esteemed *Three Godfathers* so highly. The film's message has seemed heavy-handed to some viewers—which is perhaps why Ford injected so much humor into his remake—but the sensitive performances of the principal actors and the mise-en-scène of Boleslawski's rendering are perfect.

In 1959, Chester Morris was one of several actors invited to celebrate Walter Brennan's thirty-five years in Hollywood at a Hollywood Chamber of Commerce luncheon. Morris could not attend but sent this message: "I have made 80 pictures since 1928 and of all of them, the one we made together; '3 Godfathers', will ever remain my favorite. Please tell him this for me and give him a big kiss on both cheeks. A wonderful guy!" Nearly ten years later Walter recalled, "[W]e were very happy, the three of us. We had a lot of fun."

Three Godfathers gives Brennan more screen time than he enjoyed in any previous film, and he had an opportunity to act his first important death scene—which he does with great simplicity. Eschewing all histrionics, he offers up a simple prayer, remembered from his childhood, for the protection of the child. And then he walks, utterly exhausted, out into the desert and to his death, leaving behind the stolen money, the child, and Doc's last will, bestowing everything on Bob. Brennan would have more showy, award-winning roles, but none that outshines the quiet dignity of this outlaw, humbled to the point of annihilation, yet affirming the human spirit that will prevail, against all odds, during Bob's dogged trek with the baby to New Jerusalem, where he drops dead.

Critics were beginning to pay attention, noting that the picture marked the "further development of Walter Brennan in the superb old-timer cowboy character." The "ease with which he cleans up in all departments of this feature is easily the most outstanding acting contribution," one reviewer asserted. Since both Lewis Stone and Chester Morris are brilliant as well, why Brennan was the standout requires some explanation. He is the focal point, the go-between in the dialogue between Stone and Morris. Brennan's Gus is partial to Doc and yet respects Bob. Gus functions as a sort of mediator—almost as a broker—whose openness to experience gives him an appeal that neither Doc nor Bob can rival.

During this period, as Brennan's roles became more important, he acquired the services of a stand-in. Years later, he recalled learning from his first stand-in, Dick Dickinson, about lighting and blocking. An alert stand-in observes everything on the set, functioning sometimes as an acting coach. "Watch out," Dickinson warned Brennan. "The dame can walk right in and cut you to pieces if you don't back up an inch or two as you deliver the line."

At this point, Brennan, under contract to Samuel Goldwyn, had certainly earned larger parts, but Goldwyn, an independent, could not generate pictures at the rate of major studios such as MGM, which under Joseph L. Mankiewicz had produced *Three Godfathers*. So Brennan got tucked into Goldwyn's pictures and loan outs to other studios. Like Old Atrocity, Brennan's characters dating from this period virtually ferry stars to their destinations. In *These Three* (March 18, 1936), he jauntily delivers Miriam Hopkins and Merle Oberon in a taxi to the site of their dilapidated school, where they encounter Joel McCrea, their love interest. In *The Moon's Our Home* (April 10, 1936), a Paramount production, Brennan plays a sublimely deaf sleigh driver and justice of the peace who marries Henry Fonda (an adventure writer) and Margaret Sullavan (a movie star). Brennan has plenty of competition and support from Beulah Bondi, who from an early age specialized in playing to perfection old ladies that matched Brennan's meticulously impersonated old men. She was "perhaps the most consummate of all character players," in James Robert Parrish's estimation. Just as significant in *The Moon's Our Home* is Margaret Hamilton, best known as the Wicked Witch of the West, but also remembered for her accomplished performances of acerbic characters.

Brennan's best small role is in Fritz Lang's *Fury* (May 29, 1936), another MGM production. Brennan plays "Bugs" Meyers, a deputy who locks up Joe Wilson (Spencer Tracy), falsely accused of murder, and is almost lynched. Brennan's portrayal goes way beyond the scope of what is actually in the film's script. He plays a new modern type, an ordinary man suddenly elevated to importance because he plays a small but highly visible part in a widely publicized crime story. In short scenes, Bugs's ego expands as he becomes recognized as an "authority" on what happened. Brennan's conception of the character is profoundly original. Bugs becomes a creation of publicity—and, suddenly, a figure of significance to himself—and his enjoyment of his new, expanded role, is palpable in the joy that suffuses Bugs's face with the excitement of being—or rather act-ing like—he is in the know.

Brennan outdoes other stalwart character actors such as Walter Abel, who is good as a district attorney full of himself, and Bruce Cabot, who delivers a satisfactory performance as the town bully. During his moment of glory, Bugs remains Bugs, diffidently doling out his inside informa-tion, as he gradually assumes an air of authority. Brennan is so good in *Fury* that it is surprising Lang did not find more scenes for him. In fact, Lang wanted to do more with the character, but Brennan became ill, and his courtroom scenes were transferred to George Chandler, who portrays Milton Johnson. When Lang had an opportunity to cast Bren-nan again, he did so, making Brennan the surprising choice to portray a Czech professor in *Hangmen Also Die!* Lang had his pick of émigré actors used to playing Old World Europeans on the screen, but he was proud of his insistence on choosing Brennan for the part.

When Spencer Tracy dropped out as the lead in *Come and Get It*, Howard Hawks paired veteran character actor Edward Arnold, playing Barney Glasgow, with Brennan—this time making Brennan, as Swan Bostrum, part of a triangle involving Lotta Morgan (Frances Farmer), a dancehall chanteuse. Barney is smitten with Lotta, but then drops her when he decides to marry his boss's daughter in order to further his am-bition to be become a timber tycoon. Swan, a simple Swede who lacks Barney's drive, ends up marrying Lotta and fathering a daughter, also named Lotta (and also played superbly by Farmer). Naturally, Barney becomes infatuated with the second Lotta when he makes a reunion visit to Swan, now a widower, who has remained in the old timber camp town in which the two men started out. In the end, Barney realizes that he is old and cannot compete with his son (Joel McCrea), who is in love with the younger Lotta.

Farmer, in her first major role, was understandably nervous, and at one point seemed unable to do a scene. The wording was not right, and she was having trouble with her lines in a scene with Brennan. Fortu-nately, she had a director specialized in making sure his actors said their lines in a way that suited their delivery. After conferring with Hawks and Brennan, Farmer worked out a solution that satisfied all of them. Wal-ter confided to his son that he did not like Farmer. She never took care of herself. "She would come to work and smell like she hadn't taken a bath." Walter told his son.

The bulky Arnold was a somewhat odd choice for the lead, but his character transitions from lumberman/foreman to timber tycoon in a way that suited the actor, who often played burley corporate types and government office holders. Oddly, neither James Robert Parrish's nor Twomey and McClure's books about character actors even mention *Come and Get It* in the paragraphs they devote to Arnold, who so often played "two-faced smoothies or bombastic bosses," to use critic Manny Farber's memorable phrase. Beginning with *Come and Get It*, Arnold perfected roles as the "large and seemingly good natured" fellow who turned out to have a sinister side. As David Thomson notes, this aspect of Arnold's style is best developed in films such as *Mr. Smith Goes to Washington* (1939) and *Meet John Doe* (1941), where as the fascist newspaper tycoon D. B. Norton, Arnold again acts as a foil to Brennan. Like Brennan, Arnold gets to explore his range in *Come and Get It*, playing a character who is smooth and overblown, but who cannot cope with aging as his pal Swan does. *Come and Get It* is one of those rare films in which Brennan got to age in his part, gaining in wisdom.

Anyone coming from a fresh viewing of *Barbary Coast* will notice that Walter Brennan cleans up very well. No trace of Old Atrocity is visible in one of *Come and Get It*'s first scenes, in which the wiry, acrobatic Swede leaps into Barney's arms, wrapping his thighs around the rotund Arnold's midsection as though about to take his buddy out for a ride. For once, Brennan plays a man near to his own age with his six-foot-one frame—no stooping over or cringing; no hopping about with a limp. And his Swedish accent sounds authentic and charming. As usual, Walter had done his research and insisted on working with a dialogue coach. But to his ear, the Swedes he heard talk each seemed to have a distinctive pronunciation. So rather than trying for a literal Swedish accent, Walter went for a more generalized singsong that movie viewers already associated with on-screen Swedes. Characteristically, Walter knew what would *play*.

If Swan is a simple soul, he is also a sensitive man. As Swan grows older, he recognizes that Barney's ambition has made him a bitter man. As a result, Brennan's portrayal of Swan's sweetness is all the more appealing. The role had a certain poignancy for Walter, since he based his reading of Swan on his father, who died during the production of *Come and Get It*. Ruth worried about her mother-in-law's reaction to the film, because she believed that her husband had so perfectly captured his father. Walter never said much to those outside his family about William Brennan, but even in the few fugitive comments Walter did make, it was clear that he thought his father lacked a certain drive. Like William Brennan, Swan is a diligent worker but no match for the dynamic Barney.

When Walter's mother saw *Come and Get It*, to her it seemed as though her husband, not her son, was on the screen.

Since bringing his parents to Pasadena and building a home for them, Walter had watched his father go blind but remain active, operating an elevator for an engineering firm and continuing to work in his home workshop, making things by touch. Mike remembered his grandfather being quite stubborn. William would not listen to Walter when his son kept telling him he should not sell his patents. Of his grandmother, Mike had nothing much to say—although by the look on his face when he mentioned her, I'd say this woman he described as "ordinary" perhaps wanted to be treated as something special. William died of cancer, diagnosed in a hospital after it was too late for treatment. Mike remembered accompanying his father to see William on his deathbed. William peered out of the corner of one eye and said to his son, "Do you still have your red hair, Walter?"

William Brennan did not live to see his son, now a remarkable transformative actor, win his first Academy Award, for *Come and Get It*, the first time the award for supporting actor was given. Edward Arnold's superb performance of a less than sympathetic character was not even recognized with a nomination. Walter said he was surprised at receiving the award and had not planned to attend the ceremony, but his studio insisted, giving him evening clothes when he said he did not have a dress suit. As a result, he remembered, "I stepped up to receive that unexpected Oscar in tux Number 34 from the Western Costume Company."

Arnold and Brennan also starred in the one-hour Lux Radio Theatre adaptation of *Come and Get It*, broadcast on November 15, 1937, in which much of Arnold's harder-edged character is softened, while Brennan's Swan loses the zesty and then troubled qualities that the actor was so good at showing on-screen. In a brief conversation with the actors after their performance, Walter stayed in character as Swan, delighting the studio audience with his Swedish accented repartee.

The Academy Award set a pattern for Brennan, who had perfected a persona that could be crusty, ornery, and outspoken, but also charming, comical, and always in the service of the hero as companion, conscience, and counselor. Brennan's Swan has a sweet nature, and the sentimental side of this "crazy Swede," as Arnold calls him in the film, endeared itself to audiences and Academy voters, many of whom as extras and bit players had watched Brennan advance year-by-year in their profession. Brennan did not escape criticism for what some viewers consider overacting, or as *Variety* (November 18, 1936) put it, "exerting too much pressure now and then." *Come and Get It* still has its enthusiasts, but others second Donald C. Willis's verdict in *The Films of Howard Hawks* that Brennan is "too cute as the Swede."

Brennan seems more authentic in *Banjo on My Knee* (December 11, 1936). He plays Joel McCrea's father, a wizened old river denizen and musician who goes off in search of his son, who is himself looking for his estranged wife (Barbara Stanwyck). Brennan dominates scene after scene. He becomes iconic, the very spirit of the fiercely independent and rugged river people. William Faulkner was assigned this picture, and though he was taken off it early, the spirit of the novelist's country people seems to suffuse Brennan's performance. He plays a character thirty years older than his actual age—not through makeup or mannerisms, so much as with his reedy voice, semi-toothless grin, and adroitly mussed and thinning hair, all of which projects an age-old and indomitable presence. When Brennan gets to Memphis, just north of Faulkner's Jefferson, Mississippi, he becomes a hit performer after a club owner discovers him. Brennan's performance on banjo, harmonica, drums, and various other instruments—while also singing the "Saint Louis Blues"—is pure vaudeville, which is to say, pure Walter Brennan. And it's worth noting that the scene is also a ruse, since Brennan played no instruments; six musicians actually produced the sound that seems to be coming out of his nimble fingers.

That Brennan became his character is evident in a story Buddy Ebsen liked to tell. Ebsen, who does a wonderful dance routine in *Banjo on My Knee*, and decades later would star with Brennan in *The One and Only, Genuine, Original Family Band*, remembered the day the picture wrapped. "I'll see you at the preview," Buddy said to Walter. "You will," Walter said, "but you won't know me." A puzzled Ebsen asked, "What do you mean?" Brennan said, "You'll see." At the preview, a "nondescript young man" approached Ebsen, who expected another autograph seeker. But this one said, "How are you?" Ebsen asked, "You know me?" Brennan answered, "I'm Walter Brennan."

Like *Barbary Coast*, *Banjo on My Knee*, was almost sabotaged by censors, and like Samuel Goldwyn, Darryl Zanuck had to rescue his picture from the petty moralism of the Breen office. Fox receive an eight-page letter objecting to "unacceptable drinking and drunkenness throughout," and to what the censor saw as continual sexual innuendos. On August 24, 1936, an exasperated Zanuck had a letter hand delivered to Joseph Breen. The letter began: "I can only come to the conclusion that someone in your office is of the opinion that we are trying to produce a picture to be shown in brothels. Your reader has injected smut and sex where none was ever intended." And to the censor's negative assessment of Walter Brennan's character, Newt, whom the censor deplored as a drunk in an unseemly hurry to have his son bed his new bride, Zanuck countered that Newt "is not interested in sex; he is not a drunk character; he is merely a poor, old backwoods-man who longs for children, who longs for an heir to carry on his name, because all of his other sons have been killed in the river." And as to drinking, the characters "will only drink when the story demands that they do—not promiscuously as I can imagine nothing more disgusting that a picture of drunks." Zanuck's letter proved effective. Breen backed down, saying the letter "covers our concern on this particular point." Zanuck's representatives conferred with the Breen office and agreed to make a few minor modifications, but the picture survived intact— fortunately, since it contains one of Brennan's greatest performances. *Film Daily* (December 1, 1936) called Brennan a standout, and the *Hollywood Reporter* (December 1, 1936) was even more effusive:

> The hit of the picture is unquestionably Walter Brennan as Newt Holley. It's one of those performances that come up once in a long time and one that sends the audience shouting praises for the artist. Brennan takes an exceedingly difficult part, far from being actor-proof, and fashions it into one of the best pieces of acting see on the screen in some time, and one that will earn him a producer search for material to give him feature billing in the future.

Nothing much changed in Walter Brennan's domestic life even after he won his Academy Award and received rave reviews for both *Come and Get It* and *Banjo on My Knee*. He remembered hurrying home with his gold statuette, strutting in his borrowed tuxedo, and asking his wife how it felt to be married to an Academy Award winner. Ruth gave him a look and said, "Turn out the lights and go to bed. I lived with you when you didn't have a dime." His rare moment of bragging caught her off guard, and he had never spoke of stardom. It all seemed just work to him—or so Ruth supposed. Years later, she admitted she had not taken in the honor bestowed on her husband.

Sam Goldwyn, who had Brennan under contract at that time, was not much more enthusiastic. No congratulatory telegram, no party—just a one-sentence acknowledgment when Brennan bumped into him: "Hey, Walter, that's a pretty nice thing you did winning that." In retrospect,

Brennan had to laugh: "Can you imagine! The academy award and he acted like it was a prize in a box of crackerjacks." Actually, this was a typical Goldwyn ploy. He always worried that actors under contract would begin making demands after they became successful. When David Niven was assigned his first role on the Goldwyn lot, he arrived to find another young hopeful, Dana Andrews, dressed in the same outfit that Niven was to wear. When Niven asked what was going on, the perplexed Andrews could only say that Goldwyn had directed him to show up on set in the clothes provided for him. Goldwyn later confessed that he was sending a message to Niven: "You can be replaced!"

On the Goldwyn lot Walter still liked to talk to everybody, including the floor sweeper. Walter asked him what he was thinking about when he swept. Nothing, the man said. But when Brennan said he might play a worker like the sweeper, the man said, "Well, I'm thinking I'm damn lucky to have a job because I know a lot of fellows who wish they had a job now. Most people don't realize when they're well off." Walter liked to sit around the set, gabbing with the gaffer, grips, and prop men.

What did change is that Walter Brennan became the subject of personality profiles and fan magazine articles. Typical is Jeanne de Kolty's *Silver Screen* piece (August 1937), which reprised Brennan's early career:

[H]e is happy and grateful for his success, but not one bit surprised. He has plugged along year after year, in the face of discouragement and disappointment, always knowing that some day the break would come. He has tremendous faith in himself. Perhaps his dogged determination can be traced to his New England ancestry. His story is that of the plodder who refused to give up under any conditions.

Home life was simple and quiet in a Mexican farmhouse and the land surrounding it in the San Fernando Valley, complete with walnut trees, roses, horse corrals, and barns. On this ranch the Brennans cared for two horses, three cows, a dog, and a cat. The family liked to ride out to the desert and cook breakfast over a campfire. Walter seemed to find the drives soothing. He suffered from an ailment Mike called "nervous indigestion." Someone else might say Walter had a case of nerves. In effect, whatever Walter suffered, it was stress related. He had come a long way from his beginnings, and those beans cooked in the basement of his Swampscott home. In December 1937, he made a return trip to Swampscott, the first time he had returned home since leaving in 1920.

By this time, Walter Brennan had perfected what he called the "old man with a heart of gold." Old coot might be a better term, because his characters were usually pretty shabby, if ultimately redeemable. One of his studio biographies reported that he had a collection of ninety hats to pick from when playing old timers. Brennan relied on his own costumery as a way to mold characters that otherwise lacked individuality. Inevitably, owing to the quality of the script and direction, some of these characters were clichés, like Ote O'Leary ("Oats") in *She's Dangerous* (January 24, 1937), a cook and all-around handy man working for Dr. Scott Logan (Walter Pidgeon). Oats's routine is disrupted when the doctor takes in a woman (Tala Birell), a fugitive from justice. She is actually innocent, but she is suspect in Oats's eyes simply because she is a woman who cleans up the kitchen and interferes, as all women do, in a man's "method of doing things," Oats tells her. But in the end he stands by her, even dresses up as a sign of respect when she is about to be executed. She is proven innocent at the last moment, when the real murderer (Cesar Romero) is tricked into a confession. On November 19, after shooting for eighteen days, this Universal picture came in five thousand dollars under its $150,000 budget.

When Love Is Young (March 28, 1937) softens the Brennan image into Uncle Hugo, who is there mainly as a sentimental source of support for the heroine, played by Virginia Bruce, as an aspiring singer leaving her hometown to make good in New York. At this point Brennan's salary was $600 a week for a total of $2,500. Hal Mohr, better known as a cinematographer, was directing his first full-length film for Universal and proceeded at a very slow, deliberate pace, completing thirty-nine days of shooting on February 5, 1937, and bringing in the project at $254,000—$54,000 more than the original budget.

In *Wild and Wooly* (July 19, 1937), Brennan is restored to his cantankerousness as Gramp, a retired town sheriff who provides some relief from the obstreperous Jane Withers, who perfected the role of a Depression-era tomboy spending her time straightening out the affairs of her world. In this case, she has to contend with her grandfather Hercules (Brennan), the town's former sheriff, and his feud with Edward Ralston (Berton Churchill). After going on a drunk, Hercules redeems himself by capturing a gang of bank robbers and reconciling with Ralston.

Brennan had a starring role in *The Affairs of Cappy Ricks* (May 24), a Republic Pictures programmer. The studio specialized in turning a profit on B pictures and offered Brennan the opportunity to play character leads, dominating later pictures such as *Brimstone* and *The Showdown*. Working conditions were austere but pleasant and efficient, allowing Brennan to go about his business without fuss or interference. Its only A-list star would be John Wayne, although in 1937 he was still two years away from his breakout role in *Stagecoach*.

The Affairs of Cappy Ricks is a slight story. As a crusty old sea captain, Brennan is opposed to his family's efforts to modernize his ships and to merge with his arch competitor. He deceives them into taking a voyage that strands them on an island, where he hopes to make his relatives come to their senses. The *Daily Variety* reviewer blamed Brennan for not being "strong enough to pull the piece through." But it is surely poor writing that dooms this contrivance. Republic was much better at action pictures that appealed to rural audiences, notes film historian Ronald Davis. The neat editing and straightforward plot lines of the studio's best pictures perfectly suited Brennan's own sensibility.

A much better role materialized in Cecil B. DeMille's *The Buccaneer* (February 4, 1938), one of his extravaganzas featuring a huge cast and impressive battle scenes. Brennan is Ezra Peavey, a scout attached to Andrew Jackson during the War of 1812. To watch Brennan, done up in buckskin, with his face scrunched up during society scenes set in New Orleans is the most enjoyable part of this historical drama in which Fredric March overacts as Jean Lafitte. Peavey, the battle hardened veteran, follows Jackson (Hugh Southern) everywhere, like a bodyguard sniffing out trouble among the high society types. Peavey is thoroughly unimpressed with these rich folk, and Brennan plays him as the epitome of the common man, assured of his own rights and dignity and the very emblem of what the war for independence and the subsequent war with Britain was all about.

According to Brennan, DeMille, who could be quite autocratic and hard on actors, treated him "royally." May Robson, who worked with Walter on *You Can't Buy Everything* (1934) and *The Adventures of Tom Sawyer* (February 11, 1938) had told him, "Oh, [DeMille will] swear at you. He'll treat you miserably. He'll do everything." Walter told her, "He'll only do it once, May." Walter enjoyed the work. His verdict on DeMille: "a kind of ham but he made good pictures, good, clean, pictures." Whenever DeMille saw Walter, he would ask, "How's Mr. Peavey today?" Brennan became quite fond of the director. "He was a gentleman," Walter concluded. His pay rate now reflected the demand for his talents. For *The Buccaneer*, Brennan was paid $1800 on execution of an agreement, with a guarantee of $2,516,67 for his work.

In David O. Selznick's charming color film, *The Adventures of Tom Sawyer*, Brennan plays Muff Potter, an old sot wrongly accused of murdering the town's doctor. In fact, the true villain is Injun Joe, played by Victor Jory, an actor Walter admired—especially in the graveyard scene they did together, in which Jory knocks Brennan out and puts a knife—the murder weapon—in Brennan's hand. Although Brennan plays Muff well, the character as written is mainly a collection of reaction shots, emphasizing Muff's bewilderment that he should be accused of a crime he cannot remember committing. Unlike Ezra Peavey, Muff is given no opportunity to thrust himself into the main action as a kind of commentator as well as participant. Muff is by definition a victim. The better character roles go to May Robson, as the strict Miss Polly, and Donald Meek, as a punctilious Sunday school superintendent. It is a pity these superb performers do not have an opportunity to interact with Brennan.

Brennan and Robson do have scenes together in *The Texans* (August 12, 1938), a Randolph Scott western set in Reconstruction era Texas. Brennan is Chuckawalla, a Mexican War veteran who is now a retainer for Granna (Robson), who owns a large ranch with ten thousand cattle that Kirk Jordan (Scott) wants to drive to Abilene. Kirk's love interest, Granna's daughter Ivy (Joan Bennett), wants to drive the herd to Mexico in a harebrained scheme to unite with the Mexicans against the United States that is fomented by her fiancé, Alan Sanford (Robert Cummings). Most of the interest comes in watching the cattle herded through rivers, windstorms, snowfalls, and sandstorms. The poor script gives Brennan very little to do except act the loyal sidekick, spouting lines such as "Women are like horses. Some take to rawhide, and some don't"—a reference to Ivy's stubborn resistance to Kirk's sensible plans. Why the screenwriters did not capitalize on the Robson-Brennan duo, when there is an obvious opportunity to exploit their strong, quick sensibilities in a master and servant comic interplay, is mystifying. Brennan scorned such films because they were so unrealistic. He looks grimy enough in his role, but Scott's hair is never mussed, and his buckskin is pristine—not to mention Joan Bennett's makeup, which, thanks to Max Factor, never fades. Still, for Walter, work on the film reflected an increase in his pay: $2100 payable on execution of agreement, and $700 per week with a guaranteed total of $2800. Another bonus came from reviewers, who still found him refreshing in another otherwise trite film.

The Cowboy and the Lady (November 17, 1938) is another picture that squanders Brennan's talents. He appears as part of a backup crew for

Gary Cooper, courting Merle Oberon, who is—no surprise—the lady. This film is a jejune remake of earlier Westerns that try to have their fun with an aw-shucks cowboy holding his own in high society. "A terrible picture," was all Brennan had to say about it later on, when reminiscing about his career. His fondest memory of this film was the photograph Cooper gave him on the set, a memento that Walter treasured in part because of its inscription: "To Walter, Two guys sitting on a fence thinking of the good old days, doing extra work, Gary. 1925, 1938." Brennan and Cooper did have some fun on the picture. When Fuzzy Knight, playing a Cooper sidekick in the picture, showed up drunk on the set, Cooper said, "I'm going to screw him up good since he screwed us up." So Cooper changed some of the lines around, and Fuzzy got even fuzzier.

Then Brennan finally was awarded a bravura role, winning his second Academy Award for his Technicolor performance as Peter Goodwin in *Kentucky* (December 30, 1938). Goodwin is an unreconstructed Confederate who can never forget that a Unionist killed his father. Loretta Young and Richard Greene are the ostensible stars of this horse opera, but as the *Newsweek* reviewer put it, the romance is a "synthetic affair." Young's biographer, Bernard F. Dick, observes that the horses—followed by Brennan—are the main attraction. Dick is hard on the Academy Award winner: "And for all the accolades heaped on Walter Brennan for his portrayal of Peter, he gave a performance in one key, in a voice so petulant that he would have been a prime candidate for anger management classes if they had existed in 1938." To put it another way, what worked for Brennan as a character actor does not play quite so well when he is the virtual star of the picture. Although Brennan would give much subtler performances in later films, it is likely that Academy voters were impressed with his let-out-all-the-stops rendition of a lost cause survivor, a type often sentimentalized in Hollywood films.

In this case, the lost cause is a horse. No one believes he will win the Derby except for the testy Goodwin, who triumphs in the end even as his heart gives out, so that in winning he loses his life. This poignant ending, perhaps more than anything else about Brennan's performance, won the actor his prize. If the film has not worn well, in part that is because it does not have the rich repertoire of character actors who often endow slight and sentimental films with a depth of personality and interest they otherwise lack.

The reviews of *Kentucky* boosted Brennan to an even higher level in the Hollywood echelon. The *Hollywood Reporter* (December 15) summed up the sentiment of the time: "Walter Brennan, who has already carved a large niche for himself in the movie hall of fame, has himself a really grand and glorious triumph as a Kentucky gentleman and horse breeder. A real persona and thoroughly lovable one, he wraps up the picture neatly with his capable acting and beautiful characterization and is a tribute to the South. And Hollywood gossip columnist Louella Parsons did not mind campaigning for Brennan, calling his performance a "standout" that "might well earn him an Academy Award."

More personality profiles followed Brennan's *Kentucky* triumph. Most noted that off-screen, the forty-two-year-old actor did not resemble his disheveled characters. Indeed, Brennan showed up for one interview in a natty "dark green gabardine shirt, paisley scarf, and plaid sports jacket." His steel rimmed glasses, white and gold, made him look like "an old fashioned school principal." He enjoyed his anonymity and seemed contented that he was "not a glamor boy" who got the girl. He was also an intensely private man who wanted to lose himself in the makeup and the clothing of his roles, so that no one became unduly interested in his life outside the movies. The second Academy Award, Brennan told a reporter, could not match the thrill of the first one—or even of his breakthrough role in *Barbary Coast*. "I've been through so many disappointments I guess I don't get nervous and excited any more." Of course, the award pleased him when he thought of those long years when he "waited for the phone to ring and then shook so when it rang for fear it wasn't a job. 'I couldn't answer it,'" he confessed. Now he was working nonstop.

While Walter was at work, Ruth took care of business. When Walter's mother ran out of money, his brother Irvin, deeply in debt, on February 19, 1939 wrote not to Walter, but to Ruth:

> I have not written to you before about something you should know because Mother has forbidden me to mention it. Some of the Flanagan pride. It concerns my application for a pension for her.
>
> You are probably unaware that she has practically no money left. Preliminary inquires I have made disclose the fact that if an application is made the two sons will be called on the carpet to show why they are not supporting their mother according to the law. I should hate that kind of publicity but I may have to risk it soon as these things take time . . . . I wish you would drop me a note about this if you care to and don't above all let her know that I spilled the beans.

Ruth wrote a curt reply, saying, "Walter has already informed Mother that she may have all the money she needs to live on." This letter is the only family correspondence in the Walter Brennan papers at the National Cowboy & Western Heritage Museum. Ruth was Walter's buffer, and she made sure that nothing got between her husband and his work. Irvin's letter also goes a long way in explaining why his younger brother did not want to deal with him directly. Irvin's letter could be interpreted as a kind of shakedown, an implicit warning that Walter better take care of their mother, or else. Asked about Irvin, Mike Brennan said, "He pulled some shenanigans. And he was a womanizer." Andy was on the set of one of father's pictures when a telegram from Irvin arrived. He had shot himself in the leg. Surgeons wanted to amputate the leg, and Irvin was asking Walter to give his permission. To Walter, it seemed like a suspicious setup, and he could see lawsuits resulting from his involvement in his brother's troubles. He did not answer the telegram. Mike can't remember seeing Irvin more than one or two times. "If I saw him today, I wouldn't know him." Irvin had two children, but Mike has no idea what happened to them. Walter shunned his brother as if Irwin were contaminated with a disease.

When not working, which usually meant just a few days between pictures, Walter liked to drive down to the Santa Monica beach at the end of Pico Boulevard. "He'd get down in the water and have fun with us kids," Mike remembered. Walter also liked to relax on his two-acre farm, which had a few Herefords. All his children were members of the 4-H club. As his son Andy later wrote, "It was the picture business that made a devout westerner" out of his father. He wanted it noticed that he was a man of the land who really had nothing much to do with the town where he worked. As one admiring journalist put it: "The Brennans are the direct answer to the oft-repeated question, 'Are there ANY normal people in Hollywood.'"

A reporter spending an afternoon in the Brennan's San Fernando home sat in an inner veranda, its walls "hung with gay sombreros, dried maze, and long strings of red peppers. A huge native water jar hung from a low branch of the central tree. Coal glowed in the barbecue pit where a huge chunk of beef was simmering and inside the house Mrs. Brennan was showing the cook how to make hot barbecue sauce." Outside near an old horse barn and corral, the three Brennan children were sitting on the fence of a corral containing three snorting horses. They were listening to Bill Steele, a movie cowboy and an old crony of their father's, tell them tall tales of the West—although he did not mention the good old days when their father, still looking for movie work as an extra, had to borrow two dollars from his old crony.

All the Brennans had taken up photography. In fact, Walter had just returned from a 155-mile trip to photograph desert wildflowers blooming in response to winter rains. To the reporter, Brennan looked like a country doctor. Instead of the stooped sodbuster sort of characters he played, he stood erect at just over six feet, wearing glasses that gave him a studious look. Naturally gregarious, Walter nevertheless disliked parties and claimed never to have frequented such establishments as the Trocadero and the Cocoanut Grove. He did not go near hot spots. He didn't even own a tuxedo. He could afford a new luxury car but drove an older model. He called Hollywood "a city of $100 Millionaires."

Even as Walter's salary increased, he retained a rigid control over family finances—and over his children. His oldest child, Mike, was now in high school and wanted spending money. He was given no allowance; instead Walter put him to work on various odd jobs, and Mike had a milk route. Walter was quite proud of the sense of responsibility he instilled in his children: "I remember Andy borrowing $130 from me to buy an old car when he graduated from high school. He was to pay back $10 a week from his earnings, and he never went out on a weekend until that $10 was paid. He tried to slip through a couple of times, but I held him to it. And I don't think he's any the worse for it today."

Brennan did not see his sons as movie material. Andy, seventeen, and Mike, fifteen, seemed tied to the land. Walter joked about them as "two clunks" tending horses and cows of their own. "Andy got a load of alfalfa for his cows from his thoughtful father," wrote Lucie Neville in a June 4, 1939, *Washington Post* profile titled "He works Anywhere To Earn an Honest Academy Award." But Walter thought that his daughter, Ruth, fourteen, did seem talented enough to pursue an acting career. Brennan did not expect or want his sons to work in Hollywood. It was never a place he felt at home. He brought his lunch to work and came home from work at the end of the day. In fact, the studio world often annoyed him. While he almost always got along well with his fellow actors, he hated the overbearing studio brass and their assistants, who gave extras a hard time—which is why he belonged to a union, despite his conservative politics. But Walter Brennan was hardly a typical union man. Mike remembered an incident that occurred on a very cold day when the heaters used to warm the set were not turned on. The union man who was supposed to turn on the equipment had not shown up, and Walter proceeded to push the button to warm up cast and crew. When the union man showed up, he asked, "Who turned this on?" Walter answered, "I did." "Why," the man wanted to know. "Look here," Walter said, "you're paid to be here on time and by God you better be here."

To say that Ruth Brennan was at the center of her husband's life is no understatement. He never disparaged her supporting role, never spoke like some men do of "the wife," as if referring to a possession, even an encumbrance. Marriage was not a joking matter to Walter, ever. His son Andy remembers his father's response to a dirty joke about an actress. Walter didn't laugh, but instead paused and said, "My wife is the most wonderful woman in the world. When things were really rough and I was out of work—and at times disappointed but never discouraged—there was never a word of criticism. She'd say, 'Try again tomorrow.' I'm so lucky that I found someone like her."

Before becoming Sam Goldwyn's prized possession—and during a decade and more of taking roles that put him out there to be seen and perhaps noticed—Brennan did play characters who disparaged women. But what happened when he was offered the plum role of Jeeter Lester in John Ford's production of *Tobacco Road* (March 7, 1941) is revealing. Erskine Caldwell's best-selling novel had been a huge hit when it was adapted for the Broadway stage, and now the prestigious director was casting the film version with several actors—including Ward Bond, Gene Tierney, and Dana Andrews—whose careers would benefit from Ford's attention. In *Tobacco Road*, Jeeter is the shiftless family patriarch. Not only does he lack ambition, his jokes, to Walter Brennan, seemed offensive. Ada, Jeeter's wife, is demeaned just for laughs when he says she "never spoke a word to me for our first ten years we was married. Heh! Them was the happiest ten years of my life."

Sam Goldwyn had a long-standing business partnership with Twentieth Century-Fox, the studio making *Tobacco Road*. As a contract player, Walter had to do what he was told. The system usually suited him. He was never one to gripe about servitude; indeed, he always seemed happy to serve. He might imitate the autocratic Sam Goldwyn, calling up Gary Cooper and convincingly fire the studio's star in Goldwyn's voice. But Walter also told a reporter, "Sam was class. We used to consider the Goldwyn studio the country club of the motion picture industry. He did nothing cheap. Everything was first class. So I have a soft spot in my heart for Sam Goldwyn."

And yet Walter Brennan defied Goldwyn when it came to appearing in *Tobacco Road*. "I know all the words and all the jokes," Walter told Hedda Hopper—but he was not about to repeat them on-screen. The penalty for refusing a role was usually suspension, and why Goldwyn did not take Brennan off salary I do not know. Walter wouldn't even take his wife to see *Tobacco Road* when the studio requested he do so. "You can fire me, but I'm not going to the premiere. I got a little principle left," he declared. "If there was anything shady in a show," Mike recalled, his father would say, "Now that's out, boys."

For sure, there was always money to be made loaning Walter out for other projects, including *The Story of Vernon and Irene Castle* (RKO, March 29, 1939), *Stanley and Livingston* (Fox, August 18, 1939), *Joe and Ethel Turp Call on the President* (MGM, December 1, 1939), *Northwest Passage* (February 23, 1940), and *Maryland* (Fox, July 19, 1940). Brennan appeared in Goldwyn's own grand production *They Shall Have Music* (August 18, 1939), featuring the renowned violinist Jascha Heifitz.

In the Astaire-Rogers biopic musical about the pre-World War I dance team of Vernon and Irene Castle, Brennan is Irene Castle's manservant, and there is something distinctly odd about his performance. He seems strangely out of place, especially when he accompanies the Castles to Europe and becomes an integral part of their establishment, almost like a house slave. In fact, Irene Castle's manservant was black, and Castle, a technical advisor on the film, disliked casting Brennan. But Hollywood protocol would not have permitted a black actor to be as outspoken and yet subservient as Brennan is—except in a picture like *Gone With the Wind*, in which the black mammy, by tradition, is allowed to have her say. For once, Walter Brennan did not really know what to do with a role because, perhaps, it was so inauthentic. Edna May Oliver plays the great character role as the Castles' blunt but sensible manager. As Philip K. Scheuer noted in the *Los Angeles Times* (April 5, 1939), "Walter Brennan has, at any rate, an opportunity to be clean-shaven. His role is disappointingly negligible." Still, Brennan has his moments, especially in the first part of the film when he rebuffs Astaire's efforts to woo Rogers. An IMDb user review recommends, "Watch the scene where he [Brennan] is watering the grass and ignoring Astaire's comments."

Motion picture producers were well aware of audiences who now looked to Walter Brennan to spice up the action, to do *something* that would entertain them in pictures that were otherwise commonplace. Even in a major A film starring Spencer Tracy as the explorer Henry M. Stanley, Brennan was added for comic relief—in effect because he was Walter Brennan, screenwriter Philip Dunne recalled. When Brennan and Tracy, both Academy Award winners, appeared on the set of *Stanley and Livingston*, the huge assemblage of extras applauded both men.

Although Brennan had appeared in *Fury* with Tracy, they had only a few scenes together there. Now, however, they appeared as a companionable pair. "I knew Spencer Tracy was all right the moment I saw him chatting easy-like on the set . . . with a prop man," Walter observed. "He treats the office boy who brings us our mail with the same courtesy he does Kenneth Macgowan, who is the associate producer of our picture." Tracy's decency meant a good deal to Brennan, with his memory of what it was like to be ordered around as an extra.

A studio publicity release reported that the actors were on good terms and admired one another's performances. Brennan watched Tracy do a scene and said, "Shucks, I wish I could act like that fellow does." Tracy, in turn, praised one of Brennan's close-ups, confiding to his stand-in, "He's the most natural actor in the world, barring none." But in the arena, as publicity chief Harry Brand put it, the two actors became hecklers:

> "That was a swell performance of yours in that last scene, Walter," Butch Tracy will say. "Only why did you lisp?"
>
> "My son," Killer Brennan will reply, "I couldn't help lisping after I saw how you were ruining everything by twisting up that mug of yours. Can't you play just one scene straight?"

Director Henry King had to referee, restraining "Haymaker Brennan" from scratching imaginary fleas during one of Tracy's serious monologues, and attempting to control "Battling Spence," who reciprocated by blowing his nose during one of Brennan's "more sublime moments." Their rivalry culminated in a scene during which Tracy undercut Brennan by lowering his voice, with the result that Brennan grew even quieter. Henry King yelled "Cut," and then asked, "Say, boys, is this a whispering contest?" Brand, employing mock studio hyperbole, called the incident part of the "battle of the century."

In *Stanley and Livingston* Brennan plays Jeff Slocum, Stanley's sidekick—but that is the problem with the film. Brennan is just *there*, and even though he is beside Tracy during the trek across Africa, he is given little to do—and nothing, really, that is essential to the plot. The fun is supposed to reside in thrusting Slocum, who has been Stanley's guide through Indian country, into the "dark continent," as it was then called. This Brennan character dates badly. As one IMDb user review puts it, "he is corny beyond belief," with his complaints that about the lack of flapjacks and the like. "You can safely skip 'Stanley and Livingston' unless you want to go to the theatre to get cooled off," Russell Maloney wrote in the *New Yorker* (August 12, 1939). This is a harsh but under-standable verdict, given the picture's hokum about Stanley deciding to give up journalism in order to perpetuate Livingstone's humanitarian mission. Nothing of the sort actually occurred. Very little in the picture resembles reality, in spite of some of the location shooting. How little Brennan's performance means to the film is obvious. Tracy's biographer, James Curtis, does not even mention Brennan's role. Tracy never seems to have thought much of the film. . After seeing the completed work in a projection room, Tracy pronounced, "Might be entertaining, not great."

With the exception of *Bad Day at Black Rock*, Brennan and Tracy were never given material as good as the pictures Brennan and Cooper did together. A case in point is *Northwest Passage*, in which Brennan is wasted playing a sidekick for the bland Robert Young, while Tracy plays a west-ern hero in a role better suited to John Wayne or Randolph Scott. As Major Robert Rogers, leader of Rogers' Rangers, Tracy seems squat and hardly roughened enough for outdoor duty. In fact, Tracy had "ballooned to 189 pounds," according to James Curtis. As a journalist boldly braving the wilds of Africa, Tracy was passable, but as a frontiersman and soldier? He was not keen to do another adventure picture, but "there was no get-ting out of it," Curtis notes. Six weeks of location work in July a hundred miles north of Boise near the Oregon border—with a cast of well over one hundred extras (local lumberjacks and miners) and stunt men, not to mention 450 Indians who were given their own encampment—com-bined with physically demanding action scenes, did not constitute Tracy's idea of fun. Expecting bad food, he brought a box of chocolates with him. His trainer and masseur also accompanied him, but their efforts made no difference in the figure Tracy cut in this picture. As a result, it is hardly credible that he would earn the respect of the rugged rangers he is supposedly guiding. He looks more like the guy from the front office sent in to ride herd on the boys. Tracy was "well taken care of," his direc-tor, King Vidor, drolly commented. "I guess in the long run it was more important that he remain well than anyone else."

Walter Brennan, who had consorted with lumberjacks and always looked the part, is introduced in promising fashion as Hunk Marriner, an outspoken woodsman first shown in the stocks, being punished for his acerbic comments about the rich and powerful. But then Hunk does no more than shore up Robert Young, another rebel and a Harvard Col-lege dropout, who eventually learns the ways of the wilderness when he signs on as Rogers's cartographer for their trek across country killing Indians and searching for a new trade route. Unfortunately, Brennan's character just fades into irrelevance. When Rogers drives his men mercilessly and seems fanatical to no good purpose, hardly a peep is heard from Hunk—who is given one good moment, when he acknowledges that Rogers is always right, but adds that it isn't good for a man to be always right.

Walter Brennan complained about his part and about the director's misguided and dangerous efforts to make an adventure film. "They thought it was going to be this great picture," Walter recalled, "and they were going to make a sequel. . . . I said, 'Well, just include me out.'" Brennan was undone by King Vidor's direction that he and the rest of the cast lug boats over a hill to avoid the detection of several French ships (this is 1750s) that block the way of the Rogers expedition, which, with fewer than 150 participants was too small to engage in battle. "Rogers Rangers only lugged those boats over the hill once," Walter told the director. "We lugged them over ten times, and they were real boats." But it got worse. The most harrowing scene in the film occurs when the Rangers have to cross rapids, and Rogers commands them to form a human chain to get across the hazardous waters. Even though the scene was shot on a studio lot in a special tank designed to look like a river, it proved perilous, as Brennan, Tracy, and the rest of the cast contended with five feet of water roiled by motors, propellers, and fans. "When you went across, you went across with nothing to walk on," Walter remembered.

> And you had a pack, and you were holding a rifle up. I stepped off of that bag, and boy, I come up a half a mile down the ways down there. I said to Tracy . . . when we started going across . . . "Gee, this looks pretty tough."
>
> He says, "It looks tough."
>
> I said, "Oh, it's not that tough, or they wouldn't let us do it."
>
> And then when I come out of the water, here's Tracy waiting for me.
>
> He says, "What do you think now?"
>
> I said, "You're right, it's pretty tough."

But the studio thought only of the epic nature of the film, employing Idaho National Guardsman to play 225 British soldiers, hiring in total over fifteen thousand bit players and extras— not to mention the hookers who showed up to provide services for the unsavory characters who became part of the picture business.

Off-screen, Tracy demonstrated the grit he was supposed to show in the film—at one point throwing a plate of powdered eggs to the other side of a camp tent and refusing to work until everyone got something decent to eat. After watched Tracy during this episode, Robert Young said admiringly, "That's power." And Tracy kept it up, threatening to go home. To keep Tracy happy, Vidor hired an attractive young woman to coddle the star.

Tracy gives a convincing performance when he nearly breaks down, but such moments are few, and the rest of the cast is not given enough to do. Tracy later said that Kenneth Roberts, whose best-selling novel formed the basis of the film, threatened "bodily harm if I so much as entered the state of Maine." *Northwest Passage* was enormously expensive to produce, and though it did well in theaters and with the critics, it lost nearly a million dollars for MGM. A plan for the sequel never materialized.

Such disappointing results did not deter Walter Brennan. He was not the kind of actor who worried much about misfires. He was "about the most untemperamental actor in Hollywood," as columnist Erskine Johnson reported in "Behind the Make-Up." Even when he had the flu during the *Stanley and Livingston* shoot, Brennan managed to carry on. Somehow, a dressing room had not been provided for him, and so he "sprawled out on some padding in a corner of the sound stage." Brennan told an apologetic assistant, "Don't get yourself heated up, son. I'm right comfortable here."

Walter Brennan was always in demand and gave the lie to the Hollywood cliché that you are only as good as your last picture. He never delivered anything less than a competent performance, but he never deceived himself when he was playing in lousy pictures. He was plot proof. Indeed, the pleasure of watching him in a long forgotten film such as *They Shall Have Music* has nothing to do with the sentimental Goldwyn extravaganza that has renowned violinist Jascha Heifitz meet the equivalent of the Dead End kids. One delinquent, Frankie, gets religion—that is, the desire to be a classical musician after hearing Heifitz perform. A kind music conductor, Professor Lawson (Brennan) mentors Frankie. The professor is unworldly and inspiring in his wholehearted devotion to teaching poor children how to play and sing the world's classics. It is a treat to watch the scenes with Heifitz playing and Brennan conducting, commanding the children to perform while expressing his joy in the creation of something wonderful. The movie was a dud at the box office but nevertheless enhanced Sam Goldwyn's prestige as the producer of tasteful and uplifting motion pictures. Although the making of *They Shall Have Music* received much press attention, the *New York Times* reviewer, who only had praise for the music, could not resist the quip, "All is not Goldwyn that glistens."

And yet the film enhanced Walter Brennan's reputation as versatile character actor. He plays Professor Lawson as a noble soul, a type he revisits in *Joe and Ethel Turp Call on the President*, in which he appears as Jim, an old postman in peril of losing his job because he has opened and destroyed a letter. Joe and Ethel (William Gargan and Ann Southern) seek the intervention of the president (Lewis Stone), explaining that Jim acted only out of kindness for a woman he once loved whose troublesome son, Fred (Don Costello), has caused her much grief. Jim is unwilling to make her situation worse by delivering the dreadful news that Fred has died during a prison escape attempt. This aspect of the Brennan persona—honorable and humane—would reach its ultimate form in Fritz Lang's *Hangmen Also Die!* (1943), where Brennan plays a Czech professor who is the moral center of the picture, a position Brennan also occupies in *Maryland*, a faintly disguised remake of *Kentucky*.

In a memo dated April 22, 1942, concerning a script conference about *Maryland*, Darryl Zanuck rejected the idea of making a radical change in Brennan's screen persona. Brennan simply could not be presented as "a prospective bridegroom—even though in real life he is a man about 38." Such a persona would be "completely wrong since Brennan is a most unromantic character . . . the audience would never swallow him in any romantic complication because of his unattractiveness." Instead, the producer suggested that the screenwriters build interest by concentrating on Brennan's character and his fluctuating fortunes. They did so by having him play another horse trainer, William Stewart, who is at odds with Charlotte Danfield (Fay Bainter) because she has forbidden her son Lee (John Payne) to ride horses after her husband is thrown from his horse and dies in the midst of a fox hunt. As one IMDb contributor notes, Brennan is "less shrill" in this role and gives a performance that is more subtle and believable than his Academy Award winning bravura acting in *Kentucky*. Brennan's William Stewart is just as outspoken as Peter Goodwin in *Kentucky*, but Stewart is not an unreconstructed rebel like Peter. Even though *Maryland* perpetuates many of the black stereotypes that infected Hollywood films of the 1930s and 1940s, Stewart is not obliged to express the nastiness that undergirds *Kentucky*, which endorses white supremacy in the post-Reconstruction South.

Walter Brennan knew it was the writing, more than anything else, that determined how much he could accomplish on-screen. And he had yet to be given a script with the kind of human complexity that would catapult him beyond the ranks of accomplished character actors. At this point in his career he seemed fed up after working virtually nonstop for Goldwyn on six pictures since 1937—not to mention all those in which he served as the producer's prize loan-out to other studios, such as Universal, Republic, Fox, Paramount, RKO, and MGM. Brennan rarely commented publicly on studio bosses or Hollywood politics, but in a column, "Behind the Scenes in Hollywood" (March 25, 1940), Harrison Carroll reported, "Walter Brennan has served notice on Samuel Goldwyn that he will make no more pictures like 'Maryland' until he gets a long vacation . . . . he is tired out." To columnist Frederick G. Othman, Brennan complained of being "punch drunk." And on the set of *Maryland*, he protested, "I got up this morning at five, as usual, for my regular call, and got dressed. So when the call came at 5:30, it said I didn't have to show at the studio until eight. I just dropped down to the sofa and when my wife came down later she found me snoring, with my hat and overcoat on."

And yet there was no letup, and Walter Brennan kept working, as a contract actor must. And in truth he wanted to do so—especially since he was preparing for a performance that made Gary Cooper, Hollywood's highest paid star, wonder if he could hold his own with his old pal.

CHAPTER 4

The Apotheosis of Walter Brennan

(1940)

GARY COOPER WAS WORRIED. UNDER CONTRACT TO SAMUEL GOLDWYN, HE was told his next assignment was to star as the cowboy Cole Harden opposite Walter Brennan as Judge Roy Bean, the colorful and ornery hanging judge and icon of the Old West. Much had changed for Walter Brennan, who was no longer delivering messages to Cooper in *The Wedding Night* or buried in the credits of *The Cowboy and the Lady* as a Cooper hanger-on.

The film's working title was "Vinegaroon," the name of the town Bean dominated like a law unto himself. From the start, in other words, Cooper would be fighting to establish himself on Brennan's terrain—not an enviable position for an A-list actor to occupy. "I couldn't figure for the life of me why they needed me for this picture," he claimed. "I had a very minor part." Even so, why would Gary Cooper fear appearing with Walter Brennan? He knew, at a minimum, that every two-shot would favor him. And indeed they did, since director William Wyler frequently chose to shoot Brennan from behind, looking at Cooper, who is almost always shown in three-quarter profile.

To be sure, Brennan had won two Academy Awards, but Cooper was a huge star who dominated the screen by seeming to do nothing at all—so said director Lewis Milestone in his unpublished autobiography. Cooper seemed positively listless. "Why stand when you could sit?" he liked to say. "Why sit when you could lie down?" Cooper quipped as he draped himself on anything that would support his languid figure. And yet, on the screen, even in the day's rushes, Cooper's charisma conquered all, an awed Milestone observed. No leading lady—certainly not Merle Oberon in *The Cowboy and the Lady*—could rival his appeal. Indeed, the picture builds on Cooper's power to draw the viewer in by making this beautiful woman pursue him. Early in his career, Cary Grant got the roles that Cooper cast aside, learning along the way that his best work resulted from scripts that had his leading lady latch on to him. In fact, Cooper had established such a formidable precedent that Grant, who had come to Hollywood as Archie Leach, picked the name Cary because it rhymed with Gary.

So how could Walter Brennan possibly dominate Gary Cooper? It would be virtually unheard of in Hollywood to reverse the natural order of things and have a character actor outshine the star. Who would want to do that? What director or producer would take such a risk? It just wasn't done, unless that character actor possessed that rare quality that could translate to leading roles. Even then, why build a picture around Brennan? As Walter Brennan told columnist Sheilah Graham, "My part is such that it cannot help but steal the spotlight."

Both Cooper and Brennan got their start as extras. Like Brennan, Cooper had learned his craft by roaming around movie lots, absorbing the atmosphere and watching how things were done—especially the subtle interplay between actors, and between the best actors and the camera lens, which always picked up details that not even the most perceptive directors could spot before they were projected onto a screen. And like Brennan, when Cooper got his first two minutes of screen time, he was prepared. Watch him in *Wings*, playing an aviator about to go to his death, enter a tent and converse with the film's two stars, Buddy Rogers and Richard Arlen, who are immediately fascinated by his bluff allure. He is a hero without bravado. He is for those two minutes the picture's star, the very embodiment of what Hemingway called grace under pressure. Cooper's ability to convey composure just before a dogfight, to act with such quiet courtesy and aplomb, stuns Rogers and Arlen—and just that quickly Cooper takes the picture away from them.

And just that quickly Walter Brennan could do the same to Gary Cooper. That is what Gary Cooper knew and did not want to say. If Brennan had not already done so in *The Cowboy and the Lady*, it was only because the picture saddled the character actor with two other buddies, thus diluting through inane dialogue and action any opportunity to wrest the moment away from the picture's two principals, Cooper and Oberon. But in *The Westerner* Cooper would have to confront not only Judge Roy Bean, but also Walter Brennan, the most popular extra ever to rise to stardom. Brennan knew not only how to handle stars, he knew how to handle crowds. He been one of them, and he would remain, among the extras, their most popular and esteemed success story.

For all Cooper's fame and success, he was as insecure as anyone in Hollywood, where you were judged not by your body of work but by what you had done lately. He was a contract player, part of a studio system that, in effect, owned him. Don't do the part, and I'll sue you, Sam Goldwyn told Cooper. William Wyler—who had his own conflicts as a contract director working for Goldwyn—was assigned to *The Westerner*. The director saw the humor and the fun of pitting Cooper against Brennan—especially when Niven Busch rewrote the script not only to build up Cooper's role, but also to exploit a sentimental vulnerability in Bean, who is besotted with the English actress Lily Langtry. Cooper, as Cole Harden, sentenced to hang, tricks Bean into believing that the cowboy knows the stage star and can arrange for Bean to meet her. Thus Harden delays his hanging and embarks on a trip with the credulous judge to accost his idol. Watching the wizened old judge become giddy over the very idea of sharing a moment with his beloved Lily turns *The Westerner* into a powerfully amusing take on how a devotion to stardom can overcome even the hardest case. It would all be such fun, Wyler assured Cooper.

Cooper was not convinced and did the picture under protest. He was not even swayed by Wyler's argument that by underplaying scenes with Brennan—who was obliged to be rather frenetic in order to stay in character—Cooper would, as always, come out on top. But in effect, with Lily Langtry as Cole Harden's bait, Cooper would turn Brennan into his suitor. Indeed, in one comic scene, Brennan and Cooper share the same bed, with Brennan's arm, at one point, draped over Cooper's. It is tempting to see Lillian Hellman's hand in such scenes, since she was assigned to do rewrites of Busch's script. She specialized in the sexual ambiguity of the ménage à trois, as in *These Three* (1936), a Goldwyn production that featured two schoolteachers in love with the same man. In *The Westerner*, it is the off-screen Langtry who links Brennan and Cooper. Her aura envelops Harden and dazzles Bean, especially since Bean has to work overtime to pry out of the laconic Harden luscious details the judge slavers over. Accompanied by Brennan's moist patter, Cooper dryly doles out his delicacies, including a lock of Langtry's hair (actually taken from the daughter of a homesteader who has fallen in love with Harden). During the Lux Radio Theatre production of *The Westerner* (broadcast September 23, 1940), Cooper's droll delivery evoked more laughter than Brennan's stridency.

Much of the credit for the Brennan/Cooper romance is due to their friendship. Brennan loved to reminisce, but he noticed that certain stars hated to be reminded of their struggles, and Brennan's tone of familiarity sometimes irked them. Not Gary Cooper, Walter affirmed: "He sits down and swaps yarns about how tough the going was. He's regular and I admire him for being honest with himself." But there was also, perhaps, some good-natured mockery in Brennan's mimicry of Cooper's style. A reporter once watched Brennan pull out a package of cigarettes, poke it with a finger, draw a cigarette from the pack, and stick it in his mouth. "Slowly he reached into a pocket for matches. There was a flourish and finesse as he lit the cigarette. A flick of the wrist and the match went out. With great deliberation, perfection of motion, he put the matches back and stowed the cigarettes." It was trademark Cooper. "When Cooper lights a cigarette, it's a rite. When Brennan imitates him, it's a riot," the reporter concluded. So when Judge Bean eyes Cole Harden across the bar and Harden gives the look back to him, Walter Brennan and Gary Cooper are playing out their understanding of one another.

Wyler was not very articulate when explaining to actors his conception of their roles. He could discourse on the great possibilities of a script, but he was nearly hopeless when it came to suggesting to an actor the kind of business that would bring a role to life. Wyler knew great acting when he saw it, but he would do two dozen takes before he was sure the camera had captured a superb performance. In other words, whatever Wyler actually said, it was not enough for Cooper and Brennan. They knew it would be up to them to supply the goods.

As soon as the actors got down to work, they became engrossed in the job at hand. Brennan was an old hand at inventing bits of business, things Wyler would never come up with himself, but which the director deeply appreciated. At the same time, Brennan played Bean straight—that is, the judge is perfectly serious about his love for Lily Langtry. Brennan refuses to simply play his character for laughs. Rather than resorting to the broad gestures he learned in vaudeville, Brennan expresses the judge's excitement by leaning in to Cooper for confidential conversations across the bar. Cooper's casual reclining on the counter, holding his right hand to his jaw as he dreamily conjures up the glorious Lily, is matched by the rapt gaze Brennan fixes on his interlocutor. It's as if Langtry were in the room with them.

Whatever misgivings Cooper had about entering the ring with Brennan, he also realized that Walter was too good an actor and had too refined a sense of ensemble acting to do anything other than make Cooper look good. It was all good, as a matter of fact. Wyler was able to shoot the film on location in Tucson, Arizona, benefitting from Goldwyn's million-dollar budget, which allowed for the construction of a replica of the opera house that Lilly Langtry appeared in. For Wyler, Brennan, and Cooper what mattered was the work.

On the set Wyler's wife, Talli, watched Cooper in action—or rather in what looked like inaction, since he seemed about as lively as a block of wood—and was astounded at the magnetism that came through in the rushes. Walter Brennan almost never needed prodding from Wyler. Cooper, a far less confident performer, got the soft touch from his director, who would walk over and murmur something to Cooper that no one else could hear. It probably did not matter what Wyler said. Wyler himself admitted that he did no more than point out the comic possibilities of a scene that might call for a "funny look" from Cooper. And yet the director assumed exactly the kind of quiet authority that Cooper got credit for in his performances. Wyler took Cooper into his confidence, making their asides a crucial part of their routine and leaving the impression that the star would always be able to deliver. If Wyler ever conferred with Brennan in this way, such instances have not been reported.

In all likelihood, Walter, like the judge he played, was on his own. Becoming Roy Bean was an all-consuming project. Walter worked late into the night "making the old fellow come alive." Weeks of preparation went into his performance. "I have literally become that man and will never for a single instant compromise with his character," Walter insisted. "He must always be himself and never his brother or his uncle. I find myself eventually thinking like him." Brennan had to see it in his own eyes as he watched himself on the screen. Had he made Judge Bean come alive? "I always say that an actor is no better than his last day's rushes," he said. You cannot fool the camera, Brennan liked to say. "The camera picks up what you think and not what you say or do. The reason I'm proof of that is because I've seen me give some lousy performances, and I said, 'I wonder what I was thinking when I did that.'"

Brennan had the best lines in the script. Dispensing justice from his saloon bar, he declares, "Don't spill none of that liquor, Son. It eats right into the bar." Walter relished his character's dispensation of justice:

JUDGE ROY W. BEAN. Shad Wilkins, you've been tried and found guilty of the most serious crime west of the Pecos, to wit: shooting a steer. Do you got anything to say for yourself before the sentence of the court is executed?

SHAD WILKINS. I told you they shot at me first. I didn't mean to kill that steer on purpose. I was aiming at the man.

JUDGE ROY W. BEAN. It's your bad luck you missed him. That's the trouble with you sodbusters . . . you can't shoot straight. Shad, may the Lord have mercy on your soul.

There is a childish aspect to Bean's character that Brennan captures with gusto and sensitivity. When asked about the film years later, he commented, "Of course, we're all little boys at heart, you know."

The picture was Brennan's, but it was no good to him if Cooper, his co-star, did not hold his own. It was characteristic of Walter Brennan to want Cooper not only to be happy making the picture, but also to feel that the two of them had something in common—in this case, their servitude to Sam Goldwyn. Employing his powerful gift for mimicry, Brennan called Cooper and, in Goldwyn's voice, said, "You're so lousy I want Brennan to have top billing in this picture." Sooner or later Brennan broke down and cackled over the irate Cooper's responses, and Cooper laughed, too. The point Brennan always made to his fellow actors was—as he had learned during his years as an extra—that they were all in the business together.

Brennan later took issue with the customary laconic image of Cooper: "Mention any subject that might interest any adult, well-educated he-man, and you can have a conversation with Cooper. Mention horses or cattle or guns, and he'll out-talk you." But then, that was Walter Brennan talking, a man who seemed always to have the right word for his friends, and who was so approachable that conversing with him was nearly always a delight. In fact, this is what happens in *The Westerner*, where Brennan plays to his strengths, initiating one conversation after another with Cole Harden.

Walter Brennan knew that in Judge Bean he had "everything an actor could ask for." The role won him his third Academy Award and surely his most deserved accolades to date. Some of his greatest roles, however, lay ahead.

CHAPTER 5

Primal Brennan

Gary Cooper, Humphrey Bogart, Frank Capra, Jean Renoir, Howard Hawks (1940–44)

BY 1940, WALTER BRENNAN HAD BECOME A NATIONALLY RECOGNIZED figure. He was also well on his way to developing the all-American, down-to-earth persona that would catapult him into even greater fame in the television age and designate him, at one point, "grandfather of the year." The *Lynn (MA) Item* (May 5, 1940), reported that Walter Brennan, on a "flying trip home . . . remembered as a tackle at Swampscott High. . . . declared the old town hadn't changed much." The same could be said for him. Indeed, he liked to look up the "old gang" when he made short visits to Lynn and Swampscott.

Walter always played down his urbane, sophisticated side, and claimed to have few interests outside work. But somehow this story got into a studio biography:

> Brennan's pet hobby is rugs and furniture, which resulted in a Hollywood architect being driven to distraction. In the midst of building an additional bedroom on the Brennan home, he [a Hollywood architect] had to stop work, pull out the walls and build it all over again. The reason: Brennan had bought at an auction an Oriental rug, size 18 by 27 feet. There was no place for Brennan to put it but in the new bedroom, which was being built to the dimensions of 14 by 25 feet. The architect had to rebuild the room to fit the rug.

By contrast, most of Brennan's screen characters had simple tastes and motivations—just like Hector, the lovesick mailman in a Deanna Durbin vehicle, *Nice Girl?* (February 21, 1941). Durbin had a pleasing lyric so-prano voice, and she made a fortune for Universal Studios playing the proverbial girl-next-door. Hector, the equivalent of a town crier, brings a special delivery letter to Professor Dana (Robert Benchley) announcing the visit of a scientist (Franchot Tone). This is spectacular news for the small town about to celebrate July 4, its only exciting event other than Groundhog Day, according to Dana's daughter Jane (Durbin). As soon as Dana reads the letter, he hands it to Hector, apparently assuming that the mailman will broadcast the visit as breaking news. And he is right to assume as much, since earlier Hector is shown making his rounds, telling people what is in their mail before they have read it.

Hector is smitten with Cora (Helen Broderick), the housekeeper/cook, who he accosts in the kitchen. She kindly but firmly deflects his attempt to kiss her. He is dressed up in his band uniform to impress her and has come bearing a heart shaped cake that says "Cora." After the arrival of the scientist, who is enjoying a flirtation with Professor Dana's three daugh-ters—especially Jane—the scene shifts again to the kitchen, where Hector is playing cards with Cora. After losing a game and sixteen cents, he grabs her hand and says, "This is the only good hand I've had tonight."

Hector's main purpose is to lead the band during the July 4 celebra-tion. On the bandstand, he introduces Professor Dana, who is about to give an address even as two boys in the audience engage in a scuffle. Hector interrupts them to say they will have to stop enjoying themselves while the professor gives his talk. After Dana's mercifully short speech (he acknowledges no one really wants to listen), Hector starts to conduct the band, but then spots Cora dancing with a rival. When he asks the band if they can play without him, they yell, "Better!" So Hector cuts in to dance with Cora. Like the Andy Hardy movies, starring the irrepress-ible Mickey Rooney and Lewis Stone as the fatherly Judge Hardy, Dean-na Durbin productions were wholesome, sweet, and mildly entertaining, enlivened by the middle-aged eroticism of the courtly Walter Brennan, who would soon reprise this type of role as an octogenarian with a some-what sharper romantic edge in *Rise and Shine*.

Walter Brennan was now making as much as $5,000 a week, an in-credible sum for a character actor, and he was in a position to fulfill a cherished dream. He bought a twelve-thousand-acre ranch near Joseph, Oregon, for $72,800, with a down payment of $15,000 and the remain-ing $57,800 secured by a mortgage. Walter had first heard about the land from Mike's North Hollywood High School "Ag" teachers (Agricultural Education Teacher), who brought Mike's class out to the family's San

Fernando home. Mike does not remember what the class did, but Walter and his son's teacher became absorbed in a conversation about buying a ranch. The teacher, who had taught in Enterprise, Oregon, six miles down the road from Joseph, told Walter, "You ought to go to Wallowa County. That's better than Jackson Hole, Wyoming." Ruth liked to tell the story of their first trip to Wallowa County, driving the thousand miles or so from Los Angeles. It was a three-day trip that took them through the High Sierras, some of it on unpaved back roads. They arrived late at night and checked into a room a few floors up in a hotel in Enterprise. She said, "We woke up the next morning and opened the curtains, and here were these fabulous mountains. We were amazed." Somehow they had just not been prepared for such a sight, which seemed to emerge out of the darkness of their journey. They would soon learn to appreciate the county's topography: the mountain valley, the canyons, and on the top, a huge high prairie. Walter grew to enjoy his role as rancher, and that's how people treated him—without the Hollywood fanfare he wanted to escape. In fact, no visitors from Hollywood ever showed up—except for Andy Devine, a friend for life who had begun, like Walter, as an extra. Other than a hand cranked phone, a wood stove to heat the house, and a gas generator for lights and the laundry, the Brennans did without most modern conveniences in a ranch house surrounded by beautiful apple trees with access to spring water. These were the days before modern sprinkler systems, when a rancher used flood irrigation, digging a canal-like ditch that would serve as a conduit to the fields below.

Walter bought Lightning Creek Ranch from Ray and Bessie Pogue. Walter tended to drive hard bargains, and Mike suspects that Ray, who was suffering from rheumatism and could not take care of the ranch, thought he was getting "taken." Walter, relying on the advice of an attorney, was a very careful purchaser and wrote long letters to the Pogues inquiring about their property, the buildings on it, the cost of range improvements, purchasing their livestock, and the monthly expense of running the ranch. It was often said that Walter was frugal. Vivian Strickland, who did some cooking at Lightning Creek, recalled that her ranch hand husband thought he deserved a dollar raise, especially since wages on Walter's ranch were lower than the prevailing rate. Her husband was sure he could talk Walter into that raise, but he never did. When I told Mike what Vivian said, he laughingly remarked, "Dad worked for such little money when he was a kid that he couldn't get the idea that today I'd pay a housekeeper fifteen dollars an hour. He'd say you'd have to work awful hard for that kind of money."

All the same, as the correspondence between Brennan and the Pogues shows, Walter remained on good terms with them and helped them out financially. Before actually taking possession of the ranch, Walter and Ruth visited the Pogues, staying with them. Ray reported on rainfall and the state of the grass—so important to raising fat cattle. Pogue also complimented Walter on his performance in *The Westerner*, but he could not help adding that the film's cattle and grass just did not measure up to Wallowa County standards. The Brennan family no longer owns the ranch, but it remains intact—including the rattlesnakes, the Indian caves, and the petroglyphs.

Walter became increasingly concerned with portraying the West and his characters as authentically as possible, even though he realized Hollywood had a tendency to prettify the picture. "Raising kids on a ranch is a healthy way of bringing them up," Andy remembers his father saying. "They get to know how to take care of themselves." All three children were members of the 4H Club. The Brennan children learned how to care for a herd of Hereford cattle. "Dad purchased a three-hundred acre farm near the ranch to raise hay for the cattle," Andy recalled. Early July was usually the first cutting, and then there would be a second cutting as soon as it grew back. Depending on the weather, a cutting early enough in June might mean getting a third by the end of summer. Haying could be hazardous. Even today, you don't step out of a vehicle on the ranch without making sure you know what is under your feet. "There's a dead rattlesnake there, right down in the draw," ninety-two-year old Mike pointed out to me. Mike had no interest in an acting career. "That job was dog eat dog," you know. "We kidded about it." But Walter didn't care about his children working in film. "I could have doubled for my father and been a stand-in," Mike mused. But only Andy actually entered show business. In fact Andy began just as his father had, working as an extra. "I didn't tell anybody I was Walter Brennan's son," Andy said. Eventually Andy played some bit parts by getting to know directors. "I was trying to fill a pretty big shadow there." Eventually, he would go to work for Desilu in the early 1950s and work, as well, as both a stand-in for his father and an associate producer on *The Real McCoys*.

Ruth had little interest in the movie industry, and that was fine with Walter. She kept busy on the ranch with her vegetable garden and with canning. She sometimes stayed at Lightning Creek when Walter was called away to do movie work. She also kept busy with a fabric store she owned in Joseph. Judy Lamy remembered the time Walter walked in wearing a red checkered shirt and looked at the red checkered window curtains and said to the woman at the counter, "Well I guess you know where I got my shirt and where you got your curtains." He was that kind of down to earth person, Judy said.

When Brennan was asked why he bought the ranch, he simply said, "Everyone wants to be a cowboy." In another mood, he would point out that ranching was surely the natural outcome of the roles he had played. If he most closely identified with the mythos of the West, this was surely because right from the start, as a young man, he had wanted to head west, which represented boundless opportunity and the chance to be his own man. Under contract to Sam Goldwyn for a decade beginning in 1935, he nevertheless saw himself as independent—in part because so many studios used him, and he was not part of the star machine "If you're not the star, you don't get the blame if it's a lousy picture," he pointed out. "They always blame the star. They say, 'But that old man was great!' That's how I kept going." He was quite content to walk beside his friend Lewis Stone, who would get the attention of autograph hunters, while an amused Brennan remained undisturbed by movie fans.

Walter also kept himself going by keeping an account book recording his earnings, starting from the first day he showed up on a movie set. He liked to turn the pages and see the entries for $7.50 until he got to one in which he had written "with giddy gayness" $15.00 for one day's work. Subsequent pages still had entries for $7.50, but more frequently, he noted earnings of $50.00 and $75.00, after which the pay continued to increase. But he never forgot what it meant to be a day laborer, and to be, for years, on the margins of the movie business. Even at his most successful, Walter maintained his identity as an outsider and cultivated a mentality that surely contributed to his role as "the Colonel" in *Meet John Doe* (May 3, 1941).

The Colonel proves essential to Gary Cooper, playing an injured baseball player called Long John Willoughby. Willoughby is impersonating the "John Doe" that columnist Anne Mitchell (Barbara Stanwyck) invents in order to appeal to readers of the newspaper recently purchased by tyrannical tycoon D. B. Norton (Edward Arnold). Willoughby just wants enough dough to fix his pitching arm, but Mitchell persuades him that he can do more good by acting as the common man who is fed up with the corruption of modern life. His protest will culminate in his suicide, which will take the form of a dramatic plunge off a skyscraper. Brennan's "Colonel," spouting the rhetoric of a Henry David Thoreau in rags, is Willoughby's second, decrying the materialism that ties men to their jobs and families, and to society itself. The Colonel constantly urges

Willoughby to be true to himself, not to the image the newspaper and radio have carefully crafted with articles, speeches, and public appearances. Sounding a good deal like a libertarian, Brennan comes as close as he ever did on-screen to exemplifying his own deep distrust of governmental institutions and middle class liberalism, which he felt deprived the individual of his ability to thrive through his own efforts. When the Colonel departs, disgusted with his partner's celebrity (the movie is also a surreptitious attack on the discrepancy between the "star" and the real person), Cooper's "John Doe" loses his way and has to be shown by Brennan's substitute, Connell (the accomplished character actor James Gleason) how D. B. Norton is manipulating the John Doe clubs in order to further his own ambition to be president. In a scene that reminds critic David Thomson of Lear and his fool, the Colonel returns when Willoughby recovers himself, denouncing D. B. Norton and reclaiming the allegiance of the John Doe clubs that have rejected politics as usual.

James Gleason, a feisty Irishman, often played tough detectives, politicians, and soldiers, and he always received good notices from important critics such as James Agee and Manny Farber. Gleason's Connell is as pivotal to this film as Brennan's Colonel, because Gleason, as the newspaper editor working for nefarious D. B. Norton, is the "inside man" who complements the Colonel's distrust of corporate institutions. Gleason wants to publish real news, not the trumped-up hokum of the John Doe story, and his authenticity bolsters Brennan's even as the star, Gary Cooper, wavers between telling the truth and playing the sham hero. It is Gleason who takes effective action as Norton's nemesis and thus prepares for the Colonel's return just as Cooper reaffirms his opposition to Norton's takeover of a populist movement. Cooper's sincere effort to commit suicide, and to be the John Doe he had only pretended to be, is thwarted when members of a John Doe Club arrive to tell him he will do more good alive than dead.

This ending defies the logic of the film, as Frank Capra understood. The director said he tried alternative endings, including one that turned the picture into a tragedy rather than a story of redemption. Capra explained, "We see Cooper on the roof about to jump. And we cut down to Brennan. Suddenly Brennan hears something, turns around, and my God he sees—we don't show it—he sees the body on the steps. He rushes onto the steps, cradles Cooper in his arms, and says, 'Long John, Long John, you poor sucker, you poor sucker.' That's the end." When the director was asked if he showed this ending to preview audiences, he replied, "No, you just don't kill Gary Cooper." Scrapping this ending deprived Walter Brennan of an important moment in his film career, one that transformed the marginal Colonel into a major voice decrying the media and corporate manipulation.

Shot between July 8 and September 12, 1940, *Meet John Doe* was a huge and arduous production that required fifty-seven sets, seventy-five loudspeakers, ten amplifying systems, seventy-five thousand yards of bunting, and new editions of ten thousand newspapers for big scenes that were shot over a ten-day period. The picture had 137 speaking parts, and four thousand extras were used in late night scenes shot at Wrigley Field in Chicago, where Cooper's "John Doe" tries and fails to tell the thousands assembled about the perfidy of D. B. Norton in his efforts to manipulate and control public opinion. Two hundred plumbers kept rain falling steadily for eight nights at Wrigley Field, using over 250,000 feet of rubber hose and thirty-six thousand nozzles. In the convention scenes, enough power was used to light a city of fifty thousand for an entire week. Four huge kitchens with one hundred cooks fed everyone. Both Brennan and Cooper were ill during the production, which fell nearly a week behind schedule. Walter was used to working four to six hours a day, but working nine hours a day on this picture was not uncommon, and after one day when he was kept until 7:30, Brennan said to the director, "Why don't you keep Cooper there for half past seven some night?" When they did, Cooper showed up the next morning at 10:30 for a 9:00 o'clock call. "He never said anything," Walter recalled, "but when they kept him after, he made it up someplace else."

Did these two actors, both quite conservative, see the parallels between Norton and studio moguls like Sam Goldwyn? Did Norton's private police force suggest to these men who began as extras the incipient fascism of the system they had endured? In Brennan's case, the answer is probably yes. Years later, reminiscing about the Hollywood studio system, he told a television director that the studio guard was among "the feared men in Hollywood." Walter remembered the day he arrived in his car for work on *The Adventures of Tom Sawyer*, a David O. Selznick production. "What's your name?" the studio guard asked. "Do you have a pass to drive on?" Walter said, "My name is Walter Brennan. If Mr. Selznick asks where I am, tell him I'm at the beach." The guard asked, "Which beach?" Walter replied, "Just the beach," and drove away. Sounding like the Colonel, Brennan told a reporter, "My weakness is talking about how I'm always going to punch somebody in the nose." Sometimes he did take a swing and even cussed out "some overbearing studio hireling who picks on extras or on one of Brennan's friends of the hard luck days."

Capra's Hollywood ending pays homage to the common man and to the spirit of individuality that could still win out over corporate power. This was, after all, an era when the menace of fascism did come from outside the country, and not a time when American grown fascism would have been uppermost in the minds of most Americans. In an interview toward the end of shooting the film, Cooper summarized its message: "When human beings accumulate more than they really need, they start losing their souls. Seems to me time for friendships like John Doe's and the Colonel's, time to sit by a stream and talk alone is a pretty fine thing. But no one has very much of it these days. Everybody is too busy chasing things." This was the Cooper who made time for Brennan to reminisce about their early days in the movies.

On the eve of America's entrance into World War II, Walter Brennan embodied fundamental decency and democratic virtues that made him indispensable to Cooper's signature Everyman roles. Brennan's performance in *Sergeant York* (September 27, 1941) foreshadows the country's emergence from isolationism into a reluctant, then confirmed internationalism. Although Brennan received an Academy Award nomination for his work in *Sergeant York*, his low-key style is barely mentioned in later accounts of the film, which focus on Gary Cooper as Alvin York, a backwoods Tennessee conscientious objector who overcomes religious objections to war to become the nation's greatest war hero.

Brennan's Pastor Pile persuades York to fight for his principles, to abide by the law and register for the draft, and then to serve in the army after he is denied conscientious objector status. Alvin York's story is sentimentalized in patented Hollywood fashion, but early in the film Brennan's character establishes the basis for Cooper to excel as the down home boy who realizes that going to war is the only way to preserve the very precepts of decency and democracy that had first led him to pacifism. In one of the film's most memorable scenes, York shoots a turkey after several others have tried to kill the bird as it bobs its head up and down behind a rock. As with the uncooperative donkey that would not bray at the right time and provided Walter Brennan with employment as a jackass, the turkey could not be coaxed to lift its head above the rock—that is, until Walter was enlisted to gobble like a turkey. (On- screen, it is made to seem as though York is doing the trick.)

Look also for Ward Bond and Noah Beery Jr., who are splendid as Cooper's backcountry brawling companions. They help to define the world of rusticated masculinity that limns Cooper's character. The rugged Bond, who usually played heavies, displays a cheerful, goofy side here, as he did in *Tobacco Road* (1941), and Beery would be indispensable in the deep bench of character actors Howard Hawks employed in *Red River*. But more important to *Sergeant York* is Margaret Wycherly, playing York's mother. The British-born stage actress, another favorite of critics Manny Farber and David Thomson, grounds the first part of the film in the dynamics of rural family life that make York's later exploits all the more astounding. And yet, when Wycherly first began to deliver her lines, her dour manner seemed to disconcert director Howard Hawks. Was she going to play the mother this way throughout the film? Indeed she did, and gradually it became clear to the cast that the actress's restrained affection for her son made the scenes between Alvin and his mother much more powerful than the usual sentimentality Hollywood called for. Walter Brennan, working with Wycherly for the first time, was quite amused at her solemnity. He watched Wycherly question the young June Lockhart, playing Alvin's sister Rosie, "Are you interested in the the-a-tah?" Walter dissolved in laughter. Later he said to Lockhart, "That was one of the funniest things I've ever heard," as if doing *Sergeant York* was just play.

Brennan's performance as Pastor Pile, while impeccable in terms of the part as written, was also restrained because of the producer's careful presentation of the minister as a paragon. "I was scared, plumb scared," Brennan said on the set. "And I'll be scared until this whole sequence is filmed. Puts a lot of responsibility on an actor to set himself up as a preacher, especially one who's really living, like this man Pastor Pile I'm playing. When he sees the picture I hope he'll remember how he felt the first time he faced a congregation—and judge me accordingly." Although Brennan's statement was part of a Warner Bros. publicity release, his sincerity as a man of deep religious conviction cannot be doubted. Walter wanted to get the role right: "I want to put enough spirituality into my characterization to make him like it when he does see it," he added. "I've never before faced a challenge like this one. I have to come through." While the earnest piety of the film has troubled film critics, it is precisely what attracted Brennan to his role. Brennan also liked his part because it was a change of pace: "Ordinarily, I play hellers. Bad ones, too. Now I find myself warning Gary Cooper that the devil has him by the shirt tail, and exhorting him to wrestle him, wrestle him like he would a b'ar. I like it. Pastor Pile . . . is the most fascinating character I've ever portrayed. He has a wonderful fund of sound philosophy." Brennan's Pastor Pile exerts a gentle firmness that complements Margaret Wycherley's strict but loving mother, who never doubts that in the end her son will do the right thing.

Producer Jesse Lasky (1880–1958), one of the pioneering moguls who created the Hollywood film industry, had spent years cultivating Alvin York, coaxing the reluctant war hero to agree to a screen version of his life, and getting others, like Pastor Pile, to cooperate in the filming. The producer had to secure releases from all the principals in York's life so that they could be portrayed on-screen. Pastor Pile had never even seen a motion picture and was wary of what how Hollywood would treat his person and his beliefs. Lasky had to carefully avoid any suggestion of religious fanaticism.

The producer wanted his audience to sympathize with Pastor Pile's pacifism, which has to be reconciled with his patriotic adherence to his civic duty. Lasky sent two of his representatives, Julien Josephson and Harry Chandler, to court the minister. They reported on May 8, 1940: "We had a long talk with him [Pastor Pile] in Tennessee, and you have the letter in which John Hale says this old gentleman is enthusiastic about your plan for handling the story, which we outlined to him." In order to get Pile's release for the use of his name he had to be given every assurance in writing that he would not be made to do or say anything that would be against his beliefs and his dignity. Fortunately Lasky's representatives discovered that Pile was not a "'hell and brimstone shoutin' preacher' so typical of the fanatical mountain revivalist." There seems to be no extant record of Pile's reaction to the huge eyebrows affixed to Brennan's face. Producer Hal Wallis thought the makeup tests made Brennan look like Groucho Marx. For some reason, this distracting feature remains in the finished picture.

Brennan's third Academy Award for his performance in *The Westerner* was announced during the making of *Sergeant York*. To the actor's surprise, no one on the set said anything to him when he arrived. "I didn't expect the gang to fall all over me, but I did anticipate some congratulations," Walter said. "When nobody said a word I was first surprised, then hurt, and finally mad." Then he walked into his dressing room packed with flowers; a huge green 3 had been painted on his flower wreathed mirror.

With Howard Hawks in charge, the production proceeded slowly and deliberately as he engaged in his usual habit of rewriting the script to accommodate the way his actors wanted to play their scenes. Needless to say, actors appreciated the director's deliberate and sensitive handling of their work. Joan Leslie described Hawks as an elusive, almost ghost-like presence on a set. He would run the actors through several rehearsals of a scene and then just before a take he might say something to Leslie like, "Now would you turn your face a little more to the left"—and then disappear.

Leslie was playing a sixteen-year-old girl, Gracie Williams, whom Alvin York is courting. And Leslie herself was only sixteen years old and in awe of Gary Cooper. Before meeting him the first time she repeatedly rehearsed how to address him. Mr. Cooper sounded too formal. Gary sounded too familiar. But Cooper solved her dilemma by coming up to her and in character saying, "Howdy Miss Gracie." Like Walter Brennan, Gary Cooper made a point of putting younger actors at their ease, and it helped that Cooper and Hawks, like Cooper and Brennan, were fast friends who shared many interests, like hunting, which they did during breaks in filming.

No matter what, Hawks stopped for a full afternoon tea at 4 pm, June Lockhart recalled gratefully. It was all a part of Hawks's graceful and unhurried approach. Predictably, the picture fell behind schedule, much to the annoyance of assistant producer Eric Stacey, who was in charge of monitoring Hawks's work. The director was shooting fewer than two pages a day, when the studio expected three or more to be in the can. As Brennan said, Hawks "never hurried." One of Stacey's reports reveals how Hawks worked:

> In the last night rushes, there is considerable discussion regarding scene 122 in the Int. Pile Store. This is the scene where the men register for the draft and Alvin agrees to register, after Pastor Pile tells him he will put in an application for his exemption on religious grounds. The scene was made on Saturday and was rewritten on the set because Mr. Hawks thought it would not play as it was and when they saw it in the rushes it still did not play and it is more than likely that this entire scene will be re-written and remade. The scene as shot runs 2¼ pages, and will take, based on previous experience, the best part of a day to shoot.

Hawks's growing dislike for Stacey, one of those officious studio hirelings Brennan wanted to punch, is evident in this comment from the latter: "Mr. Hawks is very slow to give any opinion about anything that is coming up . . . . We were trying to discuss this particular set yesterday because it was scheduled to be done today when Mr. Hawks made a very sarcastic crack—something about shooting a schedule and not making any picture. The picture is now six days behind schedule."

But even the zealous Mr. Stacey sometimes relented: "Mr. Cooper reported a half-hour late, which is nothing unusual for Cooper, I assure you. . . . Mr. Hawks has been in the habit of providing tea and cake for his staff every day. This was done today, and much appreciated, and I can honestly say that no time was lost by doing so. If, however, I notice delays coming from this, will let you know."

There seems to be no record of what Mr. Stacey thought of Howard Hawks's pranks. While doing the scene in which Pastor Pile reads aloud from a newspaper carrying the news that the United States has entered World War I, Hawks said to Brennan, "Next time we take it, read a little past the headline." Brennan did so, glancing down the page, pausing, and then, without changing his voice, read, "40,000 Italians captured by two Greeks." Just then, in fact, the Greeks were mounting the first successful counteroffensive against Il Duce's supposedly superior Italian forces.

According to Brennan, Cooper also had his fun during a scene set in Pastor Pile's store, when a salesman supposed to be selling long underwear opens his case to find a "huge pair of women's silk bloomers," an item Cooper placed there so as to elicit a look of "abject terror" on the salesman's face. Cooper and Brennan were good copy, thanks to the character actor's collaboration with studio public relations personnel and the press. "Walter Brennan insists those handlebar rides he's getting on Gary Cooper's bicycle are a mutual arrangement. 'Coop wants exercise, I want rides,'" he explained in an item that appeared in the *Oakland (CA) Tribune* (May 25, 1941).

Sergeant York was an enormously popular picture, solidifying Gary Cooper's status as the common man hero and earning him an Academy Award. Walter Brennan's nomination for a fourth award likewise ensured his continuing presence in major productions in the 1940s, although some of his performances in minor features equaled and even excelled his work in A-list movies. In *This Woman Is Mine* (August 22, 1941), for example, he plays a gruff sea captain, Jonathan Thorne. He curtly tells two self-important businessmen, who are aboard his ship on a trading expedition funded by John Jacob Astor, that they are under his command. Then, quill pen in hand, he forestalls any further argument: "Now if you'll excuse me I'm writing a letter to my wife. I always do that on the eve of sailing." What begins as an abrupt dismissal softens ever so slightly when he mentions his wife. This is the first signal that there is more to this martinet than his assertion of authority. Although writing his wife might appear to be a duty like everything else, his very mention of her is surprising in a man who seems to be all business. As the two traders, played with consummate blarney by Nigel Bruce and Leo G. Carroll, exchange perplexed expressions, Brennan sits down and concentrates on his letter.

In a performance that compares favorably to Charles Laughton's as Captain Bligh in *Mutiny on the Bounty*, Brennan as Captain Thorne declares he has two gods: One he acknowledges by simply looking upward, and the other, he announces, is "discipline." To yet another trader, Robert Stevens (Franchot Tone), who has not asked permission to address the captain on the quarterdeck, Thorne announces, "Mr. Astor is the biggest man I know on shore. But at sea I'm bigger than Mr. Astor." Thorne then raises his voice to the stunned Tone,, "Now get off my quarterdeck!" When Julie Morgan (Carol Bruce),a female stowaway who has fallen in love with a crew member, is discovered, Thorne calls her presence a blasphemy aboard a "decent ship among God fearing men." The disgusted captain, calling her *"a woman"*—as if the female sex itself is an abomination—accuses her of "trying to turn my ship into a waterfront." Thorne's ship, in other words, is the one place where he can exert his strict religious code without being contradicted. At the same time, he will not turn back the ship to rid himself of the stowaway because of his "duty to Mr. Astor." Referring to Julie as a "jade" and a "jezebel" he assembles his crew to announce that no one is to speak to her, including the traders, and that she will be assigned work like everyone else. Anyone disobeying the captain's orders will be flogged, including the traders. Thorne is outraged when he catches Julie in his cabin looking at a photograph of his wife. When he dismisses her, he bows his head, no longer angry, only clearly sad as he gazes at his wife's picture. Even the way the captain walks in the next shot suggests, in Brennan's skilled performance, the melancholy suffusing his rigidly controlled bearing. Such fleeting moments brilliantly convey the anguish of a man who misses the other life he has on land.

Brennan's accomplished acting makes *This Woman Is Mine* worth watching, despite its otherwise uninspired elements. The main plot is supposed to be about Julie Morgan's love for the unworthy rascal, Ovide de Montigny (John Carroll), and about her growing affection for trader Robert Stevens. After a love scene between Ovide and Julie, there is a five-second shot of Thorne staring into the sea and then turning around toward the ship with an inconsolable look. When he catches Ovide talking to Julie, the grim captain orders Mr. Mumford to flog Ovide. The captain reiterates his determination to maintain discipline. But he does so with a catch in his throat, and then he bows his head after he hears Ovide say that Julie did not encourage his advances. Thorne turns his back on the flogging even as he tells Mr. Mumford to "lay on with a will." But the scene is really the first sign that the captain's heart is breaking. Julie rebels, refusing to wear a cabin boy's clothes and tells Thorne he will have to tear off her dress. When he cannot bend her to his will, he tells her to get out of his sight. But he relents, even allowing her to go ashore when they reach the Falkland Islands. When she does not return by the time ship sets sail, Thorne abandons her for disobeying orders, even though his expression when doing so is clearly troubled. Stevens, now becoming a Fletcher Christian, threatens to blow a hole through Thorne if he does not send a boat to retrieve Julie and her lover, Ovide. After reminding Stevens of what this mutiny means, Thorne backs down and orders a boat to be sent. As he does so, he relaxes his rigid military bearing and leans against a ship rail, a subtle gesture that is accentuated by his softly spoken command, "ease your helm down."

As soon as Julie and Ovide are back aboard, Stevens surrenders his rifle to Thorne, who puts Stevens in the brig for mutiny and locks Julie in a cabin. When Ovide tries to resolve matters by offering to marry Julie, Thorne is outraged, because Ovide explains that he feels forced to wed. He does not share the captain's regard for marriage as a "holy and beautiful thing," a sentiment Walter Brennan clearly shared with the character he played. Thorne is aghast when Ovide suggests that Thorne has deeper feelings for Julie than "maybe you let yourself understand." The captain, with a look of horror on his face, summons Julie from her room. She tells Thorne she does not want to marry Ovide. Thorne asks her, "You've changed your mind since you've come aboard?" She agrees and goes back to her room. Then Thorne dismisses Ovide, and with head bowed, gives Julie her freedom by giving her the key to her room. As soon as the ship reaches its destination and trading commences with the Indians, Thorne acquires clothes for Julie. Rather breathlessly, the captain gives her permission to live on land. When he escorts her ashore and she dashes off to join Stevens (with whom she is falling in love), Thorne breaks his formal pose and inadvertently turns toward her, then watches her depart before resuming his customary bearing. After the men begin fighting over her, she returns to the ship, where Thorne, atypically shown in undress, his shirt and vest open with no coat on, receives her with surprise as she announces she feels safer aboard ship—and has cooked his dinner. Thorne glances back at her as she leaves the room, and for the first time, his mouth is open—but he is wordless in astonishment.

This Woman Is Mine culminates in an Indian attack on Thorne's ship. Thorne is thrown into the ship's hold with other injured sailors, but he manages to crawl to the ship's gun powder supply and blow himself up with the ship, giving Julie a chance to escape to shore with Stevens. This predictable denouement, in which the captain must not only go down with his ship, but also live up to the faith Julie has placed in him, works because Brennan brought so much authenticity to his otherwise routine role. Some credit has to be given to the director, Frank Lloyd, most famous for directing *Mutiny on the Bounty* (1935), which won an Academy Award for best picture. Lloyd uses Brennan's performance to give some psychological and moral depth to a B picture. Edward Curtiss, the film's editor, who got his start with Howard Hawks in the 1920s and did distinguished work on *Scarface* (1932), *Come and Get It*, and *The Hunchback of Notre Dame* (1939), beautifully counterpoints Brennan's emotional development with scenes between John Carroll (a B movie Gable) and Carol Bruce, appearing in the second film of an undistinguished career.

As is the contract player's fate, of course, after this superb, visceral performance in *This Woman Is Mine*, Brennan had to make the best of playing a perfunctory, if enjoyable role in *Rise and Shine* (November 21, 1941), appearing as another Southern crank. As he said, "The greatest bugaboo in Hollywood is being 'typed.' And that's exactly what I want to avoid. It's just as easy to be typed in the role of old man as, say, a villain." Walter dreaded doing a role that he thought would "finish him off" in a preposterous story about a dim-witted college football player (Jack Oakie) who cannot stay awake, let alone study for his exams— and is then kidnapped by a gambling cartel. Allan Dwan (one of Hollywood's great directors dating back to the silent days) had a good cast to work with, including George Murphy, Linda Darnell, Milton Berle, Sheldon Leonard (who specialized in playing heavies), and the eccentric Donald Meek, who contributes so much good local color to *Barbary Coast*. Berle, playing a dumb henchman, whinnies and is called Seabiscuit. Meek plays a college professor obsessed with magic tricks. Murphy does his patented song and dance routines. And Darnell, playing the down home girl, supplies the love interest. Brennan postures as eighty-year-old Grandpa, his oldest character yet, still fighting the Civil War, with a "fatal weakness for blondes" and "given to wild bursts of senile rug-cutting," to quote Harry Brand's Twentieth Century-Fox publicity release. Brennan gave his absurd role his usual careful preparation, which included removing his upper bridge to muffle his diction and to create more wrinkles around his mouth. Hours of practice before a mirror satisfied him that he was "letter-perfect in the squint of age." He was given the hairpiece and beard he wore in *Kentucky*, and his acerbic asides are clearly meant to recall Peter Goodwin's. "Can't you talk?" he asks Oakie. "Sure I can talk," says Oakie, whose mouth is full of food. "Well, let's hear you say something," Brennan demands. "Well, I ain't got anything to say," Oakie admits. "Fine, you and me's going to get along fine," Brennan tells him. "It would be a great world if people who didn't have anything to say would make up their mind to shut up." A flummoxed Oakie stares at Brennan, while the dog eats Oakie's food and Meek does one of his magic tricks, appearing to insert a long needle into his bald head and draw it back out. Although Grandpa hits on the blonde next door, he does it with such charm and perkiness that Brennan gets away with playing what is essentially a dirty old man part. It is worth watching the movie to see him dance with his blonde pickup, clicking his heels, and then sitting her down at a table and showing her his $32,000 bank account—actually just a little notebook, although he claims to have the money (which turns out to be Confederate currency) hidden under his bed. When his date rejects his advances, he says, "The night is young. Why don't you be like the night?" When she pleads to be taken home and is willing do anything he wants in return, he says, "Then what's the use of going home?" But of course his role dictates that he resign himself to playing the grouchy guy who drives her home. Brennan's lines came from one of Hollywood's greatest screenwriters, Herman Mankiewicz, who wrote *Citizen Kane*. In the end, Grandpa serves as Murphy's sidekick in a successful effort to rescue Oakie so he can play in the big game, which the gamblers expected to win by preventing the star player from appearing.

After seeing the completed film, Brennan thanked Goldwyn for persuading him to do it. "It's stories like these," he told Hedda Hopper, "that make you realize it isn't all beer and skittles in the life of a producer. I don't mean our people should be mollycoddles and do things against their will, but they should listen to men who back their own opinions with their own cash." Brennan always had a healthy respect for businessmen and liked to think of himself as one, too. After the production wrapped on *Rise and Shine*, he was finally able to spend some time with his family at Lightning Creek.

Between *This Woman Is Mine* and *Rise and Shine*, Brennan gave a stirring performance as an outcast in *Swamp Water* (October 23, 1941). As

Tom Keefer, unjustly accused of murder and taking refuge in a swamp, he becomes a second father to Ben Ragan (Dana Andrews), estranged from his crusty father, Thursday (Walter Huston). Ben happens on Keefer while searching the swamp for his dog, Trouble. The young man learns the ways of the swamp from Keefer, and he also realizes Keefer is innocent. Their bond is strengthened further when Ben falls in love with Keefer's daughter, Julie (Anne Baxter).

Ward Bond has a key role as Tim Dorson, the real murderer, now aided by his brother, Hardy (veteran character actor Joe Sawyer). Tim and Hardy terrorize Ben, but are led to their doom when they pursue him into the swamp. Keefer traps Sawyer in quicksand and drives Bond into the wilds of the swamp, where he will surely die. Rounding out this impressive cast of character actors is John Carradine, playing the craven tool of the Bond-Sawyer duo. Carradine knows Keefer is innocent but is afraid to tell the truth.

Jean Renoir, working on his first American picture, created beautiful, lush shots of the Georgia swamp, although much of the film was made in the studio. But Brennan remembered the cottonmouths and was grateful that he had a double in scenes with snakes, since one of the reptiles (they were not defanged) bit one of the trainers. Like other cast members, Brennan found Renoir "wonderful." "Oh, what a gentleman," he recalled. "Oh, I just loved the guy. He was so gentle and nice." During one take, Walter turned to the director and said, "How was that, Gene?" Renoir said, "[I]t was good. I liked it. I have tears in my eyes." Walter said, "Oh, I thought it was lousy." A perplexed Renoir, whose understanding of English was imperfect, called for an interpreter. When he agreed to let Brennan do the scene again, he had to admit the retake was better.

Dudley Nichols's script smooths the rough edges of Vereen Bell's novel, making Keefer a more sympathetic character more in line with Brennan's screen persona as the irascible but ultimately decent and tenderhearted crank. Brennan is suitably grimy for a guy who lives in a swamp, and Keefer, like the Colonel in *Meet John Doe*, stands out as a rebuke to civilization. He is a natural man without a place in a corrupt society. The power of Brennan's most memorable characters derives from their autonomy. They operate independently of what others expect of them and will not compromise their convictions. In this case, the swamp becomes a mysterious and sacrosanct domain where evildoers like the Dorson brothers are bound to perish. As Dudley Nichols put it in his report to Darryl Zanuck, "The swamp is a world in itself . . . it has an added factor,

a sort of religious atmosphere, casting shadows of eternity over the people who dwell near it, giving depth and meaning to their lives." Ben says
as much when he calls the swamp "another world," and Keefer, spot-
lighted in the darkness surrounding a campfire says, "I hear stars is other
worlds too. Big rafts shining in the ocean of God's night . . . . Livin' in this
swamp is just like livin' on another star." Brennan delivers the lines with
an ease and pleasure that tempers their otherwise factitious insertion in
the dialogue. Keefer has had plenty of time to think in the swamp, and
now that he can actually articulate his observations to another human
being, he is profoundly happy.

Swamp Water was a huge hit, especially in the South. Much has been
made of Darryl Zanuck's editing of Renoir, who preferred longer takes
and atmospherics to Zanuck's taut plot construction and melodramatic
character types. But the authenticity of the performances—especially
those delivered by Brennan, Andrews, Huston, and Baxter—override the
script's sentimentality and make this film a neglected classic.

Brennan's identification with the land, and with a persona that seems
as solid and enduring as the earth itself, made him the natural choice to
play Karp in *The North Star* (November 4, 1943). Karp, a Ukrainian peasant, is unbowed by the brutal German assault on his village at the beginning of Hitler's invasion of the Soviet Union. Counterpointed with Brennan, Erich von Stroheim exerts all of his aristocratic bearing as a German
surgeon disdainful of his second-in-command, played by Martin Kosleck
(himself a refugee from Hitler's Germany who often played Nazis). Brennan's daughter, Ruthie, working under the name Lynn Winthrop, made
her screen debut as Karp's granddaughter, who takes up arms against the
invading Germans. She ended her career early when she married. When
I mentioned the film to Mike Brennan, he immediately said his father
did not like it: "It had too much Commie in it." Directed by Lewis Milestone, and written by Stalinist Lillian Hellman, this three-million-dollar
Goldwyn production was, at the time, considered part of the war effort
aimed at bolstering America's solidarity with its Soviet allies.

A more welcome assignment was a ten-minute short, "To Each Other,"
promoting the war effort. Sponsored by U. S. Steel, the film depicts a $700
million program to build and expand blast furnaces for a "war of steel,"
Walter says, impersonating a steelworker reading aloud from a letter from
his son in the armed services. Shots of rolling mills turning out huge steel
plates punctuate the steelworker's report to his son. Whole new plants
are being built and production records broken, as illustrated in shots of
miles of steel rods and pipes, and of springs for machine guns, anti-aircraft

guns, automatic rifles, and other weapons. Wire for radios and other instruments for bombs slide along assembly lines. Women welders shape
protective armor and shells for aircraft and tanks. Steel invasion ships are
launched, as the steelman says he hates to think of the enemy having to
fight against such a mass of escort ships coming out of expanding ship-
yards—in one instance, four new ships are launched in fourteen minutes. "That's really rolling out the tonnage," Walter the steelman declares
to his son, ending with the message, "[W]e are all fighting together for
the day when you come home."

Although Brennan spent as much time away from Hollywood as he
could manage, he had films sent to his Oregon ranch, where he sat in
his own specially built projection room along with his wife and his son
Mike. Sometimes he would rerun an interesting film and even slow it
down to look at close-ups and makeup. Some directors only expected
him to play a certain type, but he was always eager to try something
new. At this point, he might well have become stuck playing provincials,
if not for a director who realized that Brennan exuded a strength of purpose and possessed a command of character that permitted him to play
virtually any nationality in any setting. In *Hangmen Also Die!* (April 15,
1943), Fritz Lang's film about the assassination of Hitler's henchman, Re-
inhard Heydrich, Brennan jettisons his avuncular and rustic persona for
a powerful performance as a Czech professor. Lang, a refugee from Nazi
Germany, specifically requested Brennan, later judging the character actor "very good"—high praise indeed from a demanding director. Brian
Donlevy, who played the heavy in *Barbary Coast*, appears as a Czech doctor whom Brennan's professor has to hide when the doctor narrowly
escapes after assassinating Heydrich in Nazi-occupied Czechoslovakia.
David Thomson's remark that Donlevy has a streak of "naive honesty" in
certain roles is especially applicable to *Hangmen Also Die!*, since the doctor desperately needs the help of the shrewd professor. Brennan handles
his part with masterly understatement, a performance that is especially
noteworthy because so many of his roles called for far more boisterous
behavior.

Gene Lockhart's extroverted performance as a Czech collaborator
makes a fitting contrast to Brennan's circumspect but principled professor. "I rate Gene one of the best craftsmen in our business," Brennan
said. "I always run his pictures two or three times." Lockhart had tricks
worth "watching and stealing." Brian Donlevy, the hero who assassinates
Heydrich, is all the more impressive because he is not merely presented
as the noble anti-Fascist, but as a doctor committing a counterintuitive

act that he barely manages to accomplish. In this case, the actors had the benefit not only of Fritz Lang's sophisticated direction, but also of Bertolt Brecht's nuanced script, although the ultimate product was also given some Hollywood polish by screenwriter John Wexley.

Brennan's offbeat role in *Slightly Dangerous* (April 1943), with Lana Turner and Robert Young, is much more fun to watch than his predictable parts in A-list pictures such as *The Pride of the Yankees* (July 14, 1942), starring Gary Cooper, and *Stand by for Action* (December 31, 1942), a vehicle for Robert Taylor. In the Lou Gehrig biopic, Brennan plays Sam Blake, a journalist who becomes the right-hand man for Gehrig (Cooper), the legendary baseball player who had died the previous year of amyotrophic lateral sclerosis (ALS), a progressive neurodegenerative disease that affects nerve cells in the brain. Blake, a journalist, is there to cover and comment on Gehrig's sensational career, which included 2,130 consecutive games, a lifetime batting average of .341, and four Most Valuable Player awards. Blake is loyal and proud, a sentimental antidote to the cynical newspaperman Hank Hanneman, a role performed with the right edginess by the always reliable Dan Duryea. Sam Wood's saccharine direction is labored, although Teresa Wright as Gehrig's wife performs at her usual high level. As Brennan said of her, "[S]he's a truly great dramatic actress. She has that inner fire, sincerity, imagination, and self-discipline that are the trademarks of true genius. It isn't in that girl to give a bad performance." Gary Cooper has the right sensibility for his role, but he is too old in the early scenes and is not given much to do except seem humble and noble next to the equally irreproachable Blake.

Similarly, in *Stand by for Action*, as chief yeoman Henry Johnson, Brennan can't do much more than provide some ballast for the lightweight Robert Taylor, playing a callow officer who has to learn a thing or two from seasoned Lieutenant Commander Martin J. Roberts (Brian Donlevy). Brennan's part could be cut out of the film without altering the plot in any significant way. It is a pity that Charles Laughton, playing an admiral, never goes head-to-head with Brennan. *That* would have been wonderful to watch.

But in *Slightly Dangerous*, in a role that Brennan claimed did not suit him, he makes a spectacular entrance that entirely changes the tempo of a slight, silly, and perfectly enjoyable film. Lana Turner romps through this light comedy as Peggy Evans, a working-class girl who jettisons her job and decides to provide for herself by assuming a new identity as an amnesiac heiress, Carol Burden, so that she can claim the fortune belonging to the long missing (and presumably kidnapped) child of tycoon

Cornelius Burden (Brennan). Turner does not have Carole Lombard's flair, but she has enough of Lombard's feisty sexuality and cunning that is matched, surprisingly, by Robert Young's gifted, implosive performance as her employer, Bob Stuart, who wants to expose her ruse. Young dances well and demonstrates a knack for physical comedy and double takes in scenes that show his world collapsing in on itself as he is stymied in his quest to reclaim his employee. Playing Durstin, a newspaper proprietor, Eugene Pallette, a character actor easily recognizable by his stout figure and stentorian voice, almost whispers, "This is a great moment, a sacred moment"—presumably because the grieving father will be reunited with his daughter.

A photographer is on hand as businessman Cornelius Burden (Walter Brennan), in three-piece suit and wide-brimmed hat, enters. Brennan bursts into the plot by charging into the room where Turner is supposed to prove her bona fides as Carol Burden. As the camera flashes, Burden grabs it and hurls it right at the center of the screen in a shot that is followed by a cut, then a shot of the broken windowpane, marred by a hole shaped like the flash attachment of the camera. Such is movie magic. "Now which one of you muck raking buzzards is Durstin?" the menacing Burden asks. As Burden explains how he has broken all of his business competitors and exposed other women pretending to be his daughter he flicks his finger across Durstin's nose and says, "I'll break you like a dried twig." The forceful, lean Burden calls the credulous, porcine Durstin, a "beer barrel," who has been terrorizing his staff, but is now reduced to stammering out a defense of his motivations. Burden is stopped from further dominating the scene by Peggy's decision to reverse course now that she fears exposure. When Burden says with gusto, "Let's get started," she blurts out, "Wait," and tells Durstin, "He's not my father." The disappointed Durstin asks for an explanation. "Well," she considers, and then says, "his face." Brennan's reaction is reminiscent of his work on *The Westerner*. He reflects surprise by raising his eyebrows in a facelift that resets his emotional temperature, so to speak. For once, the powerful, cynical businessman is caught off guard. "What about my face?" he asks, squinting, as if for the first time he is not confident he can see through this new pretender. "It's a face you couldn't forget, especially if you'd been exposed to it as a child," the cross Peggy answers. Remarkably, it is the imposter who is offended, as Burden looks on in genuine puzzlement, his eyes now open but giving her a penetrating look. Suddenly the momentum of the scene shifts to Turner, as Brennan looks on, a spectator now resigned to watching Durstin persuade his protégé to prove her identity. When Burden's lawyer threatens to get the district attorney involved, Peggy agrees to submit to Burden's request that she meet with the nurse who took care of his daughter. A thoroughly disconcerted Peggy declares, "If I turn out to be your daughter, I'm going to run away from home." "And I'll help you," Burden retorts. Out of the office, she is handed over to Ward Bond, playing Brennan's bodyguard. The rest of the cast—Dame May Whitty as Baba the nurse, Alan Mowbray as the English gentleman who befriends Stuart, and an extraordinary large ensemble with many familiar faces and bit players—reflects director Wesley Ruggles's meticulous coordination of character types and faces.

Brennan's first scene is his best in the picture. Gradually, he is shown to have a sentimental side that has been carefully hidden so as not to be hurt by all the claimants to his fortune. But enough of his humanity is shown in that first scene so that when he does, in fact, learn that Peggy is not his daughter, we can believe he has become so emotionally invested in treating her as his offspring that he cannot accept her admission that she is a fraud. None of this is credible, of course, and yet in the emotional universe of this marvelously put together movie, probability does not matter. What does is that Bob Stuart, like Cornelius Burden, comes to love Peggy, who is a perfect realization of their desires. Plot and subplot, father and daughter, daughter and her lover-pursuer, are thrown together in a final scene in which make believe trumps reality. She has found a father who accepts her, and a suitor who cares more about her than about exposing her fraudulent claims. Shopgirl Peggy Evans's wish for another life and the power of her imagination are what ultimately drives the movie and moves these men into the power of their love for her.

An MGM promotion piece in *Lion's Roar* (April 1943) noted that in *Slightly Dangerous* Walter Brennan is kissed on-screen for the first time. In fact, Turner kisses him six times, and Brennan claimed he "couldn't be comfortable in a role" that involved "a manicure, stiff collar, freshly scrubbed appearance, daily shaves, starched shirt, tails and a top hat." Strictly an unshaven blue-collar actor with grubby clothes and broken teeth, he had to redo a scene because of so much lipstick on his face.

It is unlikely, though, that playing dress up bothered him as much as showing so much of his real face to the camera. He did not want to be recognized, he admitted. He would later turn down the part of a magazine publisher in *Gentleman's Agreement* because he didn't "feel right in those dress-up parts." Some scenes with Turner bothered him, too. He thought the cinematographer was showing a little too much of her bust and so advised the cameraman, "Make sure you cut that shot pretty high." Even in interviews, Brennan preferred performing to divulging his own identity: "He amused and amazed us yesterday by slipping from Southern dialect into Irish brogue, to Scotch burr to Texas twang. He claims, jokingly, that if he were two feet shorter, he'd make the best Japanese butler in Hollywood, and he rattled off a barrage of pidgin English to prove it," a Richmond, Virginia, reporter noted. Nearly two decades later, Brennan reveled in stumping the *What's My Line* panel by speaking in a Japanese accent.

Off-screen, Walter Brennan wanted nothing more than to go home and have dinner with his wife and enjoy their Oregon ranch, where he returned during the Christmas holidays of 1943. Running into blowing wind and snowdrifts on Christmas Eve resulted in quite an adventure. As Walter wrote to Ray and Bessie Pogue, the drifts got so deep he and a friend got out and stood on the car's right fender, not wanting to bother with chains. As they struggled to the top of a rise, the car's driver shouted:

> "Hang on!—if I make it this time I'm going to hit out across country," so when he got moving I made a dive for the right running board and grabbed the door handle and we were off on a cold ride, Ken bouncing on the back fender with only the rear light to hang on to and me hanging on to the side with my fingernails and eyebrows. When Grant saw a suspicious mound in front of him, he'd swerve around it, thus causing deep mental cruelty to Brennan [referring to himself in the third person], who expected to fall off any minute. Well, we finally made it, and it was the first time I was ever out of breath from just hanging on."

Ray Pogue enjoyed Walter's account of his adventure, but also said it was just one of those "everyday occurrences" at Lightning Creek, where life was never monotonous. February 1944 in California was also hazardous, owing to a thunderstorm that caused a two-day power outage that shut down the Brennan breeder, and Walter and Ruth had to bring thirty chicks into the house. They were placed on a tile shelf by a breakfast room window, next to a telephone where their peeping made communication almost impossible. The other news, Walter informed Ray and Bessie Pogue, was that Mike would be inducted into the army on March 13. He was hoping to see Andy soon, if a furlough from the Navy came through.

Walter spent no time on politics or associating with actors in the causes that agitated the country in the 1930s and early 1940s. The abbreviated references to his private life seem part of his carefully couched rejection of phoniness. To pretend to be someone else as a profession suited him, so long as his work was shown to have virtually nothing to do with him as a person. And yet his on-screen roles are often about characters like Brennan, who cannot abide phonies. He never played himself, to be sure, but he could not be himself unless he played roles with conviction. And he did everything he could to maintain the same integrity on-screen and off. As one of his grandchildren recalled, he would never work with anyone that he could not bring home to dinner. But which actors or actresses his father did not like was not given voice at home. Walter Brennan did not gossip, his son Andy recalled. "He never said anything about these people."

It is doubtful, for example, that Brennan would have brought Ward Bond home to dinner, although the two appeared in nine pictures together, and Brennan had a very high opinion of Bond's talents: "He's so good they ought to star him." But Bond was a roaring drunk and part of director John Ford's stable of actors, palling around with John Wayne, and acting, as Wayne's biographer Scott Eyman puts it, the part of Javert in the rightwing campaign against communists and their sympathizers in Hollywood. Brennan sympathized with Bond's anti-New Deal diatribes, but he wanted no part of Bond's society outside the studios. Hollywood was more of a moral problem for Brennan than a concern with subversives infiltrating the movie industry. Bond and his ilk were bullies. Brennan would play such characters, but he would not seek their company off-screen.

Brennan's ability to play the patriarch, the man who can take the world in hand, made him the best choice to play J. F. "Thunder" Bolt in *Home in Indiana* (June 15, 1944), yet another horse racing picture. But this time, he is not the crotchety horse breeding Southern malcontent of *Kentucky* who is vindicated in his choice of the winning Derby horse, or the fiery autarchic horse trainer of *Maryland* who comes out of retirement to watch his horse ride to victory again. Instead, Brennan plays a loser, a broken man, a harness racing driver busted by a falling out with his partner. He is also a failed contender for the winning stake in the state's most important harness racing event. He has lost nearly everything and lives on a land filled with empty stables, with only memories that drive him to drink during the horseracing season. Like *Kentucky* and *Maryland*, *Home in Indiana* is a color film celebrating a lush pastoral landscape. In place of Loretta Young and Brenda Joyce, this third equine drama features the charms of a "dazzling blonde," June Haver, and tomboy/horse girl Jeanne Crain, attracted to "Sparke" Thornton (Lon McCallister), whose mission is to restore J. F. Thunder's desire to race again.

Unlike the previous two equine pictures, Brennan, under the direction of Henry Hathaway, is allowed to bring a startling degree of realism to his role when he learns that Sparke, his adopted son, is about to breed Lady, a blind once-upon-a-time champion. Brennan looms in a doorway, hands at his sides, in a low angle shot that makes him look especially menacing. It was one of the few times that any director took advantage of his six-foot, one-inch height. As Thunder's wife screams at him not to "beat the boy," Thunder advances on Sparke, saying "I'm goin' to lick you boy." He slashes away at Sparke for a frightening seven seconds, talking to the boy as though Lady were a woman that Sparke had been fooling around with. Brennan gives McCallister nine strokes across the head, as the boy tries to protect himself with his arms. As Brennan delivers the last slash he is overcome not just from physical exertion, but also from the brutality of what he has done. He just stands there heaving for more than thirty seconds, as Sparke quietly offers his apology, saying he wanted to tell Thunder about the horse the night he heard Thunder walking up and down the floor overhead. Sparke is referring to a scene in which Hathaway shoots only Brennan's shoes shuffling in drunken steps on the floorboards, an eloquent synecdoche for the disintegration of the whole man. Brennan might have had this scene in mind when he described Hathaway as a "good mechanic. Not only a mechanic, he puts little stuff in it besides the mechanics of making pictures."

The beating Sparke takes marks the turning point in the picture, when Thunder and Sparke emerge as partners in a horseracing scheme as Thunder's perplexed wife mutters, "Men." Of course, from this point on, the picture follows a predictable course, with Brennan perking up, Haver dazzling McCallister, and Crain mooning after her jockey boy, who wins his first race and suddenly becomes Haver's favorite. Brennan shifts the picture's mood again when he stands still, concerned as the experienced Thunder would be, that Sparke, his young protégé, may not have seen enough "dirt" in his first race—meaning Sparke does not realize the competition will resort to dirty tricks to prevent him from winning the next contest. Sure enough, Sparke is "framed" in the next race—that is, boxed in. When Sparke tries to ram the other racer, his horse goes down in a tangle, injuring Sparke's right leg, a serious and potentially devastating setback, which, after an anxious period, Thunder is able to remedy.

In the next race, Sparke loses the first heat when he is framed, making him afraid to break out of the pack. In the second heat, Sparke passes his rival, tricking him into thinking his wheel is loose. The stakes are raised when the groomer reminds Sparke that he has brought Thunder back to his former self. Now all depends on Sparke winning the third and deciding heat to redeem Thunder. But Sparke does not realize his horse is almost blind, a worsening condition that Thunder has kept from the boy. Sparke wins, but then the horse crashes into the rail, revealing what Thunder has kept secret. The horse's blindness seems, though, simply the sign of a debility, the fear of failure, that Thunder has overcome. The ending is of course too neat, but also necessary by Hollywood standards. Indeed, it helped the film win the affection of reviewers as a "warm, modern yarn." Alton Cook of the *New York World-Telegram* (June 21, 1944) summed up the verdict on Brennan, affirming that there was no "wavering" in the actor's art. Several viewers note that the film, set in contemporary America, seems encased in a time capsule, making no reference to the war. Today's viewers, judging by the responses on IMDb, find *Home in Indiana* tame entertainment, which is nonetheless valuable in a nostalgic sort of way.

The film seemed to have the same nostalgic appeal for Brennan. Around horses again, he wrote to the wife of William Weston, Walter's former employer in Swampscott, where as a thirteen-year-old he had driven a horse drawn express wagon for three dollars a week. When Mrs. Weston received a still from the picture Walter had sent her, telling her he remembered the Weston horse, "Camden Boy," she responded by sending him three pewter cups engraved with Camden Boy's name and title as the grand trotting champion of the Gentleman's Riding Club of Rockdale, Massachusetts, in 1904, 1905, and 1906. The cups took their place on the mantelpiece in the Brennan home.

A far more important role than Thunder, but one that again explored Brennan's character's triumph over his own frailties, is the "rummy," Eddie, in *To Have and Have Not* (October 11, 1944), starring Humphrey Bogart and Lauren Bacall. In December, 1943, Howard Hawks met with Brennan for a pre-production conference, a sign of the director's keen desire to get the supporting role exactly right. Brennan's name in the credits would appear in type 60 percent the size of that used for Bogart, and Goldwyn would get $2,500 a week for the actor's services during nearly a three-month period that stretched from March to May of 1944. This was now the standard agreement for a Brennan loan out.

A month before production began, the Breen office signaled its discomfort with the film's lack of moral hygiene:

> The general unacceptability of this story is emphasized by its overall *low tone* and by the suggestion that your sympathetic lead, Morgan, is a murderer, who is permitted to go off unpunished.
>
> The characters of Morgan, Eddy [*sic*], Marie, Helen and Amelia should be *softened* in order to get away from the present "scummy" flavor which their activities throw forth.
>
> The scene of the battle between Renardo, Coyo, Morgan and Eddy [*sic*] should be shot in such a way as to make certain there be no unnecessary brutality or gruesomeness about it.
>
> Please omit the words "God-forsaken."

Surprisingly, the sexually suggestive scene between Bogart and Bacall aroused no objections—except in Ohio. The censor there saw the finished print and was disturbed when Bacall's comments, "It's even better when you help," after Bogart finally kisses her back (her first effort does not seem to stimulate him).

Alongside Humphrey Bogart, playing Harry Morgan in *Casablanca* mode, Eddie behaves as if the self-contained star needs him, even though, as "Slim" (Bacall) tells Morgan, "You wouldn't take anything from anybody." What Eddie has to give is affection and loyalty, qualities in short supply in Vichy-controlled Martinique. When Mr. Johnson, who has hired Harry's fishing boat for a day, says he does not see why Harry keeps "that rummy around." Harry replies, "Eddie was a good man on a boat before he got to be a rummy." But why does Harry look after Eddie? Johnson asks. "Is he related to you, or somethin'?" Harry replies, "He thinks he's looking after me." In fact, Eddie does think of himself as Harry's protector, and when Harry kicks Eddie off his boat, Eddie senses Harry is in trouble and stows away. "You can't fool me," Eddie tells Harry, who has been trying to keep Eddie—who talks too much—out of trouble.

Eddie doesn't want anything from Harry except some acknowledgment of their bond and another drink, which Morgan carefully rations so that Eddie remains sober enough to do his job aboard Morgan's boat. Harry at first reluctantly puts the boat at the disposal of a French resistance leader seeking a way out of Nazi-patrolled waters. But Harry does not have much in common with the character in the Hemingway novel the picture is supposedly based on and wants no part of politics. He would prefer to stick to his business as a hired fisherman. But as soon as the Vichy authorities begin to get in Harry's way, he sides with the Resistance, just as the disaffected Rick does in *Casablanca*.

The shambling walk Brennan perfected for his role suggests a man always on the verge of the shakes. Gerald Mast observes, "Walter Brennan's quirky, jumpy, jittery performance as Eddie—one of the very best of his very distinguished career—took its cue from a single descriptive sentence in the Hemingway novel: 'He walked with his joints all slung wrong.'" No other actor in Hollywood could shuffle himself into greatness. The unsteady Eddie seems the last person in the world that Harry should rely on, and yet, in one of the film's key scenes, Eddie steers the boat straight through the night, enabling Harry to concentrate on outwitting a Vichy patrol boat. Filmed on location, it was not an easy scene to finesse. Walter had trouble with his lines, trying to perfect both his delivery and his jitters. Hawks stopped shooting and conferred with Brennan for about ten minutes before rehearsing the scene again. Still not satisfied, actor and director talked some more about the scene, and then did a take. Brennan, still shaking after Hawks called cut and said it was "fine," said, "I've got 'em, and not from rum."

Everyone except Slim treats Eddie like a pathetic hanger-on. What she sees is Eddie's endearing humanity and loyalty to Morgan, whom Slim has, of course, fallen in love with. Eddie, too, loves Morgan, who safeguards his fragile sidekick (Brennan is almost as gaunt here as he was as Old Atrocity), and by doing so makes Eddie strong enough to collaborate in a plot to save the lives of a French Resistance fighter (Walter Szurovy) and his wife (Dolores Moran). Brennan, steering Harry's boat out of trouble during a shoot-out with Vichy authorities, remains in stride with Bogart and Bacall—memorably so in the film's last scene, which shows him hobbling in tune to the music heralding the romantic couple's successful escape from Martinique.

Critic Nicholas Spencer observes just how central Brennan's Eddie is to the ideology of *To Have and Have Not*, a film that heralds and sanctions America's entry into World War II: "Harry's loyalty to Eddie highlights the importance of being true to one's allies when they are in trouble." Eddie turns out to be good with a gun and transforms himself, as Spencer notes, from "incompetent alcoholic to freedom fighter." No other character actor in Hollywood history rivals Brennan in the pivotal roles he played in so many films.

In retrospect, at least, Brennan's role here seems even richer than later critics like Spencer suppose. During a world war, when fascist ideology idealizes strength and ruthlessness, Eddie represents an entirely different worldview and moral code. He is not an example of the survival of the fittest, but instead is a weak man who overcomes the overwhelming odds set against him. A greater failure than any other character Brennan ever played, Eddie draws strength from Harry and is redeemed. He is the common man, the little man, the derelict, the hanger-on, the socially marginal—in short, everything the Nazis deemed worthy of extermination. He is a fool attached to a wise man. Eddie is the underside of society that fascist ideology dismissed as unworthy to exist. He is unhealthy and dependent on charity, and yet he is an indispensable part of the humanity that Harry Morgan cannot detach himself from.

Eddie is not beautiful like Bacall, who plays her important part in treating Eddie with decency and even affection, turning Eddie's querulous refrain, "Was you ever stung by a dead bee?" on Eddie, who then realizes she is on his side. And why not? Bacall, after all, plays a woman who cons men (she is a pickpocket), until she meets a man like Harry who cannot be conned. With her throaty low-pitched voice, Bacall seems, in fact, a feminine Bogart, "tough and taciturn," as Otis L. Guernsey described the actor in his *New York Herald Tribune* review (October 12, 1944).

Slim loves Harry, in part, because of his attachment to Eddie, not despite it. The scenes between Bacall and Brennan are tender and perhaps influenced by their friendship. In reminiscing about his work, Brennan said little about Bogart, except that he was "all right . . . a nice guy." They apparently got on well in a joking sort of way. Bogart made fun of Brennan's drinker's nose reminiscent of W. C. Fields, and Walter retorted: "There's a difference. He had fun getting his." But Walter knew Bacall before Bogart did. When Hawks saw the teenage model Betty Joan Perske on a magazine cover, he wanted to do a screen test with her and Brennan, who explained what happened:

I said, "Why don't you get one of these guys to take it?"

He says, "Well, you'd make her feel at ease."

I said, "Gee, Howard, I don't know whether Goldwyn will let me do this."

And Bob McIntyre [Goldwyn's casting director] called me up, and he had this deep voice, he said, "You can't do that. We got to pay you."

I said, "Well, I'm going to do it for nothing. I'll do it for Howard Hawks." And so I did it. She really shook. If you ever get to talk to her, she'll tell you how she shook.

It is not hard to imagine why the newly named Lauren Bacall treats the shaky Eddie with so much sensitivity. As John T. McManus put it in his review (*PM*, October 12, 1944), "*To Have and Have Not* has a healthy, democratic flesh tone, and it is not only skin deep." But so entranced were the reviewers with Bogart and Bacall that Brennan's superlative achievement was given only glancing recognition, as in Alton's Cook's salute to the actor's drawing on his "endless variety of resources," and, in *New York Times* critic Bosley Crowther's remark that Brennan's work is "affecting" but "pointless"!

This powerful film about redemption is as good as any film Brennan appeared in, and his performance here outranks all his others, except for his tour de force role as Judge Roy Bean.

CHAPTER 6

Western Brennan

Bob Hope, Henry Fonda, John Wayne,
John Ford, Howard Hawks
1944–48

IT SEEMS AS THOUGH IN THESE YEARS WALTER BRENNAN SPENT ALL OF his time on movie sets—sometimes several at a time. During the making of *To Have and Have Not*, for example, Goldwyn borrowed him for work on other productions, while Hawks, fourteen days behind schedule, shot scenes with the other actors. And yet Walter did have a life, however fitful, outside his production schedule. During a three-day blackout that occurred in the midst of a storm, he fretted over the fifty eggs that were about to hatch on his farm. He moved the eggs into his library and proudly announced to the cast of *To Have and Have Not* that not a single chick had been lost. "They should be prize winners," he said. "I had the eggs right close to my three supporting performance Oscars." Such comments seem to put his Hollywood career in perspective. "I rarely go to the movies," Brennan told Warner Bros. publicist Bill Rice. "I get nervous when I see my own pictures. Gable, for instance, is Gable in pictures. . . . But I never play myself. . . . always someone else, covered with layers of makeup and hair. I am afraid to go into a motion picture theatre and see myself on the screen because I don't know who I'll be next. It disconcerts me." The ranch was more than a getaway, it also seemed a way of exerting control over his own life. "First returns of the Spring calf crop from Walter Brennan's Oregon ranch have netted the actor 500 young Herefords," Rice reported, adding that Brennan told Humphrey Bogart "he'd need at least ten cowhands for the late spring roundup. He keeps four on the place the year round."

Mike took over running the ranch when he returned home from military service in 1946. He began working on the land during his last year in high school, and, except for two years in the army, he has lived in Wallowa County ever since. It had been Walter's idea for Mike to run the ranch after Walter caught the manager stealing food for his family. Mike wasn't sure he could do the job, but Walter said he needed someone he could rely on. Walter also called on his friend, Cub (Stanwood William Begley), a down-to-earth, honest friend and business associate who accompanied him on trips to Montana to buy cattle. Cub would go out to the ranch to see how Mike progressed. "Now what are you doing with the hay? And what are you doing with the horses?" Cub would ask, and he would let Walter know everything was on track. Mike tried various kinds of "tricks" as a rancher, and some were not successful. But others were, and to Walter it was clear his son had taken to work that often meant fourteen and sixteen hour days. Mike liked to talk about ranching, and Walter liked to listen to him and to the old timers in Wallowa County who shared their experiences with him.

When Mike married in 1943, his wife Florence, a native of Wallowa County, began to take care of housekeeping for Ruth. "He was awful good to me and my wife," Mike said. "He thought the sun rose and set on my wife. She could cook anything. He would come up in the morning, and she would say, 'Well, Dad, do you want me to cook you some eggs?' And he'd say, 'Oh yes.' He'd tell everybody the only person who cooked eggs right was my wife."

Mike made many improvements to the ranch, building a Quonset hut barn and employing Roy Daggett, who did a lot of work on the ranch, building roads with bulldozers. Mike dug for water wherever he found the greenest grass, the site of underground springs. The creation of ponds (forty-three in all) supplied water year round. Walter wanted his children and grandchildren to bond with the land and to understand the cycles of nature. Of course, some of the Brennan brood took to the life better than others. Andy stayed only about a year on the ranch before leaving and deciding on a career that led to work as a producer on his father's films and television programs.

Walter would fly from California to Pendleton, Oregon, where Mike would meet him and drive the 120 miles to the ranch. For Walter the ranch was for relaxing, not for much actual outdoor work. "My dad and I did a lot of walking," Mike recalled. Although Walter liked horses, he did not do much riding on the ranch. He had spent his time around motion picture horses. "You could light a firecracker under them," Mike declares, "and they'd just look around as if to say, 'What the hell are you doing?'" Walter and Ruth did participate in branding cattle and took an active interest in the cattle business. "We had about two hundred cows," Mike recalled. "Dad liked to come out here to ride around with me to salt cattle. We used to do it with horses packed with a hundred pounds of salt way out on a ridge. You'd drive a few cattle there, and they'd lick on that salt." In those days ranchers bought and picked up bulls in Colorado, loaded them into a train car in Denver, and rode along with them to La Grande, trucking them the sixty miles or so to the Brennan ranch.

Mike spent very little time visiting his father on movie sets. Andy, on the other hand, seemed fascinated by his father's work. A Warner Bros. publicity release for *To Have and Have Not* reported, "Walter Brennan almost collapsed . . . when his sailor son, Walter, Jr. [Andy], walked into the Warner Bros. sound stage and greeted him. When the actor last heard from young Brennan, he was in the South Pacific. His telegram, announcing that he was coming home on furlough never was delivered. The twenty-year-old sailor has been serving with a Navy gun crew on a merchant ship." Walter Brennan had done his own form of service in *Stand By for Action* and would do so again in *Task Force*.

Howard Hawks once said that Walter Brennan was always a joy to have on a set. He lightened the atmosphere. And he liked to invent "business" for his characters, little ticks and gestures that make an indelible impression on-screen. Not all directors want to hear from actors, of course—especially when such suggestions change the shooting script and throw off the schedule. But Walter was economical with his added bits and usually got along with directors of all dispositions, such as Fritz Lang, Howard Hawks, and William Wyler. "I've had very few people that I couldn't have a good word for," Brennan said late in his career.

One of Walter's favorite directors was David Butler, who directed him in *Kentucky* and again in a Bob Hope vehicle, *The Princess and the Pirate* (November 17, 1944). Butler and Brennan became close friends, and sometime after Brennan won his first Oscar they considered working on a project that would bring Brennan's own story to the screen. Darryl Zanuck was reported to have assigned a team of writers to do just that, but there seems to be no record of what happened next, except for a newspaper article announcing that Butler and Brennan had decided to turn the autobiography into a stage play, to be titled "The Old Character." Brennan would play himself, "returning to the footlights for the first time since he put away his makeup box in 1918 after two years in France in the 26th Division." What became of this project is also a mystery, although Mike Brennan says, "I think that stage play kind of soured him. He liked it, but things had gone too far in the movie business. He didn't care about it." The story, so to speak, had been worn out, Mike thought.

But the Butler-Brennan collaboration splendidly informs *The Prince and the Pirate*, a Samuel Goldwyn million-dollar Technicolor production that spoofs the swashbuckling pictures of the 1930s that made Errol Flynn a star. Butler seems to have given Brennan free rein in bringing to life one of his most exuberant and ribald roles. As Featherhead, a scuzzy pirate, he convinces the malicious Captain Barrett, "the Hook" (Victor McLaglen) to spare a female gypsy fortune-teller, impersonated by "The Great Sylvester" (Hope) from walking the plank. The pirate crew is perplexed by Featherhead's lascivious designs on this none too appetizing dish, but he practically slavers over his prize, which he bears away with great glee. Brennan plays Featherhead with devouring relish. But as soon as he has Hope to himself, Featherhead confesses he has known all along that she is a he. The shocked Sylvester recovers enough to say, "If you don't tell anybody I'm not a gypsy, I won't tell anybody you're not an idiot." Featherhead has appropriated the performer in a scheme to outwit The Hook and to capture a buried treasure. Brennan takes out his teeth for this role, and either through added weight or makeup, presents a rubicund complexion and a robust, rounded face that is startlingly different from the gaunt and rickety Eddie of *To Have and Have Not*.

Featherhead is one of the few Brennan characters possessed of a sex drive, although it is a put-on to put off his fellow pirates. This conceit perhaps explains why *New York Times* reviewer Bosley Crowther called the performance "curiously disturbing." Brennan has a good time leering at Hope and conning a con man, since that is really what Hope is in his role as Sylvester, a character who will feign anything if it will earn money or get him out of a scrape. If Sylvester were not so malleable, he would be of no use to Featherhead, who plays the dunce but is the cleverest figure in the picture. It is pity that Brennan does not have more scenes with the fetching Virginia Mayo, who as Princess Margaret is the damsel in distress that the besotted Sylvester is trying to rescue not only from The Hook, but from the pirate captain's boss, Governor La Roche (Walter Slezak), who imprisons the princess in his West Indian redoubt in the hopes of collecting a ransom from her father. What would Featherhead do with a truly luscious prize? Instead, she is stuck with the cowardly Sylvester. "Why don't you die like a man?" she asks Sylvester, who answers, "Because I'd rather live like a woman."

If he'd had a few more scenes with the principals in *The Princess and the Pirate*, Brennan might well have received another Academy Award nomination. Columnist Erskine Johnson reported that the actor was "being talked up for his fourth Oscar for his role as a toothless idiot." The review in the *Hollywood Reporter* (October 11, 1944) understood his achievement: "Walter Brennan again plays a role utterly unlike anything he has done heretofore and does it with his customary perfection."

Brennan is not as fun to watch playing Captain Bounce in a John Wayne western, *Dakota* (December 1, 1945). Some of the comedy is dated and embarrassing, since it involves Bounce's hectoring of his lazy Negro boatswain, Nicodemus (Nick Stewart). Brennan ferries John Wayne about to various duels with the nefarious Jim Bender (played with lubricious guile by Ward Bond) and his henchman, Bigtree Collins (Mike Mazurki). On land, the out-of-it sea captain entertains the saloon girls with tall tales and barely manages to duck when he is shot at. Bounce is there mainly for comic relief and is hardly integral to the plot. You might almost call Bounce a humors character, a throwback to eighteenth-century fiction, in which a character is exclusively defined by his obsession—in Bounce's case keeping his steamboat intact while he navigates over sandbars and other obstacles. He is truly in a world of his own and cannot quite factor in what happens on land. *Dakota*, a Republic Pictures production, supervised by the efficient Joseph Kane, unfolds in a tight eighty-two minutes, scripted by Carl Foreman with just enough character development and action to fulfill its modest ambitions. A brief review in the *New York Times* (December 17, 1945) sums up the picture well: "When John Wayne gets through with Ward Bond and his hoodlums in 'Dakota,' the good farmers of Fargo are sure of getting a square deal from the invading railroad people." A refreshing departure from the typical western is the provision made for Wayne's wife, subtly played by Vera Ralston, who keeps subverting the hero's plans and exhibits quite a mind of her own. She seems in command much of the time, as befits the Czech-born actress who was married to the head of the studio. The *Los Angeles Examiner*, *Los Angeles Times*, and the *Motion Picture Herald* all gave Brennan good notices. But his performance seems one noted—in part because the script gives him much less leeway than he enjoyed in *The Princess and the Pirate*. The *New York Daily News* (December 16, 1945) gave him one of his rare negative reviews, saying his "comedy role is one of the film's chief weaknesses." Similarly, William Hawkins in the *New York World-Telegram* complained that Brennan "is called on to do a great deal of shouting which isn't very funny." And the reviewer in *Daily Variety* (November 2, 1945), put it only a little more tactfully: "Brennan is inclined to over-emphasize his comedy."

If Sam Goldwyn read the reviews of *Dakota*, he might have taken some satisfaction in Walter Brennan's critical drubbing. Walter had decided not to renew his contract with the producer. The actor, mimicking Goldwyn's accent, later joked that while under contract to the producer, he would be met with "Valter, you are the greatest actor in the vorld." But fifteen minutes after the contract expired, he heard Goldwyn on a studio street talking to Ned Depinet, a movie executive: "You know, Ned, that Valter Brennan is the most overrated actor in the vorld." Brennan told such stories with affection, concluding, "Well, that's Sam for you, and I love him." After all, Goldwyn had, in Brennan's words, "protected me. I could still be doing bits if he hadn't watched out for the kind of parts I played."

Now a freelancer, Brennan accepted the role of Eben Folger, a crusty old New England lighthouse keeper in *A Stolen Life* (July 6, 1946), a Bette Davis showpiece. She plays identical twins, Kate and Patricia Bosworth, who fall in love with the same man, Bill Emerson (Glenn Ford). When the sisters are caught in a storm at sea and Patricia perishes, Kate, who had lost Bill to Patricia, impersonates her dead sister in order to possess the man she loves. Brennan supplies the local color, playing a character he knew well from his earliest days in Swampscott. The small part would have appealed to him because Eben, for all his roughness, is a God-fearing Christian. He is the only witness to the shipwreck and tells Kate (who has been taken from the sea to the lighthouse, all the while pretending to be Patricia), "There ain't no arguing with the will of the Lord." This line foreshadows Kate's eventual realization that she cannot live a lie and will have to own up that it is Patricia who drowned. Although Eben plays no part in the denouement—during which Kate tells Bill of her ruse, and then realizes he loves her after all—the forthright Eben nevertheless provides Brennan with a certain moral authority that resonates elsewhere in the film.

Altogether, Walter's work on *A Stolen Life* amounted to three weeks, stretched over three months (March to May) because of delays in location shooting and days lost during Bette Davis's illness. Then he returned to his Oregon ranch for a few months before beginning work in September on Otto Preminger's Technicolor musical production of *Centennial Summer* (July 10, 1946), set during the Philadelphia Exposition of 1876. Brennan is unusually well outfitted with tailored suits and a handsome beard for his part as Jesse Rogers, the head of a family involved in planning and running the celebration. "This character is likely to cost me the title of 'worst-dressed man in pictures,'" Brennan declared. "Especially when folks see me in that Louis the Fifteenth outfit—satin knee-breech-es and a gold brocaded coat that weighs fifteen pounds." (This was a getup for a costume ball.)

Preminger was notorious for his cruelty to actors. But judging by Brennan's account of one incident involving the director, the actor more than held his own. At one point in the action, Brennan took the reins of a rockaway carriage to drive his family (played by a distinguished group that included Linda Darnell, Jeanne Crain, Constance Bennett, and Dorothy Gish), and the anxious director asked, "But do you know how?" Incredulous, Brennan answered, "Do I know how? Why in World War I, I drove an ammunition supply wagon with a team of four under shellfire." He could have also have mentioned driving a delivery wagon in Swampscott and a horse and wagon in *The North Star.*

Walter Brennan is not given much to do in *Centennial Summer.* He is cast below his abilities, as Preminger biographer Chris Fujiwara notes. With Jerome Kern's music, and delightful leading ladies, the film is pleasant and predictable, and a sentimental favorite of viewers on IMDb. Brennan's character is first seen shouting, "Louder! Louder!" as he re-fuses to be shushed while President Grant mumbles his address at the opening of the exposition. "Thunderation! I can't hear!" Jesse exclaims. Outspoken and refusing to stand on ceremony, Rogers argues with a by-stander, "Are you suggesting, sir, that I pretend to hear what I do not?" Even his wife has no influence over this man, who declares, "There is nothing in the Constitution that prohibits a man from opening his mouth wide and saying what he has to say!" This is, of course, a Brennan persona, by now well ingrained in the moviegoer's imagination. But the film trades on that persona without developing or enriching it in any sig-nificant respect. Rogers, a railroad yardmaster, is an inventor determined to develop a new clock that will show at a glance all the time zones in the country, but his invention is really just a prop for a character with a quirk. And it all gets quite silly when Rogers's wife interrupts him so that he can sit at the piano and sing "I'm happy on the railroad" with one of his daughters.

It is mildly amusing to watch Brennan play Rogers making a fool of himself over his wife's visiting sister, Xenia (Constance Bennett). When she tells Rogers he is more handsome than she expected and gives him a fulsome kiss, he reacts with embarrassed pleasure, touches his tie as if to compose himself, puts on his hat, and clearly feels elevated in Xenia's estimation. At the costume ball, it looks as though Rogers is about to have the vapors when Xenia asks him if he has kissed another woman since he married his wife twenty years ago. "It never came to my mind," he blurts out as it now comes to his mind. "But it's on your mind now," Xenia says slyly. He draws a breath and then lurches toward her, only to be fended off by the approach of the railroad president, who wants to buy his invention.

The role gave Brennan substantial screen time with an excellent cast and a featured drinking scene with Cornell Wilde (courting one of Rogers's daughters). But *Centennial Summer*, designed to compete with the enormously popular *Meet Me in St. Louis*, was a flop, even with another romantic subplot involving Linda Darnell and William Eythe. In the end, Brennan could not do much with his hapless character, whose clock makes him prosperous—but only because Xenia has used her charms on the railroad president.

Brennan experienced a different kind of pleasure working on *Centennial Summer* with his daughter, Ruthie, who had just been signed to a long-term contract with Republic Pictures. Since 1945, she had appeared in bits—uncredited roles—following the same trajectory as her father. Claudia, Ruthie's daughter, remembers that her mom loved acting:

> Someone confided in her that, after watching her in a scene, my grandfather's eyes filled with tears as he said, "She really is great at this, isn't she?" But my grandfather considered the industry pretty dirty by then . . . sleeping with a director could guarantee a pretty young thing a part in a film. He didn't want to help her make it. He wanted that to be her own doing. My mom told me all this. But I also think, looking back now, that my grandfather also felt that anyone's accomplishments should be earned by them—it builds character. At any rate, he knew she was good but didn't pull strings to get her parts.

Ruthie became good friends with Gary Cooper. "I look back and wonder if it wasn't a bit of a crush," his granddaughter, Laura Schaffel, said. "He used to play the piano for her. He was as he was in movies—soft spoken, almost shy and a real gentleman."

Altogether Ruthie would appear in fourteen movies before deciding to relinquish her career for a home and family. Walter Brennan seemed a little nettled when he said, "Why is everybody so confoundedly surprised that I have a daughter who can act? The surprising thing is that she has a father who can sing." When asked about his daughter, he could become unusually loquacious on the subject of his profession:

To hear people talk, you'd think that the ability to act was like the measles—something that could be given by one person to another. But if the acting germ isn't in your blood to start with, nothing will ever develop. So I can't tell my daughter how to act. That's something she'll have to learn by herself, and by experience. About the only advice I can give her that might be worthwhile, is "Just keep your head." There's a lot of luck in this business. Sometimes it's good, and sometimes it's bad. The trick is to take both kinds in stride. If you've ever noticed, most people don't lose their head when the breaks are tough. They try all the harder. But I've seen plenty of promising young players lose their heads over a little success. They forget that maybe the breaks have been good. They start thinking that they, themselves, are good—especially with a flock of people ready to tell them so. They begin to behave accordingly. They relax. And pretty soon the smart ones, who never stop trying to improve, pass them by.

Brennan never used the term star system, but he was clearly thinking about how talent could be corrupted in Hollywood, and he wanted his daughter and other aspiring actors to avoid the excessive self-regard that could canker a career. In his own case, he was still finding new ways both to develop his screen persona, but also to act away from it, so to speak, as he did in his next project.

In *My Darling Clementine* (December 3, 1946), Brennan created one of his most memorable and original roles, one that he would repeat in subsequent films for both dramatic and comic effect. When Brennan, as Old Man Clanton, cattle rustler and all-around criminal, confronts Henry Fonda, playing the legendary Marshall Wyatt Earp, neither man blinks. Faced with Fonda's impassive stare, Brennan's penetrating eyes resemble those of a bird of prey, even as he smiles, Iago-like. When you pull a gun, be sure to kill the man, Brennan advises one of his blundering sons, who gets shot during a confrontation with Fonda. The line is delivered in a matter-of-fact tone that is also an expression of contempt and disgust so economical that Brennan is almost out of camera range as he walks past his wounded boy and out into the world to commit more crimes. Later, during the legendary shoot-out at the O.K. Corral, as Old Man Clanton awaits the arrival of Earp and Doc Holliday (Victor Mature), a low angle shot catches him in the dawning light, his habitual hard look erased by a blank expression as he is captured in a vulnerable moment, seemingly anticipating his fate. As critic Wheeler Winston Dixon concludes, "the real star of the film, other than Fonda, is Walter Brennan . . . as convincing a mob leader as the American screen has ever portrayed."

In the only picture Brennan ever did for the legendary director John Ford, the character actor worked well beside Ford stalwarts such as Ward Bond, playing one of Earp's brothers. Indeed, what is most remarkable about this film is the contrast between Clanton and his boys and Earp and his congenial brothers, the youngest of whom is killed when the Clanton gang rustles cattle the Earps have been driving to California. Brennan personifies the authority of evil, as he does in *Brimstone* (August 15, 1949), where he again bullies his boys into driving out homesteaders. It is almost as if in each subsequent film—especially in Westerns—Brennan is building a persona that is like a suit subjected to constant alteration without ever losing its basic contours. He would essay yet another version of the dominating father with sons in tow in *Shoot Out at Big Sag* (June 1, 1962), an independent production organized by his son Andy, in which Walter plays a pusillanimous preacher who has let down his wife and family by not defending them. But he ultimately redeems himself when he realizes he has lost the respect of everyone, including his daughter, who in the end proves to be his salvation owing to her unwillingness to accept her family's defeatist mentality.

Brennan stayed in character, even when the cameras were not rolling on *My Darling Clementine*. "Don't whip me, Pappy, please!" the actors pleaded. John Ireland, who appears as one of Clanton's sons, said that off-screen Brennan was like the character he played. Walter Brennan, on-screen and off, almost always knew his own mind, an attribute that sometimes resulted in an inability to appreciate other points of view. He simply shut them out, like the single-minded Ike Clanton.

Brennan seems to have met his match in director John Ford. Scott Eyman, a Ford biographer, reports that the usually easygoing Brennan allowed the irascible director to get on his nerves. "Can't you even mount a horse?" Ford shouted at Brennan, when the actor had trouble saddling up. "No, but I got three Oscars for acting," Brennan shot back. Eyman speculates that perhaps Brennan, who was unusually solemn on the set, transferred his hatred of Ford to his maniacal performance as Old Man Clanton. At any rate, Brennan vowed never to work with Ford again.

What miffed Brennan about working with Ford was the director's lack of respect for fellow professionals. Unlike Howard Hawks, Ford was not much of a collaborator. He never gave Brennan the feeling that they were in a project together. Hawks, on the other hand, treated Brennan as a crucial part of a film's success. In *Red River* (September 17, 1948),

Brennan gets nearly as much screen time as John Wayne and co-star Montgomery Clift, in the epic story of a cattle drive from Texas to Missouri that is diverted to Abilene during the lawless days following the Civil War. In one version of the film, Brennan actually narrates the story, making it his own by trading on what was now a character that transcended individual films and seemed, in effect, the voice of the West. In another less powerful version of the film, narration is delivered through the rather clumsy device of turning pages in a book. For the Lux Radio Theatre one-hour adaptation (March 7, 1949), not only was Brennan restored as narrator, he also becomes a dominant voice mediating between Dunson and the other characters.

The opening sequence features two rugged men, Wayne and Brennan, setting out on their own, leaving a wagon train that hours later is massacred in an Indian attack. Wayne and Brennan kill the Indians who attack their camp, showing how necessary they are to one another. Indeed, their ensemble playing reflects critic Thomas Schatz's evaluation of Brennan's work in *The Westerner*, *Sergeant York*, and *Meet John Doe*: Each of Brennan's roles is "crucial in defining and inflecting Cooper's." In *Red River*, Brennan does the explaining—that is, he tells other characters what Wayne is about, why the land and cattle mean so much to him. At the same time, Brennan's character can be highly critical of the hero, the star who strides in his inimitable way across the screen. In other words, Brennan makes the movie real.

While Wayne is nearly always seen in motion, taking charge, Brennan is often filmed in reaction shots—sometimes just looking out at the vast western landscape, registering the immensity of the effort to domesticate and herd life on the range. After a few minutes that establish the characters of the two men and their mission of settling on a piece of land, the film flashes forward fifteen years. Wayne has not aged, but Brennan has fewer teeth and sounds more sibilant and garrulous—again anchoring *Red River* in reality, even as Wayne becomes larger than life in his seeming imperviousness to the passage of time. Actually, director Howard Hawks wanted Wayne to age in the role, even asking Brennan to teach Wayne an old man's walk. As Wayne told his biographer Maurice Zolotow, "Brennan showed me his idea of an old man walkin' and talkin'. His idea of it was kinda shufflin' and totterin'. And mumblin'. I was supposed to be tough and hard and walk like that? Hell, I was thinkin' about those old cattle guys I knew when I was a kid around Lancaster and there wasn't one of them that didn't stand tall. I played Tom Dunson my own way, standin' tall. Oh yeah, Hawks and I had a few fights along the way, but he accepted me as an expert, which I was, and we did not have any more trouble." Walter Brennan concurred. "When I see a good Western," said Brennan, "I just sit there. I was thrilled with *Red River*, because I believed in it. Wayne was so good; I believed in him." Wayne's only concession to time is his greying hair.

Red River is especially rich in supporting players who interact well with Brennan, especially John Ireland as a gunslinger in competition with Wayne's adopted son, played by a youthful Montgomery Clift. Ireland, who plays the Clanton brother who is killed in *My Darling Clementine*, here gets to perfect a stylish, cold-blooded killer, who has a surface geniality that makes him all the more frightening—and a fitting foil to Brennan's ornery and yet inviting humanity. Walter Brennan was never happier than when he was with a company of great actors, and he looks especially vibrant in *Red River*. He shared a tent with Montgomery Clift, a newcomer to Westerns, and showed the neophyte how to roll a cigarette for a scene in which Clift has to make his own and hand the lit cigarette with authority to Wayne. Brennan, impressed with Clift's work, said, "Monty is one of the finest young actors I have worked with. His timing is almost perfect, and if he isn't one of the top actors in Hollywood in two years, I'll be surprised." Clift and another character actor, Noah Beery Jr., found Brennan's reminiscences amusing until he began to repeat himself a third and even fourth time—as Beery and Clift sidled out of the tent.

Neither John Wayne nor Walter Brennan grew up in the cowboy West, and though Brennan became a rancher, he did not pretend to be his characters the way Wayne sometimes did. Walter's son Andy remembered a story about a downpour that hit the *Red River* location shoot just as the cast and crew were sitting down to lunch: "Duke was seated next to Walter and, as everyone scurried for shelter, Wayne calmly went on eating, saying to Walter, 'This will separate the men from the boys.' Dad spooned up his rain-soaked lunch for a few minutes more, then getting up he said, 'Which way did the boys go?'" Walter had a dry wit that could be quite unlike the sensibilities of the characters he played. Andy remembered another time when a driver gave his father the finger. Walter leaned out of his car window and extended a full five fingers, saying "Take some home to the whole family."

Much of Walter Brennan's world was his work, and what he saw outside of it was filtered through his roles. Brennan said that during his contract days with Goldwyn he sometimes worked nearly every week of the year—an unparalleled record in Hollywood, which built at least twelve weeks of downtime into contracts to make sure actors were off the payroll. Brennan confessed that his wife said he was "more fun to live with" when he had an acting job. Unlike other actors worried about their place in the pecking order of the Hollywood system, Brennan's overriding reaction was gratitude: "I never wanted anything out of this business except a good living. Never wanted to be a star or a glamorous figure. Just wanted to be good at what I was doing." Brennan's absolute identification with his work accounts for the almost superhuman perfection of his output and his maniacal devotion to the job at hand—a devotion that drove other actors out of the tent.

Although Brennan's political convictions were decidedly conservative, he remained outside the political arena, which perhaps accounts for why he played no part in the controversy over blacklisting and the House Committee on Un-American Activities that would heat up Hollywood in the late 1940s and 1950s. In "Actors Split Over Right to Campaign," *Oakland (CA) Tribune* (April 6, 1948), Bob Thomas quoted Brennan as saying, "Actors shouldn't campaign because they live in another world from ordinary people. If actors got an ounce of sense with every dollar they made, it would be all right."

Brennan made everything he did look easy, but occasionally he revealed how much labor went into his roles. In *Red River*, for example, he walks with a slight stoop after the film flashes forward fifteen years. On the set, a United Press reporter watched the actor ease his apparently weary body into a chair, ordering a meal in a "semi-senile voice," and commenting, "If you knew what a job it is to assume an aged character like this, you would understand why I don't dare step out of it during the day. If I stepped out of character during the lunch hour, I would have a heck of a time getting back into it during the first few scenes after lunch. Why, I've never played myself in a film."

My Darling Clementine and *Red River* were Walter Brennan's standout performances in the mid- to late 1940s. His other, routine roles included Murph, the sour and sweet pharmacist assisting Jenny (Natalie Wood), a precocious six-year-old orphan, in *Driftwood* (September 15, 1947), and Tony Maule, a muleskinner teaching another youth, Lon McCallister, to drive a mule team and establish a successful business in *Scudda Hoo! Scudda Hay!* (September 27, 1948). Brennan had a weakness for uplifting films that would become more pronounced as he aged. The formulaic quality of these parts seems, in retrospect, to establish the grandfatherly groove the actor would deepen in the course of his television and final film work.

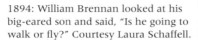

1894: William Brennan looked at his big-eared son and said, "Is he going to walk or fly?" Courtesy Laura Schaffell.

c. 1912: Walter with his brother Irvin and their parents. Courtesy of Laura Schaffell.

1915: Graduation day for Walter Brennan (first row, second from right) at Rindge. Courtesy of Cambridge Rindge and Latin School. Photo restoration Glenda Hydler.

1918: Walter in France with his army buddies. Courtesy of Laura Schaffell.

1921: Newly married Walter and Ruth in Pasadena. Courtesy of Laura Schaffell.

c. 1926: Walter's mother standing on the porch of the house he had built for his parents in Pasadena. Courtesy of Laura Schaffell.

c. late 1920s: Ruth had no need to be romanced. She was sold on Walter Brennan and never doubted he would make a success of himself. Courtesy of Mike Brennan.

c. late 1920s: Walter's father and Walter's children, Andy (left), Mike (middle), and Ruthie. Courtesy of Mike Brennan.

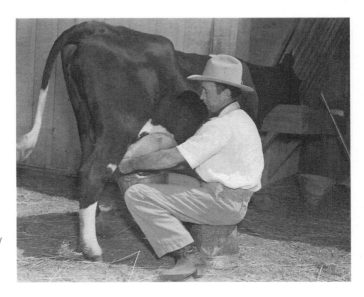

c. late 1920s: A cowboy/farmer on-screen and off. Courtesy of Laura Schaffell.

1935: *Barbary Coast*: Old Atrocity gives Jim Carmichael (Joel McCrea) the lowdown. Courtesy of Mike Brennan.

1935: *Barbary Coast*: Old Atrocity in the gambling den with Mary "Swan" Rutledge (Miriam Hopkins). Author's collection.

1935: *Barbary Coast*: Old Atrocity keeps an eye on Jim Carmichael (Joel McCrea) and bad guy Knuckles Jacoby (Brian Donlevy). Courtesy of Mike Brennan.

1936: *Three Godfathers*:
Three bank robbers—
Bob (Chester Morris),
"Doc" (Lewis Stone),
and Gus. Courtesy of
Mike Brennan.

1936: *Three Godfathers*:
Gus the gastronome
about to savor his first
asparagus. Courtesy of
Mike Brennan.

1936: *Three Godfathers*:
Gus and "Doc" with
the baby now in their
charge. Courtesy of
Mike Brennan.

1936: *Three Godfathers*: The dying "Doc" consigns the baby to Gus. Courtesy of Mike Brennan.

1936: *Come and Get It*: Swan Bostrum hops aboard his pal Barney Glasgow (Edward Arnold). Brennan won his first Oscar for playing this backwoods Swede. Courtesy of Mike Brennan.

1936: *Come and Get It*: Swan, Lotta (Frances Farmer), and Barney, who forsakes Lotta for the boss's daughter. Author's collection.

1936: *Come and Get It*: Swan promises to take care of Lotta, Barney's true love. Author's collection.

1936: *Banjo On My Knee*: Riverman Newt Holley steals the picture from the ostensible stars, Joel McCrea and Barbara Stanwyck. Author's collection.

1936: *Banjo On My Knee*: One-man band Newt Holley becomes a New Orleans sensation. Author's collection.

1938: *The Buccaneer*: Ornery Ezra Peevey tells Andrew Jackson (Hugh Sothern) a thing or two. Courtesy of Mike Brennan.

1938: *The Texans*: In this Randolph Scott western, Walter Brennan plays the family factotum, Chuckawalla. Author's Collection.

1938: *Kentucky*: Unreconstructed Peter Goodwin picks the winning horse, while Sally Goodwin (Loretta Young) is romanced by Jack Dillon (Richard Greene). Brennan won his second Academy Award for his flamboyant performance. Author's collection.

1939: *Stanley and Livingstone*: Jeff Slocum accompanies journalist Henry M. Stanley (Spencer Tracy) into darkest Africa to find the great humanitarian, Dr. Livingstone. Courtesy of Mike Brennan.

1940: *Northwest Passage*: Hunk Marriner, an outspoken woodsman, joins up with Major Robert Rogers (Spencer Tracy) during the French and Indian War. Author's collection.

1940: Walter Brennan purchases a 12,000-acre ranch near Joseph, Oregon. Courtesy of Mike Brennan.

1940: *The Westerner*: Cole Harden (Gary Cooper) arranges a meeting between the dying Judge Bean and his adored Lily Langtry. Author's collection.

1940: *The Westerner*: Walter Brennan won his third Oscar playing hanging judge Roy Bean—here confronting an angry mob of homesteaders. Author's collection.

1941: *Meet John Doe*: "The Colonel" tries to drag Long John Willoughby (Gary Cooper) away from the clutches of reporter Ann Mitchell (Barbara Stanwyck) and her nefarious employer, D. B. Norton (Edward Arnold). The pair wants to exploit Willoughby as "John Doe," an everyman, to sell newspapers and promote Norton's presidential candidacy. Author's collection.

1941: *Meet John Doe*: "The Colonel" is briefly in charge as he persuades his buddy Long John Willoughby to forsake the wiles of society and live a free man out in the open. Author's collection.

c. 1941: Walter Brennan without makeup, disguises, or prostheses. Author's collection.

1941: *Sergeant York*: Pastor Pile in full sermon mode. Courtesy of Mike Brennan.

1941: *Sergeant York*: Pastor Pile counsels prodigal son Alvin York (Gary Cooper), and York's buddies Ike Botkin (Ward Bond) and Buck Lipscomb (Noah Beery Jr.) have other ideas. Author's collection.

1941: *Sergeant York*: A chastened and reformed Alvin York is advised by Pastor Pile to register for the draft, even though doing so is against their pacifist principles. Author's collection.

1941: *Sergeant York*: Pastor Pile reassures Alvin York's mother (Margaret Wycherly) that Alvin will do the right thing. Courtesy of Mike Brennan.

1941: *This Woman Is Mine*: Brennan delivers a subtle performance as Captain Thorne, a Captain Bligh-like character opposed by Robert Stevens (Franchot Tone) and fretted by Julie Morgan (Carol Bruce). Courtesy of Mike Brennan.

1941: *Rise and Shine*: Amorous and cantankerous Grandpa. Author's collection.

1941: *Nice Girl?*: Amorous mailman Hector Titus and his beloved Cora Foster (Helen Broderick). Author's collection.

1942: *Pride of the Yankees*: Lou Gehrig (Gary Cooper) and his wife (Teresa Wright), ably supported by journalist Sam Blake. Author's collection.

1942: *Standby for Action*: Lieutenant Gregg Masterman (Robert Taylor) has to learn a thing or two from Chief Yeoman Henry Johnson. Author's collection.

1943: *The North Star*: On the set with Walter's daughter, Ruthie, who had a bit part playing the daughter of Karp, Brennan's version of a Ukrainian peasant. Courtesy of Mike Brennan.

1944: *Home in Indiana*: J. F. Thunderbolt, horse trainer, with his wife, Penny (Charlotte Greenwood). Author's collection.

1944: *To Have and Have Not*: Walter Brennan on the set with son Andy, on leave from the navy, and daughter Ruthie. Courtesy of Mike Brennan.

1944: *To Have and Have Not*: Eddie the rummy crooning with Slim Browning (Lauren Bacall) and Cricket (Hoagy Carmichael). Courtesy of Mike Brennan.

1944: *To Have and Have Not*: A watchful Eddie and a vigilant Slim worry that Harry Morgan (Humphrey Bogart) might get into trouble. Courtesy of Mike Brennan.

1944: *To Have and Have Not*: Eddie's wakeup call. Courtesy of Mike Brennan.

1944: *To Have and Have Not*: Eddie on his mission to help his pal Harry. Courtesy of Mike Brennan.

c. 1944: Walter Brennan with his soldier son, Mike. Courtesy of Mike Brennan.

1944: *The Princess and the Pirate:* Featherhead involves Sylvester the Great (Bob Hope) and Princess Margaret (Virginia Mayo) in a plot to recover buried treasure. Courtesy of Mike Brennan.

1946: *Centennial Summer*: The film is set during the Philadelphia Exposition of 1876. Brennan is unusually well outfitted with tailored suits and a handsome beard for his part as Jesse Rogers, the head of a family involved in planning and running the celebration. Author's collection.

c. late 1940s: Walter Brennan greeting Chill Wills as the latter arrives for Chief Joseph Days, an event Brennan helped to promote near his ranch in Joseph, Oregon. Courtesy EO Media Group, first publication in the *Wallowa (OR) Chieftain*.

1946: *My Darling Clementine*: Walter Brennan as mean old man Clanton. Courtesy of Mike Brennan.

1948: *Red River*: Nadine Groot tells Thomas Dunson (John Wayne) a thing or two. Author's collection.

1949: *Brimstone*: As "Pop" Courteen, Brennan plays another mean father—here with two of his sons, Nick (Jim Davis) and Bud (James Brown). Author's collection.

1949: *Brimstone*: A disappointed "Pop" Courteen learns that his son Luke (Jack Lambert) is going to go straight and marry Molly Bannister (Lorna Gray). Author's collection.

c. 1950: During Chief Joseph Days, Walter Brennan rides past his Indian Lodge Motel. Courtesy of Mike Brennan.

1950: Walter Brennan leading the Chesnimmus National Hobo Marching Band (so named by him) that went down Joseph's Main Street, headed by Brennan dressed in motley and waving a toilet plunger as a baton. Courtesy of Darlene Turner.

1955: *The Far Country*: On the way to Skagway. Author's collection.

1955: *The Far Country*: Walter Brennan as Ben Tatum, amiable sidekick of Jeff Webster (Jimmy Stewart), with Renee Vallon (Corinne Calvet) and Rube (Jay C. Flippen). Author's collection.

1955: *Bad Day at Black Rock:* Doc Velle remonstrates with Sheriff Tim Horn (Dean Jagger). Author's collection.

1956: *Good-bye My Lady*: As Uncle Jesse Jackson, Walter Brennan is pictured mentoring to Skeeter Jackson (Brandon De Wilde). Author's collection.

1957–63: *The Real McCoys*: Richard Crenna (Luke), Walter Brennan (Grandpa Amos), Kate (Kathleen Nolan), Michael Winkelman (Little Luke), Lydia Reed (Hassie). Courtesy of Linda Schaffell.

1957–63: *The Real McCoys*: Amos McCoy ready for action. Author's collection.

1959: *Rio Bravo*: Stumpy ready to dynamite the villains while Sheriff John T. Chance pins them down with rifle fire. Courtesy of Mike Brennan.

1964–65: *The Tycoon*: Walter Brennan as Walter Andrews. Author's collection.

1967–69: *The Guns of Will
Sonnett*, "A Fool and His
Money": Walter Burke play-
ing Will's old friend Charlie
Moss. Author's collection.

c. 1960s: The Walter Brennan clan, pictured with a picture of Amos McCoy on the wall.
Courtesy of Laura Schaffell.

The monkey puppet Walter Brennan used to entertain his grandchildren. Courtesy of Laura Schaffell.

1967: *The Gnome-Mobile*: As D. J. Mulroney, Walter Brennan managed to play the roles of tycoon, grandfather, and forest gnome. Author's collection.

1970: *The Over-the-Hill Gang Rides Again*: Walter Brennan, Chill Wills, Edgar Buchannan, Andy Devine, Lana Wood, and Fred Astaire. Courtesy of Mike Brennan.

Of an entirely different order is Brennan's magnificent performance as Pop Gruber, an aging grifter in *Nobody Lives Forever* (November 1, 1946), starring John Garfield as a con man, Nick Blake, who eventually goes straight after falling in love with Gladys Halvorsen (Geraldine Fitzgerald, in the prime of her beauty). The script by W. R. Burnett, one of masters of film noir, provides not just Brennan, but also George Coulouris (Doc Ganson) with more dimension than is usually accorded heavies in crime dramas.

Pop first appears on a Los Angeles street with a telescope, offering views of the moon, the stars, and the rings of Saturn for ten cents while he picks his patron's pockets. He is delighted to spot Nick, and they reminisce about their old con jobs before Nick went into the army. Pop is impressed that Nick has returned with an honorable discharge—the first hint that Nick is cut out for more than a career in crime, especially when he warmly thanks Pop for sending a box overseas to him at a time when the rest of the gang just forgot about him. Pop is perfectly perky and yet, as Brennan plays him, he also seems forlorn, masking a depression now that he is shorn of his connections in the East and past his prime. He is looking for some way to revitalize himself.

The well-spoken Doc, a desperate criminal, deep in debt and no longer attractive to women, is fiercely jealous of the handsome Blake, but Doc realizes he needs Nick to attract Halvorsen. So Doc accosts Pop in a saloon. Pop dislikes Doc and avoids Doc's intense gaze and refuses the offer of a beer, saying he has already had his allotted two. As Doc gets hysterical telling Pop about the easy two million dollars they can get off the recently widowed Halvorsen, Pop tells him to relax. And though Pop has already said Nick won't work with a has-been like Doc, the size of the booty finally gets Pop's full attention. Pop (as his name implies) takes a fatherly, if also pecuniary, interest in his protégé's success. Pop and Doc then form a makeshift syndicate to bilk Halvorsen of her fortune.

Pop shows up at Nick's palatial spread (paid for with proceeds from his successful New York club), pitching a "big one," even though Nick has already told Pop he has come out to California for a rest. "You can always rest afterwards," Pop says drily. It's a "ripe touch" that will only take a month, Pop assures Nick, who can then be on "easy street from here on." Brennan has help in this scene from Al Doyle (George Tobias, an actor Brennan admired for "doing any job well that's handed to him.") Doyle is Nick's extroverted sidekick, a role Brennan himself would have played in earlier years. But now, as Pop says, he is old and doing the best he can. The sneering Nick is about to fend off Pop, when Pop turns on him and predicts that Nick, now thirty-four, will never do any better. "When I was your age, I was on top of the world," Pop tells him. "I thought there was no end to it." Pop commands, "Look at me," and hangs his head. "That's connin' on the square there," Nick observes. "Sure, sure," Al says. Nick looks down and then glances up, obviously shaken by Pop's words, but masking his doubt with a haze of cigarette smoke. As Pop leaves, he comments about Nick to Al: "No business sense at all." Al assures him, "I'll take care of it," implying he will go to work on Nick. Al almost doesn't have to, since Nick is nervous, standing in front of his magnificent ocean view. Al, using reverse psychology, says it is just as well that Nick doesn't want to do another con, since he is out of practice anyway. "A guy could lose his touch awful quick," Al adds, suggesting that perhaps Nick, after his combat experience, has lost his nerve. But that's okay, Al says. "We have plenty of dough, *now*." And of course, Nick can't, in the end, refuse this challenge.

The more desperate Doc becomes, pestering Pop about Nick's moves, the tougher Pop's responses become; one man dreads failure, and other contemplates a comeback. Nick will "make it if it can be made," Pop says to Doc, standing up in the saloon where Pop always drinks alone. Pop towers over Doc, telling him he's never liked him: "And from now on, stay away from me, understand!" After years of seeing him stooped over in pictures, Walter Brennan's upright posture is a welcome surprise.

When Nick, now in love with Gladys, announces the deal is off, Al is upset. But all Pop cares about is that Nick pays Doc his $30,000 share, and Nick responds that he will take care of Pop as well. Pop says to Al, "Nick is too big a guy to welsh on the deal." Nick pats Pop on the shoulder, and says "correct," as Pop smiles because he and Nick understand one another so well. When Al urges Pop to talk Nick out of hexing the deal, Pop responds that he wishes he had had the same sense thirty years ago. Pop looks into his beer as if plumbing his past.

Unlike so many of Brennan's earlier character parts, in this one he plays an absolutely pivotal role in the plot, following Doc after he kidnaps Gladys Halverson in a reckless bid to finish the job himself. When Pop calls Nick, telling him where Doc has taken Gladys, Nick shows up for the noirish riverfront showdown, effectively organized by Pop. But just as Nick gets the drop on Doc, Pop shoots Doc, who is using Gladys as a hostage. Doc has just enough life left to turn around and shoot Pop, bringing their contentious connection to an end. For once Brennan, nearly always the supporting actor, gets his big death scene, saying his end is just as well. His last mumbled words are about seeing the stars "all for one dime."

Nick broods over Pop's death, and Gladys asks, "Who was he?" Nick answers, "Just an old guy, down on his luck. He said, 'Nick, life goes by so fast, you wake up one morning and find you're old.' He was worried about us wasting time." If Walter Brennan had not made another film, *Nobody Lives Forever*, would have been a fitting denouement to a brilliant career. And yet, for another decade he would continue to give superlative performances, becoming an American institution.

CHAPTER 7

Western Brennan Redux

Robert Mitchum, James Stewart, Spencer Tracy, John
Wayne— *The Far Country, Bad Day at Black Rock, Rio Bravo*
1948–58

"[T]HE LEATHER, SUN-DRENCHED FACE THAT MOST COMMONLY HELPED
tame the wild frontier was that of Walter Brennan," writes critic Manny
Pacheco. Not Gary Cooper, not John Wayne, not Randolph Scott—or
any other star—meant more to the western than Walter Brennan, who
played every sort of character, good and evil, and everything between.

In *Blood on the Moon* (November 9, 1948) Brennan is Kris Barden,
a homesteader desperately trying to hold on to his land, fighting the
machinations of aspiring cattle baron Tate Riling (Robert Preston), who
pretends to be on the homesteaders' side. Barden loses his only son, who
is also fighting for their land, in a cattle stampede. The scene in which
Jim Garry (Robert Mitchum) tells Barden about his son Fred's death is
painful but also poignant to watch. The impassive Garry tells it to Barden
straight, with only the slightest note of sympathy heard in Mitchum's
characteristically cool voice. Barden looks up at Garry, as he talks about
his loss—how high a price he has paid for defending his land—and he
looks around as though he is surveying what he has wrought, and perhaps also looking for the son he knows will not return.

In *Brimstone* (August 15, 1949), a minor western with a major Walter
Brennan performance, he is "Pop" Courteen, a rancher and an antago-
nist of homesteaders who exhibits even more viciousness than Judge
Roy Bean. Courteen rules his three sons like a tyrant, reminiscent of
Old Man Clanton in *My Darling Clementine*—although, as always, Brennan manages to escape clichés by making Courteen humorless, a man
utterly lacking the dry wit he displays as Clanton. Whereas Clanton is

almost exclusively focused on his duel with Wyatt Earp, Courteen is bent on bullying his sons into doing his bidding, reminding them constantly of his authority. Indeed, Courteen's unwavering confidence in his own judgment leads to his demise at the hands of Johnny Tremaine, played by Rod Cameron with a superb wit that shows why he eventually gets the better of Courteen. Unlike Clanton, who seems to have some inkling of his impending death, Courteen is utterly blind to his vulnerability.

In *Blood on the Moon*, on the other hand, Brennan plays to his character's vulnerability, which makes him susceptible to Garry when Garry quits the employ of Barden's adversary, Tate Riley, and joins forces with Barden and the other homesteaders. It is almost as if Garry becomes an adopted son because of the basic decency he displays when refusing to play the role of a hired gun. Brennan's role in this film is not only integral to the action, it becomes apparent even as he takes the full measure of Garry. At first, the skeptical Barden (who is told Garry is Tate Riley's friend) says, "I can buy that kind of friend for $75 a month and no questions asked." Later, Barden saves Garry's life during a barroom brawl, even though Barden is still wary of Garry's motivations. Barden tells Garry he shot the other Riley henchman in the bar who were about to plug Garry because the henchman was a handier target.

Because of the scruffy way Mitchum dressed and acted, Brennan deeply admired the star's performance. Mitchum was not the pristine western hero that Brennan despised. The West might be a myth created by Hollywood films, but within that myth, in Walter Brennan's opinion, realism still had an important role to play. Mitchum's unaffected performance and unassuming personal manner also enhanced his rapport with Brennan. Mitchum liked to say he had two acting styles, with or without a horse—a quip reminiscent of the sly question Brennan put to Howard Hawks: with or without teeth? But both actors aimed for authenticity, and Brennan was proud of his daughter, Ruthie, when she used her bit part in *Blood on the Moon* to ride down a steep boulder strewn cliff. As a Universal Pictures press release reported, "Ruth, trained since childhood to ride on her father's ranches, in rodeos and horse shows," fulfilled his boast that she was an excellent horsewoman.

Watching the nuances in Brennan's performances—especially in roles that would seem to allow for little variation—is to appreciate once again his incomparable place in Hollywood history as the consummate character actor. No star ever had Brennan's opportunities to play both for and against type, to be a hero and a villain, a fool and a wise man. Whether at the center of the action, or on the periphery, Walter Brennan made his presence count as an inevitable part of the landscape of the Hollywood western. Thus he became part of the myth of the West, one so ingrained that it seems inevitable that he became a rancher off-screen.

Brennan's non-western roles in this period are perfectly played but lack the aura that enveloped him in Westerns. The directors of pictures such as *The Green Promise* (March 22, 1949) and *Driftwood* (March 31, 1950) are simply not as nimble or as suggestive as Robert Wise in *Blood on the Moon* and Joseph Kane in *Brimstone*. Brennan's role in *The Green Promise* as an insensitive patriarch who thinks he knows better than his daughters does, however, foreshadow his television role as Grandpa Mc-Coy, who often has to be humbled into realizing his autocratic judgments require some refining and sensitivity to the feelings and ideas of others, starting with his own family. Brennan took a few risks in this role as Mr. Matthews, for at times he is not afraid to appear unpleasant, even harshly dictatorial. The film was a sort of commercial for 4H clubs, which all of the Brennan children participated in. Brennan believed that farming and ranching had developed their characters, and the organization, founded at the turn of the twentieth century, concentrated on leadership skills and citizenship that grew out of activities centered on the agricultural life of communities. *The Green Promise* was Brennan's third film with the Natalie Wood. As in *Scudda Hoo! Scudda Hay!* and *Driftwood*, she plays an outspoken child who represents a kind of antidote to the stifling world of adult authority that tries to subdue her.

Even Brennan's pairing with Gary Cooper in *Task Force* (March 31, 1950) cannot overcome the dull direction of Delmer Daves, who is more interested in the history of the navy than in his characters. For once, as an admiral, Brennan actually outranks Cooper, who plays Jonathan Scott, a navy pilot whose career is synonymous with the development of the aircraft carrier. Scott's combat experience, his duels with congressmen skeptical of new, expensive ships, and his devotion to his country's service make for some thrilling footage, but negligible character delineation. Similarly, in *The Wild Blue Yonder* (December 5, 1951), an homage to the Strategic Air Command and its development of the B29 bomber, Brennan as Major General Wolfe does not have much to do except appear Ike-like and hand out stern but forbearing commands.

The spontaneity that is so evident in Brennan's work with Howard Hawks, who allowed actors to rework lines, is absent from Brennan's performance in *Task Force*, in which he was required to stick to the letter of the script. All Brennan said, for publicity purposes, was "I'm in it just enough so that people notice me and will remember me, but not enough

so that I bore the folks who would rather be looking at the hero." A publicity release also reported, "Walter Brennan has finally got the 'crick' out
of his back. The actor, along with other members of Warners *Task Force*
company, came back from 24 days on location aboard a US Navy carrier,
with a sore back and cramped muscles from sleeping in navy shipboard
bunks." In fact, working on a troop ship took Brennan back thirty years
to his World War I experiences. The film is, if nothing else, painstakingly
scrupulous in its depiction of men and materiel. This effort at authenticity has attracted many fans, as revealed in IMDb user reviews.

Shooting went right up to Christmas 1948, which meant Brennan
could not get away to his ranch. In October, just before leaving to work
on the film, he presented each of his children with a new car. He was
very proud of them for having absorbed his work ethic and for steering
clear of Hollywood—except for Ruthie, who continued to enjoy her father's approval for gradually gaining experience in small, often uncredited roles. "Walter Brennan is having a couple of big fat geese shipped to
him from his Oregon ranch to his San Fernando Valley home for Christmas dinner," reported Carl Combs, Warner's public relations man. "The
actor had planned to get up to the ranch for Christmas, but his role in
Task Force will keep him in Southern California. He has been fattening
his Yuletide fowl since summer. Brennan's son operates the actor's ranch
while Brennan is working in Hollywood." Thus moviegoers learned
about the down home Brennan who was, in a sense, their public servant,
since it was also reported that "Walter Brennan flies to the U.S. aircraft
carrier, Antietam, early tomorrow [December 24] to play Santa Claus for
176 orphans at a party sponsored by the ship's crew. The Navy is sending
a special plane to transport Brennan to the carrier, which is tied up at
Alameda in the San Francisco Bay Area. The Navy plane will return him
so that the actor can be with his wife in Hollywood over Christmas. The
head of the studio's makeup dept went with him."

Even in studio publicity releases, Brennan made no secret of his wari-
ness of moviedom: "Walter Brennan has finally told why there is always
a bad connection on the telephone at his ranch home in northeast Oregon. 'I like it that way,' the actor said, 'because then when somebody
calls me from Hollywood that I don't want to talk to, I act as though I
can't hear them. If the call's important enough, I can hear all right.'"
But of course his very distrust of Hollywood became a Hollywood pitch,
showing off its no-nonsense product.

This last collaboration between Brennan and Cooper is also one of
their weakest. The script suffers from a kind of plodding earnestness.

Cooper's commitment to the picture seems in doubt. He knew he had a "feeble script," according to his biographer Jeffrey Meyers. On December 24, 1948, Eric Stacey wrote to the producer, "[A]s already reported many times, he [Cooper] is coming in late and leaving early, so a scheduled day's work becomes ¾ of a day at best." Like Walter Brennan, Stacey knew there was no way to hurry Cooper along: "[F]rom past experience with this gentlemen, if anybody says anything to antagonize him, he is liable to delay the company by being even later than ever."

Although Westerns usually augmented the power of Brennan's performances, there are exceptions, such as his routine appearance as a preacher/doctor in the woefully inept *Singing Guns* (February 28, 1950), and as a one-dimensional railroad engineer in *A Ticket to Tomahawk* (August 14, 1950). *Surrender* (September 15, 1950) is disappointing, especially since Brennan as Sheriff Bill Howard is compared several times to Javert in his pursuit of Jean Valjean in *Les Miserables*. Although Brennan's character is relentless in his determination to imprison Gregg Delaney (John Carroll, last seen in *This Woman Is Mine*), Brennan does not have the maniacal obsession of a Javert, and the venal Delaney hardly measures up to the suffering Valjean. The trouble in this case seems to have been that Brennan did not connect with the degree of monomania the role called for.

He was well aware of his stinkers, but he liked the work and the steady revenue that he could save and invest. Sometimes, in other words, acting was just a job. But *Curtain Call at Cactus Creek* (May 25, 1950) is something more. Never meant to be more than a B picture entertainment produced on the Universal International backlot and at the Iverson Ranch (a five-hundred-acre family property often used for location shoots), it is one of those unexpected surprises that make you want to know about everyone who had a part in creating such a diverting picture. The film has no single star, but rather an ensemble of superb actors: Vincent Price (Tracy Holland), hamming up it as a ham actor, and Eve Arden (Lily Martin) playing an aging and acerbic stage star. Their dialogue, delivered with considerable archness, is one of the film's great pleasures:

TRACY HOLLAND. I shall never forget, there were twenty-four curtain calls.
LILY MARTIN. Twenty-two curtain calls, you said last time.
TRACY HOLLAND. Later, Mr. Gould came back to my dressing room.
LILY MARTIN. Mr. Astor, wasn't it?

TRACY HOLLAND. And asked me to give a private performance of Hamlet at his estate. "No, Mr Astor" I said. "My art is for the world to see not for the few. I am not in the role of the common men"–*Henry IV* act 3, scene 1.

LILY MARTIN. Tracy . . .

TRACY HOLLAND. It was then that I decided to sacrifice my personal interest and bring great theater to this western wilderness (*The coach goes over a bump; Tracy bangs his head.*) Careful up there!

STAGECOACH DRIVER. Sorry Mr. Holland, we're in a rut.

LILY MARTIN. He can say that again.

TRACY HOLLAND. Now let me see, where was I? Oh, yes. I must bestride the narrow world like a colossus"–*Julius Caesar* act 1, scene 2.

LILY MARTIN. Tracy.

TRACY HOLLAND. Well?

LILY MARTIN. I've got news for you. It never happened.

TRACY HOLLAND. Madame, you dare to doubt my word? I who have played before the crowned heads of Europe? You attack my veracity?

LILY MARTIN. Well, that's one way of putting it.

TRACY HOLLAND. "Blow, blow thou winter wind, thou art not so unkind as woman's ingratitude!"

The script by Howard Dimsdale and Oscar Brodney, based on a story by Dimsdale and Stanley Roberts, never lets up. These were journeymen screenwriters who somehow jelled as a collective, providing Charles Lamont, a veteran director of more than 250 pictures (including Mack Sennett comedy shorts and Abbott and Costello comedies), the right material to produce a witty sendup up of both Westerns and the theater. The irrepressible Donald O'Connor (Edward Timmons) is the pivotal figure in this menagerie, serving both as stage manager and aspiring actor who is put off from performing by Holland, who hogs every scene in this traveling combination of minstrel show and melodrama. Quite aside from O'Connor's singing and dancing his famous frenetic routines, he literally links the on-stage and back stage worlds by bouncing back and forth pulling ropes, racing up stairs, and creating sound effects even as Holland emotes and Julie Martin (Gale Storm), Lily's daughter, scolds her boyfriend O'Connor/Timmons for allowing Holland to deprive him of his big break.

Seldom had Walter Brennan enjoyed such a marvelously balanced concatenation of comic characters and plot in which to perform his own droll depiction of a bank robber, Rimrock Thomas, with a hankering for the theater. Specifically, he hankers for Lily Martin, whose career he reveres in virtually the same way Judge Roy Bean worships Lily Langtry. The suggestion that Thomas is an aspiring entertainer is established from the beginning, as he is shown on horseback riding into town and singing a pioneer ballad composed by John A. Stone during the San Francisco gold rush and first recorded by Burl Ives in 1941. Singing might seem a strange occupation for an outlaw, but it is one that suits a man who enjoys an audience:

> Did you ever hear tell of sweet Betsy from Pike
> Who crossed the wide prairies with her lover Ike?
> With two yoke of cattle and one spotted hog,
> A tall Shanghai rooster and an old yellow dog.
> One evening quite early they camped on the Platte.
> They downed their blankets on the green shady Platte . . .

Rimrock stops singing, dismounts his horse, and asks his partner in crime, who is waiting for him, "How's it look?" He is told "she's loaded," meaning the bank has just received a large shipment of currency. Rimrock stoops over in pain and is annoyed when Jake, played with customary gruffness by veteran character actor Joe Sawyer, says it is rheumatism (an ailment that will later figure significantly in the action). Rimrock is disappointed when he sees a poster advertising a reward for his capture—dead or alive—because the amount offered is too small. And then he turns to see the show wagon pulling into town. O'Connor/Timmons drives in, ringing bells and distributing posters, blocking the getaway route for the bank robbery. Timmons is so green he has no idea what he is risking when he brushes past one of the robbers, who tells him to move the wagon. "I'll just be a minute," Timmons says, as he ducks under the arm blocking his way.

Rimrock reads a poster "featuring that great star of the New York stage Lily Martin." Then he turns to his gang and muses with a smile, "Lily Martin." "Never heard of her," Jake says sourly. "You ain't lived," Rimrock admonishes him. "Prettiest thing you ever laid eyes on." "What about the bank?" Jake asks. "She sure was pretty," Rimrock says dreamily. "The bank!" Jake prompts. "This ain't no time for it," Rimrock rejoins. "When's a better time?" Jake asks. "Tonight," Rimrock answers.

"With Lily Martin playing, everybody will be at the show." When Jake accuses Rimrock of going soft, Rimrock knocks him to the ground with one punch, then picks him up, having made his point.

When not thinking about Lily Martin, the brutal Rimrock speaks in a tight-lipped, grim manner. During her performance, he peeps at her through an aperture in the ceiling, even as Timmons tries to block Rimrock's view by placing a board over the opening. Rimrock finally breaks away to join the bank robbery, but is shot off his horse and takes refuge in the show wagon driven by Timmons, who has been fired for making a mess out of the theater production when he loses his concentration. After the two men converse and Timmons finds Rimrock a congenial companion, Timmons asks the bank robber (who says he has been in the banking business, off and on) if he would take a job as Holland's stage-hand/manager. In this picture Brennan begins to resemble Grandpa McCoy and finds he cannot handle all the props Timmons begins to fling at him, setting the pace for what Rimrock is supposed to do during a stage production. When Rimrock finally meets Lily Martin, he is overcome with adulation, but Holland dismisses Rimrock as a "bedraggled scarecrow" and a "lout"—until Rimrock draws his gun, and Holland hires him. When Rimrock is perplexed by all he has to do, Timmons says, "You'll get the hang of it after a while." A dismayed Rimrock advises him, "You better find yourself another expression, Son."

To Timmons, Rimrock admits what he has denied in front of his gang: Rheumatism makes it hard for him to move fast enough. Then Timmons lifts Rimrock up by his elbows and straightens out the old man's back. Here we see emerging the grandfatherly, aging hero that will grace the final years of Walter Brennan's career—a figure like his earlier old codgers, but now, as Brennan enters his sixties, performed with a certain poignancy, humor, and humanity that seems at one with the aging actor himself.

When next seen in *Curtain Call at Cactus Creek*, Rimrock is on his knees pinning up Lily Martin's dress. "Well ain't that cute," Jake says, as he comes upon his boss. Still, Brennan never loses his air of authority—even menace—as he points a gun at Timmons when he thinks Timmons has tried to turn him in to the law. With that misunderstanding cleared up, Rimrock, for all his disabilities, is now part of Lily Martin's entourage and wants Timmons to take his place as head of the gang. Naturally, Timmons cannot see himself as the brains of a bank robbing operation, and after some mix-ups that result in Timmons actually being hunted as a outlaw, Rimrock is taken into custody. The final scene, which seemed acceptable in 1950, now seems in the worst possible taste, even if it does provide appropriate plot resolution. As part of his parole, Rimrock is coerced into appearing on stage in a Mammy outfit in black face, dancing with his spurs on—or at least we are supposed to think it is Brennan cavorting like a minstrel on a ramshackle stage. The figure who appears is so entirely clothed, but with a black knit mask covering the face and neck, it could be someone else—not that Brennan would have objected to the scene, which was common enough in Hollywood films even as late as 1950.

In *The Showdown* (August 15, 1950), Brennan plays a cattleman, Cap MacKellar, who first appears in the saddle alongside Rod Main (Harry Morgan), whose gun is drawn on Shadrach Jones (Bill Elliott), who is digging up his brother's grave. MacKellar tells Jones about a report that his brother died in a gunfight, but Jones, who knows how good his brother was with a gun, believes otherwise. Upon learning that Jones has been a Texas state policeman, Main seems ready to shoot Jones. But MacKellar intervenes, and Jones bashes away Main's gun with a shovel, explaining that he is no longer part of a corrupt force that confiscated the property of men like Main. In fact, Jones's brother was about to invest in land, but was robbed of his money. Then Jones examines his brother's body and discovers he was shot in the back.

MacKellar intervenes again when his cowpunchers, preparing to take his herd to market, are about to gun down Jones, who enters a saloon looking for his brother's killer. MacKellar hires the hard-driving Jones to lead the cattle drive. Jones, a former trail boss, agrees because he is certain that along the way he will discover the murderer. MacKellar cautions Jones several times, saying that the desire for revenge will just destroy Jones's humanity, but Jones relentlessly pushes the men forward, refusing to rest until he finds the perpetrator. But when Jones falsely accuses one of the crew and realizes that his hatred has indeed damaged him, he relents and accepts MacKellar's view that retribution will be visited on the killer without Jones's intervention, suggesting there is a divine economy whereby such crimes do not go unpunished. This momentary resolution of the tension that has riven the company of cowpunchers ends abruptly when MacKellar, while freeing a calf stuck between two boulders, is gored by its mother. Mortally wounded, MacKellar asks to be put out of his misery. When Jones refuses to end MacKellar's life, the cattle boss tells Jones to look inside his vest pocket. There Jones finds the derringer used to kill his brother. MacKellar is a fraud, and he sees the irony of his own preaching to Jones, who at first wants to leave him to the buzzards, but then consents to have a cowpuncher stay with MacKellar until he dies.

The ending is a "shocker," as one IMDb user puts it, and it isn't. Brennan's character seems too saintly and a little too eager to reform Jones. All along, MacKellar has been making a study of Jones and learning how to exploit the hero's vulnerabilities. Brennan is utterly convincing as a seemingly wise old man, a tightly scripted role that suggests he could have performed Shakespeare, smiling and playing the villain. In short, largely due to Brennan's performance, *The Showdown* is one of those few Republic Pictures B Westerns that repays a second look. As another IMDb viewer notes, this noir western (many scenes are shot in the dead of night in rain) compares favorably with *Blood on the Moon*.

By 1950, Brennan was settling into a schedule that saw him making three films a year, giving him more time on his ranch and with a new business he started in Joseph, a 487-seat movie theater that opened on July 27, 1950. It was housed in a Quonset hut made out of surplus war materials also used to build the civic center. "The reason he got the theater built," Mike recalled, "was because the civic center was the same size, and they [Frank McCully and Walter] got the chance to buy two of them for half the price." At the theater's grand opening, actors Chill Wills and Forrest Tucker said a few words and signed autographs, and Joseph's mayor and other local dignitaries attended the event. A La Grande radio station broadcast the event. *Curtain Call at Cactus Creek* was the feature, following a musical short with the Nat King Cole trio.

The opening day program included thanks to the Joseph chamber of commerce, local businesses, a radio station, and the local newspapers, and listed some of the theater's features: one of the largest screens in Eastern Oregon; a stage that would be used for county and community affairs; one of the best sound and projection systems; the finest acoustics; comfortable push-back seats; well appointed and clean restrooms; an air-conditioned balcony "cry room" with a bottle warmer, bassinet, and disposable diapers at no extra charge; the latest in light fixtures; a sloping floor that left every view unobstructed; a fully stocked refreshment bar; and a lighted parking lot. The program also included this announcement:

Dear Patron

We have spared no expense in making the Rainbow Theatre Eastern Oregon's finest theatre. Fine because the people of Wallowa County are deserving and entitled to the best.

We want you to feel at all times that the Rainbow is YOUR theatre and with that thought in mind we have placed a Suggestion
Box with cards in the foyer. We will appreciate receiving your comments and criticisms on this card and deposit it in the box. Your
cooperation in this will greatly aid us in giving you the kind of
entertainment and theatre you desire.

We know you will agree—the Rainbow is as comfortable and
luxurious as any large city theatre.

We shall always strive for improvement.

Very sincerely

Walter Brennan and Frank McCully

Frank McCully was the Rainbow's first manager, in charge of taking
delivery of movies and supervising the projectionist and the concession
stand. Walter's friend Cub later took over the manager's position, even
though he had a day job as county assessor. Cub's daughter, Judy, remembers the stage in the back of the theater. She still has the upright
piano used for tap dancing classes and other activities and events. Judy
recalled the burgundy velvet drapes, heavy as lead. One of her friends
got a job running the projector while he was going to school. He'd do
okay during the first movie, but always during the second showing he'd
fall asleep, and Cub had to tell him to put the second reel on the projector. Cub sometimes had to drive seventy miles to LaGrande when the bus
did not show up with the scheduled movie.

Walter called his old boss Sam Goldwyn to report on a film that had
broken box office records. "You mean you're an exhibitor now?" Goldwyn asked. When the actor replied, "That's right, Sam," the line went
dead until Goldwyn managed to say, "Walter, I don't think I like you
very much any more." Goldwyn, an independent producer, was always
fighting with distributors to get his pictures into theaters. The thought
of an ex-employee doing well in a business that vexed Goldwyn clearly
nettled the studio executive, as Brennan surely knew it would.

Walter also became a hotelier, western style. A brochure touted "Walter Brennan's Indian Lodge Motel. The Motel of Distinction. Enjoy Your
Vacation In The Switzerland of America. Fishing—Hunting—Swimming—Water Sports—Rainbow Theater—Horse Back Riding, Joseph,
Oregon." Walter put the ever reliable Cub and his wife Geraldine in
charge of managing the motel, which remains the only motel in Joseph.
Cub managed Indian Lodge for ten years, doing the books while Geraldine took care of business during the day. Cub never had a disagreement

with Walter, according to Cub's daughter, Judy. In fact, the only difficulty she could remember arose when she was about twelve, and greeted
Brennan on the street by saying "Hello Walter." "He talked to Dad that
night and said, 'I am Mr. Brennan to the kids around here,'" Judy said.
But Walter walked Judy to the altar when she was married in a Roman
Catholic church. At that time her own father could not give her away
because he was not Catholic.

Walter enjoyed the change of scene in Joseph. "I like to fly but Ruth,
my wife, likes to drive so we generally drive," Brennan said. "It takes
about a day and a half [from his California home]. When we're really in
a hurry we take a plane up in a few hours. I've got elbow room up there.
When I go out to my mail box to pick up the mail it's practically half a
day's travel from the house." Mike remembered his father coming to stay
in Joseph every six weeks or so, whenever there was a break in filming.
On one of Walter's spring trips someone asked him how he liked Joseph,
and Walter replied, "Well, the only thing wrong is that you've only got
three seasons: winter, July, and August."

As important as Joseph was to Brennan, acting in westerns continued
to attract him, even though the work could be hazardous. In *Along the
Great Divide* (June 2, 1951), he plays an accused lyncher and murderer.
With a rope around his neck and his hands tied behind his back, suddenly, he was jerked into the air when his horse took off. Fortunately,
cast and crew came to the rescue. This was the first shot of Brennan as
Pop Keith, a wily old homesteader at odds with local ranchers. Brennan
relished such roles, saying, "I wouldn't hurt a fly, but I love to do heavies. Dirty guys. They're so much easier than nice guys. The further away
you get from yourself, the better you get." And yet neither the film nor
his performance is among his best. Pop is never really believable as the
villain, since he is shown in tandem with an adoring daughter (Virginia
Mayo) who will do anything for him, including shooting at the marshal
(Kirk Douglas) who has her father in custody. At his worst, Pop taunts
Douglas by singing a song that Douglas's father (who died because of a
mistake Douglas made) used to sing, in hopes that the marshal will break
down and Pop can seize an opportunity to escape. But not much is made
of this supposed father/son drama, since Douglas and Brennan lack the
rapport of Brennan's collaborations with Gary Cooper, Humphrey Bogart, John Wayne, and, in a few years, with Jimmy Stewart.

As Brennan said during the making of *Along the Great Divide*, "It's 90
per cent material and 10 per cent acting. Without material, the greatest
actor in the world can't do anything." The predictable, pedestrian script

gives Brennan's character no nuance. In the end, Pop is proven innocent, and Douglas falls in love with Pop's daughter. Brennan overacts, and Douglas also tries too hard as the tormented son, demonstrating no ability to understate his angst the way better actors such as Dana Andrews or Gary Cooper could have done. The picture had an important director, Raoul Walsh, but his work does nothing to remedy a weak story that does not fulfill the expectations of the film's epic title.

Along the Great Divide was Kirk Douglas's first western. It was Walter Brennan's thirty-second, with many more to come. He reveled in roles like Doc Butcher in *Best of the Badmen* (November 19, 1951), starring Robert Ryan, perhaps the only star in Hollywood with a torso as slim as Gary Cooper's. At this point in Brennan's career, it was difficult for him to avoid appearing as, by turns, an amiable or ornery sidekick. But he managed to avoid cliché when surrounded by an ensemble of good character actors, including Bruce Cabot, Barton MacLane, and Robert J. Wilke. Unlike Republic westerns, which relied heavily on process shots and stock footage, this RKO western looks authentic, the result of location shooting at several sites in California and Utah—including Kanab Canyon, where the cast got caught in an unexpected flood, the result of heavy rain that left them stranded for several hours before they could return to their headquarters. A sharply written, economical script uses Brennan as the voice of the West, narrating the film's opening scenes. He plays an ex-horse thief, ex-Confederate soldier who switches his loyalty to a Missouri-born Union officer (Ryan), who promises Brennan and a cohort of diehard Rebs a new start in life if they give up their raids on banks and swear an oath of allegiance to the federal government. At first the Rebs resist, but then relent when Union troops surround them and their Indian allies. But Robert Preston, playing a duplicitous carpetbagger akin to the part he played in *Blood on the Moon*, snookers Ryan's plan. Preston wishes to collect a reward for the Rebs, a group that includes Jesse and Frank James. When Preston's men attack the Rebs, Ryan shoots in self-defense and kills a man. Ryan is then tried and convicted of murder in a Preston-rigged trial. But then Preston's estranged wife (Clair Trevor, looking even more beautiful than she does in *Stagecoach*) smuggles a gun in to Ryan, and he breaks out of jail. Ryan takes refuge with the Rebs who have managed to escape during the shootout with Preston and his men. Ryan then revenges himself on Preston through raids on properties controlled by the carpetbagger's protection racket.

Brennan plays a key role in all this action by saving Ryan's life twice. First Brennan pops up from behind a rock with a gun leveled at Ryan's pursuers, who are about to finish him off. Brennan then manages to spirit Ryan back to the Rebs. Later, Brennan appears on the saloon stairs, gun in hand, to confront his fellow Rebs, who have discovered that Trevor is Preston's wife. She has taken refuge in their saloon/headquarters, and they are about to shoot Ryan because they believe he and Trevor have double-crossed them by alerting Preston to their whereabouts. Brennan covers for Ryan and Trevor as they make their escape. Brennan, cool under pressure and simply more intelligent than his fellow Rebs, is also given simple and effective lines. As he stands on the saloon steps staring down at the Rebs, he points his gun at them and says, "Reflect on the joys of livin'." When one of the menacing Rebs asks Brennan if he has thought through what he is doing, Brennan replies, "No." His impetuous nature has led him to take action, and his impetuous nature is going to have to get him out of this precarious situation. The line about the "joys of livin' succinctly sums up his code. Earlier, when the Union troops have surrounded the Rebs, it looks as though the Rebs might actually be foolish enough to fight to the death until Brennan, the first to drop his rifle, declares his vote for staying alive. As a wily old horse thief, Brennan's character has made a study of human nature, although the script wisely limits his wordage. He speaks only at pivotal moments in the plot. As the film's indispensable, enabling figure, he almost helps bring off the film's preposterous ending, in which Ryan—no longer pursued by the defeated Preston—joins with Trevor in declaring he will now try to clear his name.

After completing work in December 1950 on *Along the Great Divide*, Walter Brennan made the first of several appearances on Family Theater, a radio series conceived by Father Patrick Peyton, who convinced the Mutual Broadcasting Corporation to air 540 half hour dramas from 1947 to 1957. No commercial interruptions followed what was a short sermon to the effect that the family who prays together stays together. On January 24, 1951, in "A Star for Helen," Brennan played a janitor, Mr. Brannigan, a man of devout faith, who provides comfort and counsel to a young girl, Helen Jackson, coping with her mother's alcoholism. Not all Family Theater dramas had a religious message. On May 16, he starred in an adaptation of the Bret Harte story, "The Luck of Roaring Camp," on March 5, 1952, in "The Land of Sunshine," and on October 8 in "Mail Order Missus."

Brennan's next film, *Return of the Texan* (December 4, 1952), brings him still closer to the grandfather role he would perfect in *The Real Mc-Coys*. Here he plays Firth Crockett, a retired Texas Ranger living with his grandson Sam (Dale Robertson) and Sam's two young boys. Sam has reluctantly returned to their hometown after many years in Kansas City, where his wife died. Sam hopes to work himself out of debt by farming the family's old homestead, but he runs afoul of Rod Murray (Richard Boone), a peckerwood who has made good by marrying a wealthy landowner's daughter. Rod resents the idea that Sam (another peckerwood) has attracted the notice of his wife's sister, the playful and enticing Ann Marshall (Joanne Dru). Grandpa Firth complicates the tension between Rod and Sam, who is working for Rod, by trespassing on Rod's property to shoot wild game—as is Grandpa's right, he believes, because he helped settle the country so that the likes of Rod can prosper.

There is more than a little of Amos McCoy in the staunchly independent and feisty Grandpa Firth. But Brennan does not play the role for easy laughs. In fact, his presence signals the real theme of the picture, which is dealing with death and the loss of loved ones. Sam cannot let go of his attachment to his dead wife any more than his two boys can, even though Ann Marshall would clearly make a fitting new wife and mother. Grandpa tries to tell the family that death is a finality they all must accept. Otherwise, they cannot go on living. Near the end of the film, Grandpa suffers a stroke, and his own death seems imminent. When he suffers a second stroke while out hunting and realizes he will not survive, he sits down on a log as the camera tracks his two worried great-grandsons following him. As the camera gently swings round to capture Grandpa looking up to the light, he delivers a nearly three-minute monologue to his great-grandsons. "I see a million things move. Things aflyin'. Clouds sailing in the sky. Even the trees are movin'," he says, slightly swaying. "Things alive and breathin'. It's good," he affirms, nodding his head. Then as he straightens up slightly, a cut switches to a low angle shot, with his oldest great-grandson, Stevie, looking up at Grandpa, who is searching the sky and smiling slightly, acknowledging the natural cycle; "See them wild geese headin' South again." Then he slowly swivels his head toward Yoyo (the younger great-grandson), and the sound segues to another cut in which deer reappear, having been scared off earlier by the boys running through the brush. "They come back again now, a family," Grandpa announces. After another cut, a reverse angle shot shows Grandpa looking down at Stevie as his softened voice expresses an acceptance that Walter Brennan himself would articulate with his dying breath.

Here, in the serenity of the film's closing scenes, he relieves the anxiety of these young boys, still so distraught about their mother and caught up in their father's mourning. He reaches out to affectionately pat

Stevie's head, saying, "You live eighty years and more. You ask yourself a thousand times what it's all about. The only thing you're ever sure of is that life is precious. Never ought to be wasted. Hadn't ought to kill if we can help it. And never stop lovin'. And not to stop livin' when what we love is gone. That's another way of wastin' life. Lettin' the dead stand in the way of the livin'." He looks down and says, "You got to learn to let go, Stevie. Your mama's gone, but she's happy where she is. But she can't make you and Sam happy where she is." In a tight close-up, Brennan continues, "She don't care no more about this world. I reckon it's too little. It would be wrong if she hung on. She knows the livin's got to go on livin'. Now if you and Sam could let go, why things might have been different—with Ann, I mean. She would have made you a good mama and Sam a good wife. But you couldn't let go—neither of you." As another cut shows a kneeling Stevie, overcome by Grandpa's words, Brennan leans over, reaching out a hand to Stevie's shoulder: "Don't cry, Stevie, don't cry. We all get tangled up in the quick and the dead. That's what life is, I reckon. Only thing is it's wrong to waste it."

With those words, Grandpa keels over. As Stevie runs to get help, Grandpa asks Yoyo to hold his hand while he quietly dies. This scene can be dismissed as sentimental and overwritten, although Dudley Nichols, who also wrote *Swamp Water*, was one of Hollywood's best and realized, I believe, that the sentiment—including the redundant expressions in Grandpa's valedictory—are what both the boys and the audience want to hear. For after all, Grandpa himself is circling back on his own mortality. When he falls to the ground, sideways, off the log, it is like a great tree has crashed down. Indeed his body, seen sidewise, is parallel to the log he has been perched on. In his sudden silence he has become one with nature, as his own words have forecast. All along, the picture has been building to a denouement in which Sam will finally realize he cannot live without Ann, as Grandpa insisted. When Stevie rushes to tell her about Grandpa, she runs to the inevitable reunion with Sam, who realizes how right his grandfather was about the need to begin anew. Such roles enveloped Walter Brennan in a kind of piety that reflected the man himself. He embodied the continuity of family life, the bedrock values of frontier settlement, the belief that families like Sam's could begin again after tragedy struck.

Walter Brennan returned to his own bedrock values on his ranch deep in Indian country, the land of the pacific Chief Joseph of the Nez Perce. "He was not a warring Indian, but he was terribly abused," Brennan told an interviewer, admitting that so much of the true story of the West had never been filmed. "They can never make that picture. If they do, the white man's the heavy in that outfit," Brennan concluded. The actor was also instrumental in publicizing Chief Joseph Days, established in 1946 and celebrated at the end of July each year in Joseph with a parade and rodeo. On some occasions Walter would lead the Chesnimmus National Marching Band (so named by him), which went down Main Street led by Brennan dressed in motley and waving a toilet plunger as a baton. He organized local businessman and flew around the Oregon countryside publicizing the event.

And yet there was another side Walter Brennan seldom turned toward the camera, a side, in fact, that was excised from *We're Not Married* (December 17, 1952). Originally, the film featured separate stories about seven couples who learn by letter that they are not legally married because of a justice of the peace (Victor Moore, the memorable plumber in *The Seven Year Itch*) who is informed that he began performing his duties before his appointment took effect. The film, as released, starred David Wayne and Marilyn Monroe, Fred Allen and Ginger Rogers, Eve Arden and Paul Douglas, Louis Calhern and Zsa Zsa Gabor, and Eddie Bracken and Mitzi Gaynor. Who knows why the sequence featuring Brennan and Hope Emerson did not survive the final cut? Perhaps it was one story too many.

In *Hidden Hollywood*, a DVD compilation of deleted scenes, narrator Joan Collins suggests the episode was considered "too offbeat" for some tastes, although now, she adds, "it seems wonderfully funny." Brennan is first shown in the woods, watching while Lafe Beaufort goes off to work his land. Then Handsome, as Brennan is called, enters the kitchen, his thumbs resting where his suspenders hold his pants up—a necessary support for a formidable paunch (Brennan must have been wearing padding). Mattie Beaufort offers him a cup of coffee, but he doesn't see how he can accept on an empty stomach. So she ends up, inevitably, serving him a breakfast of eggs and ham. He sits down, with his left elbow on a table and his left hand supporting his neck, as he leans back to take in this robust woman. He smiles, already eating her up, as he suggests that she add some grits and biscuits to his repast. This is a flirtatious Walter Brennan, with an ingratiating smile not quite like anything that had been captured on-screen. As she carries a big tub, and he just sits there letting her do the heavy lifting, he compliments her on her strength, adding, "The things you do for that man just makes my blood boil!" In his next breath he is asking if he can have half a watermelon while he waits for breakfast. "Soon as I get my breath back," the poor woman answers. While eating, he begins his pitch: "If you wasn't married . . ." She interrupts, "Look,

Handsome, I know what you're getting at, but it ain't no use." He says it breaks his heart that she can't run away with him. "I know," she says, "but you have to be brave about it." Not only does he get her to do all the work, he also gets her to do most of the talking and to articulate what is on his mind.

Cut to the next scene, where Brennan is shown in the background, lounging on a bench and watching Emerson split a log with an axe. "You can lose your looks workin' like that all the time," he tells her. The stocky Emerson is no beauty except in the eye of her beholder. "Go on, Handsome, what looks have I got to lose?" she asks. She is talking to a scruffy backwoods type who says, "Don't go runnin' yourself down, Mattie. You ain't only a fine figure of a woman, but"—and here he opens his eyes wide so that they glisten with connoisseurship—"you must be strong as a mule, too." By the end of the sentence you can see how he envisions her in harness. He then switches to third person, as though quoting another authority on the subject: "She's all woman. Plenty of her too." Demure Mattie takes this comment as a compliment: "Awful nice of you to say so, Handsome."

The sound of a shot scatters the chickens and Handsome heads for cover. But the matter of fact Mattie tells him it is only the mailman, whose car has backfired. Mattie takes delivery of a letter, which she can't read without her glasses, so Handsome sits down to peruse it while she goes to get him more food. His eye lands on a passage announcing she is not legally married. So this should be the moment his dream comes true, but he crumples up the letter and feeds it to a hog, thus revealing that what he has been doing all along is feeding Mattie a line. When she asks about the letter, he turns to watch the hog eat it, and then he laughs, "Just another ad for Cadillacs." She laughs and says, "They sure come to the right place for it." And Handsome declares, "Why not? If you was my wife, you'd have a Cadillac." As he munches on the biscuits the cut is to the hog munching, then back to Brennan laughing and seeming to imitate the hog's snort as he chews. It has always been about the meal, not the marriage.

Was it Handsome's cheerful manipulation of Mattie that troubled the producers? Perhaps a salacious Grandpa was just too much for Twentieth Century-Fox, which had put the benevolent Brennan into films like *Scudda Hoo! Scudda Hay!* He was headed toward an anodyne grandfatherly character.

The softening and domestication of the Walter Brennan persona is on display in *Lure of the Wilderness* (July 16, 1952), Fox's Technicolor remake of *Swamp Water*, in which Brennan, now named Jim Harper, reprises his role as an outcast accused of murder. But this time Brennan is no philosopher of nature, no devotee of the wilderness, despite the picture's title. To the contrary, he yearns for home and "seegars" and sitting on the front porch. It is his daughter Laurie (Jean Peters) who is the hardened swamp denizen—even though she somehow manages to always appear in full makeup, whereas Anne Baxter, playing the same role in *Swamp Water* looks and acts like a believable country girl. Without exception, the new cast is inferior. Jeff Chandler playing Ben is no match for Dana Andrews's authentic country boy. And that menacing bully, Ward Bond, is sorely missed, although Jack Elam is passable as a wily villain and will reappear to good effect in a later Brennan film, *Support Your Local Sheriff!* But Brennan is just too damn cheerful for a man hiding out in a swamp—and too trusting, immediately taking to Ben and spending much of the picture with a daft smile on his face, signaling his hope that young'uns Laurie and Ben will become a couple.

For Brennan the worst part of making the film was taking the plunge into a water tank on the Fox lot in order to fight an alligator after Brennan is shot by one of the bad guys. As he recalled, the studio got a lobsterman to actually do the underwater scene, but not before Brennan was filmed sinking to the bottom of the tank, a feat accomplished by the lobsterman pulling him down by his feet. A cameraman was also in the tank, capturing the action. When Walter bobbed up to the surface, he cried out. One of the crew asked, "What's the matter, Walter?" Brennan answered, "I'm all out of breath. Why does a guy have to wait till he's fifty-five years old to get down under water with alligators?" Brennan claimed there were alligators in the tank, but they were not hungry. In another shot, Brennan is shown being bitten by a cottonmouth. Although he got nowhere near the snake—"it was a trick shot," he remembered—he shot up out of a chair when he saw the scene on film. In fact, the worst Brennan suffered during the shoot, some of it on location in the swamp, was a case of poison oak.

In another Family Theater production, "A Kind of Treasure" (January 21, 1953), he starred with Natalie Wood in a story about Mr. Alex, an incurable romantic, who still believes he will find the buried treasure he dreamed of as a boy. Brennan also continued to do B pictures such as Republic's *Sea of Lost Ships* (October 21, 1953), which relies on stock footage for action sequences played out amid calving glaciers. Brennan is O'Malley (his first name is never mentioned), who raises two United States Coast Guard prodigies, and then spends the picture trying to reconcile the boys after they have a falling out over their love for the same woman. Of course, it all turns out all right in this promotional piece made for the coast guard. O'Malley contrives to have both of his estranged wunderkinds assigned to the same ship, and then makes them part of a rescue team that dislodges a cargo ship stuck on a glacier. Their splendid teamwork results in a reconciliation of rivals. The poor script proves Brennan's point: He could be as ordinary as any other journey-man actor who was not given a well-written role. Nonetheless, the bad parts never diminished his own conviction that there would be, if he was patient, other good ones that would test and develop his craft. But while he waited for the plum assignments, he wanted to work. In this respect, he possessed the discipline and dedication required for the military types he often impersonated. A true veteran, he knew what it meant to gut it out.

In November 1953, on the Universal set, where he got his start as an extra, Walter Brennan celebrated thirty years in Hollywood. Jack Foley, an old friend and head of Universal's sound effects department, remi-nisced about the sound track noises Brennan produced for him—includ-ing that braying donkey Walter always brought up when talking about the not so good old days. "I can still hear the director screaming about your price," Foley said to Brennan, who laughed and said, "Had to wait until he met my price. I nicked you $25 for that one. But if I hadn't been there, they'd still be waiting for that jackass to open his mouth!" Other-wise, he was doing falls from horses for "a buck a tumble" and envious of "guys who got to double their pay by doing two falls in the same day." Brennan and Cooper used to split a candy bar for lunch.

Walter Brennan still worked on increasing his repertoire of television and radio roles. In "Lucky Thirteen" (*Schlitz Playhouse of Stars*, November 13, 1953) he is a merchant turned banker for two horse traders who don't trust one another and can't be trusted to deal squarely with him. "Brennan turns in a workmanlike job," a reviewer reported. He appeared in two more Family Theater productions "The Legend of High Chin Bob" (December 9, 1953) and "Tennessee's Partner" (September 22, 1954). In the first he stars in a western as a cowhand advising his grandson on the nature of self-confidence and faith in one's work, and in the sec-ond as another Bret Harte character, who forgives his partner's many transgressions.

Drums Across the River (June 1954), one of the revisionist Westerns of the 1950s, offered Brennan a more significant and satisfying role. With a four-week guarantee for his work that began in October 1953, he was to receive "not less than first featured credit on the screen and in paid advertising," according to Universal's weekly production minutes of October 1, 1953. On October 20, he was taken to the studio hospital. A squib (small firework) had exploded close to him, and it was thought he might have an eye injury, but he returned to the set almost immediately. The production remained on schedule and within its half-million-dollar budget. Two days later, Audie Murphy suffered a throat injury in a fight scene, but the bruising did not delay production, either. In his days as an extra, Brennan had become inured to such hazards, which even stars sometimes encountered. Most worked through illnesses and injuries, and in this case the film completed shooting in early November 1953 on schedule and $4,500 under budget.

As Sam Brannon, Brennan opposes Crown City's encroachment on Ute land in search of the gold, which will save the town from penury now that its other mining operations are played out. The actor who voiced his regret over the white exploitation of Native Americans brings considerable conviction to his argument that it is better for the town to fail than to break a treaty and plunder land and resources that do not belong to the white settlers. Brannon steadfastly opposes his own son, Gary (Audie Murphy), who sides with a group of "investors" (actually outlaws) who mean to exploit the town for their own purposes. Sam Brannon speaks the Ute language and has learned to accept Native Americans as equals, even though a Ute warrior killed Brannon's wife. It is a crime his son cannot abide—until Gary realizes that a gang of confidence men has duped him. Audie Murphy, sturdy and believable as a young man with a grievance, has a final showdown with a hired killer, Morton, played with wonderfully malign guile by Hugh O'Brien before he turned good guy in the Wyatt Earp television series. Brennan and Murphy are ably assisted by Jay Silverheels (better known as the Lone Ranger's sidekick, Tonto) as the temperate and just Ute chief. Universal used Technicolor in *Drums Across the River* to take full advantage of location shooting that included Red Rock National Park and Burro Flats in Cantil and Simi Hills, California, respectively. In the end, both Brannons broker a peace that gives the town mining rights on Ute land in exchange for Ute hunting rights on the settlers' land. The ending, of course, is too neat, but by movie standards *de rigueur*. Stirrups can be seen underneath the Ute's blankets, and Lyle Bettger, playing the head bad guy, may be the best barbered and coiffed villain in the history of the Hollywood western. Universal previewed the picture at the United Artists Theater in Los Angeles in late January 1954. "Audience reaction was good," the studio's daily minutes reported. "[I]t was the general consensus that this picture is on a par with our previous releases starring Audie Murphy."

If Brennan disliked the fakery of Hollywood Westerns, he also was drawn to them as stark dramas of frontier justice. At one point, the two Brannons stand off against an entire town, a mob keen to believe that father and son have allied themselves with the Utes in order to attack a stagecoach carrying a gold shipment. The pride the Brannons take in their code of justice appealed to Brennan; it was the same pride he took in the integrity of his own work. He lauded the cowboy's desire to "go it alone, make his own decisions, often on matters as important as life and death—his own." The courage Brennan projected onto the cowboy was a manifestation of his own fortitude.

Like *Drums Across the River*, *Bad Day at Black Rock* (January 7, 1955), is a revisionist work—this time examining the seamy side, the racism and thuggery—of postwar America. Brennan, looking much slimmer than in his previous pictures, plays a western town's veterinarian and mortician. This taut drama, featuring menacing performances by a trio of villains (Robert Ryan, Ernest Borgnine, and Lee Marvin), ultimately centers on Brennan's character (Doc Velle), who collaborates with John J. Macreedy (Spencer Tracy) to uncover the truth about Komoko, a Japanese American settler killed during the war. Doc Velle, like the rest of the town, has been cowed by the xenophobic Robert Ryan-led conspiracy to thwart and ultimately murder Macreedy after he refuses to relinquish his quest for the truth—even though he is outnumbered and apparently incapacitated because of a paralyzed arm (presumably a war wound). Brennan's Velle is no hero, but he is a man who can no longer abide his association with evil—any more than can Tim Horn (Dean Jagger), the town's sheriff. Shorn of his sidekick status and of any mannerism reminiscent of his more comic roles, Brennan emerges as the common man's powerful and utterly believable voice of conscience.

As film critic Dana Polan observes in DVD commentary on the film, much of the interior action, shot in a hotel lobby, tells the story by positioning characters as if they are on a stage. The wide frame, cinemascope screen emphasizes this theatricality of villainy. The way Brennan spreads himself out on the lobby sofa suggests Doc Velle is not as tense as the others under Ryan's (Reno Smith's) sway. Only the loose-limbed Lee Marvin and Ryan himself seem as comfortable and confident of their power to intimidate others. Brennan is the only one in the lobby tableau who is genuinely curious about Macreedy, wanting to engage him in conversation. The others are scared or hostile. When Ryan arrives,

Brennan shadows him. In the lineup of men arranged to follow Ryan's lead, Brennan is the farthest away from this mob boss and the least susceptible to his threats.

Midway through the film, Doc strides away from Smith and his henchman, signaling the eventual shift in the power dynamic from Smith to Macreedy. "Doc is going in a different direction from these people in a conformist world of evil," Polan observes. As Macready begins to assert himself, cutting down Borgnine with a judo chop, Doc—who has tried to help Macready escape—enters the hotel lobby and takes his position beside Macready. Doc commands center stage in the lobby as we near the final confrontation with Reno Smith and his gang, one in which Macreedy triumphs by lobbing a makeshift Molotov cocktail at Smith, who catches fire and capitulates.

Brennan appreciated the brooding, meditative nature of the film and the tension that mounts in the confrontation between Ryan and Tracy. It made you think, he said, a comment that revealed Brennan's awareness that many of his films did not require much mental work. "You didn't know how it was going to come out," he added. Some of the credit here has to be given to director John Sturges, whose later hits included *The Magnificent Seven* (1960) and *The Great Escape* (1963). As James Garner noted in *The Garner Files*, Sturges "knew how to take a bunch of characters coming from different directions and draw them together in one purpose. John would assemble a great cast and let them do their thing. He got the most out of actors by bolstering their confidence with a pat on the back at the right time. He was easygoing but could be tough when he needed to be. He was always fair."

Character actor Ernest Borgnine told a story about Walter Brennan that is typical of the man and his professionalism. Relatively new to motion pictures, but with a burgeoning reputation as an actor, Borgnine was surprised when Brennan approached him on the set of *Bad Day at Black Rock* and asked if Borgnine would mind if Brennan watched him do a scene. Not at all, Borgnine said, rightly taking Brennan's request as a compliment. After Brennan watched Borgnine do a take, Brennan said, "Good enough. Great."

Brennan was also impressed with Lee Marvin during a scene in which Doc Velle offers his hearse to Macreedy as a getaway vehicle. Suddenly, Marvin appears and then nonchalantly walks over to the vehicle and rips out some of the engine's wiring. The casual violence is shocking. It was the first time Brennan had met Marvin, who had a powerful effect on Brennan: "When he came out and tore the ignition out of that thing,

I could have killed him. You know, I just hated him that much. I mean, just working with him. I thought, gee, this guy's a great actor to make me hate him like that."

On the set, Walter provoked Spencer Tracy's ire. Katie (Katharine Hepburn) didn't have "good judgment" or common sense, Brennan told Tracy. Walter was referring to her attacks on Senator Joseph McCarthy. Tracy turned icy, and the next day director John Sturges discovered Tracy and Brennan were no longer speaking to one another. The estranged actors addressed one another through intermediaries. Sturges remembered this exchange:

> [Tracy to Sturges] Would you ask Mr. Brennan to not get in my key light?
> [Brennan to Sturges] Tell Mr. Tracy if he hit his mark, I wouldn't be in his key light.

At one point Brennan turned his back on Tracy and held up three fingers, signifying that he had three Academy Awards. Tracy had two.

In contrast to *Bad Day at Black Rock*, *The Far Country* (February 12, 1955) seems formulaic. James Stewart (Jack Webster) is a loner, the self-contained kind of cowboy hero that John Wayne exemplified. Even so, Webster partners with Ben Tatum (Brennan), driving cattle to market in various venues from Wyoming to the Klondike during the Gold Rush. In Skagway, Webster gets in the way of a hanging judge and his gang, who confiscate his herd and take him into custody. Since Webster's point of pride is that he accepts help from no one, how will he manage to escape getting hung or killed in the lawless West?

At first, the Stewart-Brennan combination seems disappointing. As other character actors testified, Stewart was a hard man to know. Director John Ford told Harry Carey Jr., "You don't get to know Jimmy Stewart, Jimmy Stewart gets to know you." Brennan, ever the diplomat, put it this way: "It's not that he's unfriendly, it's just he's always getting bogged down in thought." Brennan admired Stewart's economical acting style: "Jimmy's a great actor because he doesn't act. He throws things away." Off-screen, Stewart "was a wonderful companion," Brennan told Stewart's biographer Lawrence Quirk. Brennan added that Stewart was "very down-to-earth, full of good stories, fine sense of humor. He had a great talent for concentration when the camera started going—he was on top of his part every second, even kept going after Tony Mann called 'cut!'" Another Stewart biographer, Donald Dewey, describes an actor so self-absorbed and confident of his own prowess on-screen that he shared none of Gary Cooper's concern about Brennan's antics. Stewart professed only admiration for Brennan's "cleverness," telling an interviewer, "It can be entertaining, and that ends up helping the picture as a whole."

The aloof Stewart—he makes John Wayne look positively gregarious in his scenes with Brennan in *Red River* and *Rio Bravo*—hardly seems attached to Ben and never displays the slightest affection for him. And Ben, unlike Brennan's earlier sidekicks, is not an astute, acerbic companion who provides a running critique of the hero. On the contrary, Ben is gentle, doting on Webster. Ben is too trusting and too talkative. But then it becomes clear that heavyset Ben (Brennan seems to have put on considerable weight for the role) represents the very humanity that Webster has cut himself off from. Stewart is so cold in the Webster role that all he can say to the beautiful Ruth Roman's kiss is "Thank you." But when Roman and her cowboy cohort (rivals of Webster and Tatum) are caught in a landslide, it is up to Ben to tell the heartless Webster that he is wrong, and that he must do what he can to rescue his adversaries from catastrophe. Webster is restored to his full humanity only after Ben is ambushed and killed. Ben's death is, in effect, the culmination of Webster's estrangement from his fellow man. Thus, in quite a new way, Brennan's screen persona becomes absolutely vital to the moral center of the western.

Brennan himself did not see the picture so positively. He told Lawrence Quirk, "I played a grizzled old eccentric and I had some good laugh-lines and some nice situations, but I have to confess it all turned out so predictably, and it followed the well-worn Western path." But one of the chief pleasures of this picture is the contrast it sets up between Stewart and Brennan and a group of villainous character actors: John McIntire as the crafty, evil Mayor Gannon; the growly voiced Harry Morgan as one of Gannon's henchman; Robert J. Wilke, turning in another menacing performance as Madden, another henchman; and Jack Elam as Newberry, no less vicious than Madden. Elam obviously relished his roles and grew such a fan base that he was allowed to spoof himself later in *Support Your Local Sheriff!* Manny Farber was ready to recommend any performance by Harry Morgan, who could play comedy, villainy—and virtually anything in between—with his infinitely adaptable baritone. It is not surprising that he turns up again in *Support Your Local Sheriff!*, which consciously plays on the public's affection for character actors who, like old perennials, reappear every movie season. Of course,

Stewart prevails in the final shoot-out as the western hero who restores order and a sense of justice.

Walter Brennan's own trajectory toward characters who restore order and become moral exempla continued with *Four Guns to the Border* (February 18, 1955), in which he commands the action as Simon Bhumer, a retired gunslinger who has gone legit. Bhumer plans to settle on a ranch with his daughter, Lolly (Colleen Miller), but first he becomes involved in a conflict with a gang of bank robbers led by Ray Cully (Rory Calhoun), the tall, dark, and handsome hero in embryo, whose good nature is born out by Lolly's devotion. The predictable plot and stereotypical characters provide Brennan with little leeway, except to act the stern father who has to relent in his opposition to Cully when Cully saves Simon's and his daughter's lives and surrenders to the law. The film is just a reversal of the Universal pattern in *Blood on the Moon*, in which the good guy (Robert Ryan) becomes the bad guy, until the good guy re-emerges when Claire Trevor demands that he reform.

The mid-1950s were an especially productive period for Brennan on radio and television, even as he slowed his pace in motion pictures. Some roles, of course, were more challenging and more successful than others. With Edmond O' Brien, Brennan starred in *Treasure of Sierra Madre*, broadcast on February 15, 1955, taking on the Walter Huston movie role of the old prospector. In the March 2, 1955, Family Theater production of "Torkelson's Flying Circus," Brennan portrays a World War I pilot down on his luck, a self-described bum, who makes the most of an unforeseen opportunity to turn himself into a successful businessman. What is striking about the program is Walter's even-tempered voice, the virtuous expression of a soul who has weathered all manner of vicissitudes. A reviewer dispatched "Mr. Ears," a Schlitz Playhouse production starring Brennan as a kindly old man, as a "stock story." As *Variety* reported, "The Brush Roper" (November 23, 1955, Screen Director's Playhouse), benefited from some good folk humor. Brennan is a grandfather reminiscing about his bronco busting days. The episode, directed by an old Hollywood hand, Stuart Heisler, co-starring Edgar Buchanan, and featuring an appearance by Chuck Conners, later to star in *The Rifleman*, remains watchable as one of Brennan's spunky grandpa performances. He gets himself and his horse caught in a tree while roping a bull and trying to prove he still has it in him to collect fifty dollars for the runaway. In "The Happy Sun" (July 3, 1956 *Playhouse of Stars*), he is an old lumberjack whose whole family is wiped out in one night. "These softy parts fall effortlessly on Brennan," the *Variety* reviewer observed, "and he can always be depended on to give it a tearful jerk." Such programs were "more to be tolerated than enjoyed," remarked another critic. In "The Gentle Years," an *Ethel Barrymore Theater* production broadcast on September 28, 1956, Brennan is a small town newspaperman who helps a Swedish immigrant secure citizenship. In "Woman's Work" (November 20, 1956, *Cavalcade of America*), Brennan, plays a misogynist crank, but the actor's efforts were, one commentator declared, wasted in a "turtle-paced tale." But in "Vengeance Canyon" (November 30, 1956, *Dick Powell's Zane Grey Theatre*), Brennan's portrayal of an outlaw who turns a young gang member away from an act of revenge was deemed "flawless" and "believable." As the remorseful Joe, Brennan gives one of his best performances. He has accidentally shot and killed a boy in a bank robbery. Cornered by an Indian war party, he helps another man escape scalping and certain death. Then Joe greets the Indians coming for his scalp with an ecstatic expression that confirms his quest for redemption. In "Duffy's Man" (December 19, 1956, *Ford Television Theatre*), Brennan is an outcast stable hand who becomes a hero defending a town against a gang of outlaws. He plays the role "according to blueprint." As Sheriff John Larson in "Ride a Lonely Trail "(November 2, 1957, *Dick Powell's Zane Grey Theatre*), Brennan is fit for retirement, the town tells him, and he sets out to prove them wrong. The actor "did all he could to keep things moving," the reviewer noted. "But the majority of his dialogue was innocuously directed at his horse, Old Timer," with the most exciting part of the action occurring in the drama's first minute.

Taken together, *God is My Partner* (July 1957), *The Way to the Gold* (May 10, 1957), and *Tammy and the Bachelor* (June 14, 1957), exemplify Walter Brennan's wide range as an actor. In the first film, he plays a surgeon who believes his success is a gift from God—exactly what the actor himself often said about his own good fortune. Critic Leonard Maltin summed up his own reaction this way: "Sincere, hokey film of old-timer who feels he owes a spiritual obligation which he can redeem by giving away his money." But in *The Way to the Gold*, Brennan bucks his benign persona in a bit part as a maniacal and greedy criminal. In the third film, in another kindly grandfather role, Brennan bookends Debbie Reynolds's performance as Tammy by teaching her to be true, and then slapping his hat down on a log as her lover (a handsome young Leslie Nielson) comes to claim her.

In her memoir, Reynolds pays tribute to Walter Brennan:

I noticed that he wasn't looking at me while we talked. After we finished the take, I asked him where he'd been looking.

"Your ear," he replied.

"Why?" I asked in surprise.

"Because that way more of my face is on camera. Don't look at the other actors. Look in three-quarters, so your face is more prominent. Stick with me. I'll teach you some tricks."

And Walter did teach me. He shared his bag of tricks for how to make the most of a scene.

Walter was one of the greatest scene-stealers I've ever known—in the major leagues with Thelma Ritter and Walter Matthau. You couldn't turn your back on any of them. It's hard to rank them; they were all superb at their craft. I'd say it was a three-way tie for who could get the most out of their camera time.

A pilot for *Mr. Tutt*, a series produced by Desilu and based on a *Saturday Evening Post* story about a curmudgeonly lawyer, was not made into a series, but it was broadcast on *Colgate Theatre* (September 10, 1958). The *Variety* reviewer considered Brennan excellent in the part, even though the script for the pilot was subpar. Brennan's subsequent career on television might have been quite different if this role had made the same indelible impression as Amos McCoy, a part that made it difficult for audiences to accept Brennan as a sophisticated character in a series that did not have rural aspect to it.

Brennan's radio and television work in the mid- to late 1950s went well with his B Westerns, including his appearance as Doc Lacy, akin to Doc Velle and the only one in town who supports beleaguered hero Fred MacMurray in *At Gunpoint* (December 25, 1955). Viewers have relished Brennan's sarcasm and underplaying that enhanced the realism of such Westerns. He also teamed up again with director David Butler for another equine epic, *Glory* (January 11, 1956), which marked Brennan's third decade as a horse trainer, avuncular and cranky as ever. Butler, as he made clear in his reminiscences about *Glory*, was far more interested in filming races than in directing actors or working on good scripts.

In *Come Next Spring* (March 9, 1956) and *Goodbye, My Lady* (May 12, 1956) Brennan was able to rise above the pedestrian roles that followed *Bad Day at Black Rock* by perfecting the persona of the small town or rural character that emerges in films such as *Driftwood* and *The Green Promise*. Although *Come Next Spring* has been compared to *The Waltons* because of its pleasant portrayal of backwoods life, it has a core of authenticity that director Martin Scorsese has lauded. Matt Ballot (Steve Cochran) returns home nine years after abandoning his wife Bess (Ann Sheridan) and two children. Ballot lives uneasily in a fraught household with an estranged wife and in a community that despises him for leaving her. Jeffrey Storys (Brennan) befriends Ballot, works alongside him, and functions as a kind of conduit to the world that has rejected Ballot because he once rejected it. Brennan does no more with the role than is required, which means he stands for a basic decency and respect for his fellow man, a hallmark of his best work in the 1950s.

Brennan often cited *Goodbye, My Lady* as one of his favorite films. Certainly it was a labor of love in the close collaboration with the director, William Wellman, better known for his action films and for *The Ox-Bow Incident* (1943). Skeeter (Brandon DeWilde) lives with his none too ambitious uncle Jesse (Brennan) in a swamp, where they find a strange dog with a hyena-like laugh. (It is, in fact a basenji, bred in Africa). Jesse realizes the dog must have escaped from a very different environment, but Skeeter adopts the dog without thinking about the consequences should the dog's true owner show up. Much of the picture is taken up with Skeeter training the dog to hunt better than other hounds. The deliberate and careful way Wellman paces the film makes it utterly absorbing, even as Brennan delivers one of his best understated performances. With its emphasis on rapport with nature and the land and taking responsibility for other animals, the inspirational script serves as Walter Brennan's credo. And when the dog's owner shows up, Skeeter has to learn how to let go of his creation, making for an ending far more real than those of most family films. Sidney Poitier has a small role as a neighbor, and though this story is set in Georgia, there is no evidence of segregation. To the contrary, Poitier's character appears quite at home with his white neighbors, with whom he shares a bond with the land and its creatures.

Brennan's most memorable appearances continued to be in Westerns. *The Proud Ones* (May 1956), starring Robert Ryan as a sheriff going blind (who gets help at just the right moment from Jeff Hunter), also features one of Brennan's most economical performances as Jake, a jailor. Brennan has no more than a dozen lines in the film, but he is alert and does not miss a crucial moment when Ryan seems under threat. In fact, the role is a low-key warm-up for the stalwart Stumpy in *Rio Bravo* (March 18, 1959), where Brennan plays the supporting role opposite John Wayne. But Jake, unlike Stumpy, is a man of few words and nimble reflexes. The most astonishing moment occurs when Jake, seemingly relaxed and sitting in a chair against a jail wall, suddenly draws his gun in one quick, effortless motion, the result of the practice Brennan gained while working in his thirty-eighth western (not counting television work).

To *Rio Bravo*, Brennan brought his own brand of realism. He explained his reaction to the script to reporter Steven H. Scheuer:

> They tell me I'm playing a crippled old man who's got a rifle built into his crutch. Any time they get rough with him, he shoots them down with his crutch. I think about this for a little while, and then I asked them a simple question. I said, "When this crippled old man picks up his crutch and shoots why doesn't he fall flat on his dog-gone back?" They changed the script.

Stumpy criticizes John T. Chance (John Wayne), the town marshal, for Chance's inclination to go it alone and do everything himself, even when he is outnumbered and outgunned by a gang that threatens law and order. The *Red River* formula is also reprised by injecting Angie Dickinson into the plot as Wayne's love interest. Like Joanne Dru, who intervenes when Wayne seems bent on destroying his protégé (played by Montgomery Clift), Dickinson deplores Wayne's lone wolf mentality. But Dickinson is given more to do than women are accorded in most Westerns, so she is not relegated to reaction shots, but is instead fitted into the ensemble of players that includes Ricky Nelson, a substitute for Clift. The lightweight Nelson is wisely shunted away from a confrontation with Wayne, instead becoming the extra gun Wayne needs—and also the extra voice when Dean Martin (a rehabilitated town drunk), Nelson, and Brennan sing a song together in the jail where they are holed up, awaiting the arrival of the bad guys. Such scenes in Westerns are usually factitious, but Martin's easy way with a song, Nelson's cool underplaying, and Brennan's full throated contribution provide a precious moment in the film, one that reveals Brennan's robust appeal.

Greg Ford identifies why Stumpy has annoyed certain viewers: "Brennan's tetchy impetuosity, his grumbling, his cackling, his ceaseless clamoring for all the attention of Wayne and the others, transparently veiled his small child's desire for adult consolation." This childish side of Stumpy is a facet of several Brennan roles that has rarely been commented on. Part of the appeal of Brennan's old men is a boyish freshness and recalcitrance that makes the world move at their pace. This kind of feat, for a character actor, is quite remarkable, as is the audience response to it.

To be sure, Brennan has his detractors, who see him as simply repeating the same role. Examined closely, however, his best parts show him individuating the stereotype so that it leaves an indelible impression on old and young alike. Many years after making *Rio Bravo*, Angie Dickinson was told about the grandson of a friend who as a boy demanded to be called "Stumpy." His limp was "so bad," Dickinson was told, "that they had him tested many times, and sad to say, doctors could not help him. After several years of this, and I'm not making this up, it somehow was revealed that all along, he loved Stumpy so much (from having seen *Rio Bravo* so many times on DVD) that he wanted to walk like him. All that time, he was simply 'being Stumpy.'"

In the end, Stumpy is integral to the denouement of *Rio Bravo*. It is his idea to blast the bad guys out of their lair with dynamite. More importantly, each of the male leads is obliged to give an account of himself to Stumpy. Manny Farber, who judges the film second-rate Hawks, nevertheless suggests this about Walter Brennan: "Perhaps the most satisfying of underground pleasures is to see the fantastic technician . . . building with suicidal force within a stale, corrupt, losing proposition."

Howard Hawks took the credit for goading Brennan into a great performance:

> [H]e amazed me with the first scene he did. I said, "What the hell is going on here? Are you going to play that goddam television show that you've been doing, for me. Do you think I'm gonna make a *Real McCoy* out of it? This is supposed to be a crabby, evil, nasty old man." "Oh God," he said. I said to Wayne, "Come on, Duke, let's go over and play a game of checkers and let this dumbbell think up what he's got to do." So for fifteen minutes we stayed away, and he just sat there. Then he came in and he was really a bastard. It was easy the rest of the time.

Angie Dickinson has often spoken of her admiration for Brennan, and did so again for this biography:

> Brennan and I had no scenes together, and therefore rarely crossed paths. On a big set like that, if you don't work, you don't just come around and "hang out." Either for me or for WB. One day we were on the set together in Tucson, and we had a lovely brief chat, and he was so very dear, gentle and calm. But we made no other contact. I can only say that he was a sweet man, and he was brilliant

in Rio Bravo, as in everything he did. He was a true ACTOR. And by the way, I regret I did nothing to promote a friendship. . . . However, I think he was a very private man, and one just didn't do that to a legend like WB.

It was so like Brennan to be utterly accessible on a set, but also to draw a sharp distinction between work and his personal life.

Just when you think Brennan is merely repeating his shtick as crotchety sidekick, he mimics the film's star, John Wayne, in a closing scene that startles Dean Martin. Earlier, when a prisoner calls Stumpy crazy and says the deputy is going to shoot him, the maniacal Stumpy is elated, as though he just received a wonderful compliment: "You know. I'm just nuts!" Howard Hawks, the delighted director, remembered how hard the audience laughed. Critic Robin Wood, writing in Joseph McBride's *Focus On Howard Hawks*, describes Brennan's character Stumpy as the epitome of the "garrulous and toothless old cripple," who is nevertheless "remarkably complex . . . funny, pathetic, maddening, often all at the same time; yet, fully aware of his limitations, we never cease to respect him." For *Rio Bravo* this consummate performer was paid $10,000 a week for five weeks, an unusually high sum for a supporting player.

Rio Bravo is an answer to the lionization of the lone town marshal, portrayed so powerfully by Gary Cooper in *High Noon*, but *Rio Bravo* is also a deft remake of *Red River*, one that highlights Brennan's role as a moral authority and a witness to history central to the ethos of Howard Hawks's Westerns. But heretofore the Brennan persona rarely displaced that of the stars he supported. That would happen when, in the television age, the actor became, like Ward Bond in *Wagon Train* (1957–61), the locus of the action, the center around which the family and the nation revolved.

CHAPTER 8

The Real McCoys

America's Grandpa
1957–63

That's Grandpappy Amos, the head of the clan,
He roars like a lion but he's gentle as a lamb.

—FROM THE SONG THAT INTRODUCES EACH EPISODE OF *THE REAL McCOYS*

SOMETIME IN 1954, IRVING AND NORMAN PINCUS, APPROACHED WALTER Brennan about appearing in a series featuring a "West Virginia hillbilly family transplanted to California." Having already invested his time in one pilot without results, Brennan rejected the idea of another, but Irving Pincus continued to press his case. After a year or so, Brennan said yes, claiming he did so "just to get the cuss off my neck." But surely Pincus's pitch that Brennan had an opportunity to make television history by starring in the first situation comedy to feature rural characters in an endearing format was persuasive. Brennan portrayed a character that was a distillation and domestication of his ornery and affectionate screen persona—deprived only of the malevolence on display in *The Westerner*, *My Darling Clementine*, and *Brimstone*.

Although NBC took a one-year option on the show, and Danny Thomas's production company agreed to finance the pilot, the network decided not to air what appeared to be a poor prospect. When ABC finally broadcast the show, it seemed doomed from the start, since it was in the same time slot as two popular dramatic programs, *Climax!* and *Dragnet*. The first review, in *Variety* (October 7, 1957), seemed to confirm Brennan's original misgivings: "'The Real McCoys' is a cornball, folksy-wolksy situation comedy series destined to find the going tough." The *Variety* critic called the humor "forced," the pacing "sluggish," and the characters' adventures "only lightly amusing." And too many lovable characters! Brennan received due praise as a "fine actor," but the rest of the cast was just "okay." And yet, by the third week the show was number one in its time slot, compelling the *Variety* skeptic to allow, "It's all so hokey that it can't be taken seriously, and for that reason this quarter can't see any really strong reason why cityfolk shouldn't appreciate and enjoy it for what it is. The show is already big in the hinterlands." By December 2, 1957, the critic was obliged to report that the "laughs come freely." And then, for season after season, the praise escalated. The show began with an audience of ten million, but within a year the number of viewers had tripled.

None of the writers, producers, or actors was from West Virginia. In fact, Irving Pincus made it almost a point of pride to say they were all Northerners. "Take away the Cracker Barrel and what have you got?" he asked. "A script that would play just as well on *Father Knows Best*." Brennan "really, really liked my work," recalled Kathleen Nolan, who played his daughter-in-law, Kate. On the first day of rehearsals for the show, the actors read their parts, each doing a version of a West Virginia accent. When Nolan spoke, Brennan responded immediately, telling the cast, "Follow her." To have one of the best character actors in Hollywood history single her out was for Nolan "one of the greatest moments of my life."

Brennan was not looking for an authentic West Virginia accent, but rather for a certain sound, voice tone, and phrasing that would create an ensemble that was also a believable family. He took an interest in all of his fellow actors, said director Hy Averback. Brennan pointed out to eleven-year-old Michael Winkleman (Little Luke), "Why don't you turn the other way? It's better stage for you." It made a difference, the director said. Brennan watched the shows as they were broadcast, noticing his mistakes, but also his triumphs. He also watched other shows, especially *Gunsmoke*. James Arness as Matt Dillon had an instant rapport with his character and could create, in Brennan's words, "another realm." Brennan watched such shows to observe fellow actors, because to him acting was "pure and simple competition." He was also worried about mugging for the camera and told Hy Averback to stop him when he saw the actor "cut a dido" to get a laugh. One morning, Brennan recalled, Averback whispered in his ear, "You're doing it." What looks like natural delivery was difficult for Brennan: "It's a tricky business saying all those funny insulting lines that Amos is always throwing at people. Once I let Amos McCoy know he's being funny, I'm through. That's what our director watches for."

Even away from the set and in Joseph, Walter Brennan continued to police his performances—as Louise Kunz observed when he visited his wife in the hospital, where she was recuperating from an operation. At the only television set in the hospital, everyone gathered around to view *The Real McCoys*. Louise and a group of teenage kids watched as Walter said, "Oh, I did that okay. Oh, I've got to work on that, that's terrible." When the episode ended, a boy asked him how he remembered to limp. Walter said he put a tiny pebble in his shoe; otherwise he limped on the wrong foot. Diane Turner remembers the times Walter would enter the local drugstore, sit down at the soda fountain, and entertain everyone with his Grandpa Amos routines. When his granddaughter Tammy Crawford watched *The Real McCoys*, she would get upset because every episode the characters would get mad at her Grampy—although by the end of the show he would have learned his lesson.

Walter's grandson Dennis says, "It was fun to watch him on television, but he was just Granddad." Tammy adds, "We all looked forward to his visits." She recalls an old school grandparent who expected children to behave, to speak when spoken to, and to be seen rather than heard, although nothing in his treatment of his grandchildren lessened their pleasure during his visits. Granddaughter Caroline Ward remembered how he would tune up, imitating the sound of brass instruments, and drum on the table doing his impression of a marching band.

Walter liked to get up early, sometimes as early as 4:00 am, and walk around Joseph, just looking. On his way back to his motel, as he walked past Joseph Cash Market in the middle of town at about eight in the morning, a car pulled up and a guy asked, "Is Carlyle [the store owner] open yet?" And Walter said, "Well, I don't know, let's see." He pushed the door and it opened. The guy wanted a pack of cigarettes. There was no money in the till. But when Carlyle got to the store, here was Walter standing behind the counter, selling things to people, making change out of his own pocket.

"But if you had seen him on Main Street," Louise recalls. "He wore a hat my father would have thrown away. It was so dirty. And he always wore bib overalls—although he could dress up in a three-piece suit." Most of the time, Walter enjoyed being treated just like everyone else in Joseph. Mike remembered that when his father ordered his favorite meal, a steak dinner in a local restaurant, he would be asked how he wanted it done. Walter would answer, "Just knock one horn off." Dennis Brennan said many people in Wallowa County just took it for granted that Walter was a native. But every so often Dennis could hear his grandfather's New England intonation. With his grandmother Ruth, it was different. She was pure New England.

Walter Brennan's wished to be treated like everyone else sometimes had curious and amusing consequences. When he received a call from Hollywood summoning him to return for retakes, he drove to Pendleton's airport. Once when he took out his checkbook to pay for his fare, Pete Miller, the airline clerk, said they did not accept personal checks. He did not know who Walter Brennan was. Walter had urgent business, he told Miller, who remained adamant about airline policy. Finally, Walter put his car keys on the counter and told Miler to keep them. The airline would get the money for the fare when he returned in fifteen days. "But don't drive the car," he admonished Miller. When I repeated this story to Judy Lamy, whose father worked closely with Walter, she said that by the time Walter returned to the Pendleton airport, the embarrassed Pete Miller had learned who he was dealing with. "And Walter and Pete became *very* good friends," Judy added. Later, Walter arranged for Judy to get an interview with Pete, which eventually resulted in a job at United Airlines. Walter Brennan "believed in women," Judy said.

Of course, sometimes even in Joseph Walter was treated like a star. On the street a woman noticed him and said, "I should know you." She thought for a moment and then said, "Why you're Amos McCoy." She then asked him to sign autographs for her two grandchildren. Walter looked around for a place to sit and decided to sit down on the curb while he talked to the children, asked their names, and gave them his autograph. On another occasion, a man wanting an autograph approached Walter while he was eating dinner in Pendleton (about a hour's drive from Joseph). Walter said he was eating, but if the man cared to wait in the lobby, Walter would come out and sign an autograph. A young actor dining with Brennan remarked, "Why do you waste your time signing autographs?" Walter looked at him and said, "You ought to remember. They're paying your salary."

Television afforded Brennan the all-consuming focus that he reveled in—so much so that during a summer off from the series, he complained about the making of *Rio Bravo*. Camera setups seemed to take forever, and then actual shooting might not begin until the next day. He did not mind television's twelve-hour days, the long drives to the studio, and the fourteen pages of script he had to memorize for each episode. He brought a bag lunch with him and napped during breaks. Unlike motion picture production, in television there was very little standing around waiting for lighting, sound, and so on. In television, you made an immediate impact on millions watching at home at the same time every week. Altogether, making movies was a more labored, fitful, and less economical enterprise. And, of course, now Walter Brennan was the star. He was sixty-three when he started the series, and he believed that playing yet another old man would keep him young.

The show was shot on an enormous sound stage, the largest one in Hollywood, and the same one used for *Gone with the Wind*. A complete house for the McCoys was built on the set. In those days, the all-consuming grind of doing a television series meant that actors spent their downtime in little huts called "knockdown greens." They were like tents, said Kathleen Nolan. "Now you have a trailer outside, but then it was an efficient way of keeping the talent close at hand. They did four shows a week, and then took a week off, so that Brennan could rest. Working on a show started with two days sitting around the table, where the cast would discuss the script and sometimes ask for rewrites when the lines did not seem to suit their characters. "Everybody had a say, and the writers were there. Sometimes they [the writers] said, 'Just say it,'" Nolan remembered with a laugh. Then three days of shooting followed: "Everything was blocked, and the house was practical. When I made dinner, the stove worked." Brennan would sometimes take Nolan off to a corner, where they would mull over a scene. Because the show involved conflicts with Grandpa, Brennan would often discuss his character's attitudes. "He was a working actor—for what—fifty years?" Nolan pondered. Brennan's son Andy sometimes served as his father's stand-in. "I didn't think Walter treated him very well," Nolan remarked. She remembered Walter saying to his son, "Knock on my door before you come in," even though Andy was only entering one of the knockdown greens. Nolan did not think Brennan was aware of how cruel he could be to his son.

Andy's memories, however, were quite different. "I watched him," Andy said, describing his feelings about his father. Andy could see that many actors were excited but also intimidated by Walter Brennan, because he had become such a legend. Andy would observe his father take someone off to the side and say, "Now don't worry about anything. We can get through this. I'll help you out." Andy had no complaints.

Much better than its imitators, *The Real McCoys* constantly tests the unity of a West Virginia mountain family that has moved to a ranch in the San Fernando Valley. Grandpa is the ostensible head of the household, which includes his grandson Luke, Luke's new wife, Kate, and Luke's two siblings, Little Luke and Hassie. Although plenty could be

said about how the show conforms to 1950s television with its sentimen-
talizing of family life, other aspects of the family dynamic are equally
important. Grandpa is a tyrant. In the first episodes of the series he is
cruel to Kate, and it takes him awhile to adjust to her presence. And he
is always backsliding, telling everyone what to do. He could, in fact, be
downright annoying—even repulsive—if each episode did not ultimately
reveal Grandpa's realization that he has been unjust not only to his own
family, but often to neighbors and friends as well. He is incorrigible, and
yet he submits, eventually, to a more decent and tolerant view of his
own kin, and of humanity. If each episode ends happily, it does so with
the expectation that next time Grandpa will again begin in the wrong,
forced to struggle to find his way goodness. Amos McCoy gets his family
into jams, but you still root for him, realizing that he is due for a course
correction.

Episode titles reveal a good deal about how the series went about
appealing to a broad audience: "Kate's Dress," "It's A Woman's World,"
"Little Luke's Education," "Time to Retire," "Kate's Career," "Grampa
Learns about Teenagers," "The McCoys Visit Hollywood," "Kate Learns
to Drive," "Kate's Diet," "Hassie's European Trip," "Pepino's Fortune,"
"Grampa Pygmalion," "Luke the Dog Catcher." Eventually each cast
member became the subject of individual episodes. The dynamic between Kate and Grandpa is especially notable, since she not only presents
a mature woman's point of view, and as Luke's wife, she also provides
an outsider's view of the family. This was perhaps the most important
decision the writers made—making Kate a capable woman who stands
up to Grandpa's tendency to dictate all aspects of home and family life.
Walter Brennan understood Kate's crucial role in checking his tendency
to dominate and perhaps meant more than the cast realized when he
said of Nolan, "Follow her." Kate keeps the series real—that is, as real as
a situation comedy can be—by voicing her dissent, and also by finding
ways to accommodate herself to the family, even as it accommodates
itself to her.

Critic Paul Mavis praises the high quality of the writing and the acting that brought a fresh approach to what was essentially a sitcom in
dungarees:

An episode like A Question of Discipline, where Grampa takes over
raising Hassie and Little Luke, would be pitched for slapstick guf-
faws and phoney [sic], condescending bathos in a modern sitcom,
but watching this fifty year old story, you almost get a lump in

your throat from the subtle emotions that Brennan's Grampa goes through when he realizes he's the wrong kind of primary influence on the kids. And most welcome, too, is Brennan as the main protagonist; how often do we see anything on TV today that has to do with aging, with older people feeling useful, with older patriarchs and their shifting influence in a family (main elements in many episodes of this first season)?

Mavis is right to suggest that without Brennan the series would not have worked: "All bluster and whining cussedness, Brennan knows exactly when to turn soft-hearted in his eyes, and when to lower his voice a pitch, to show not meanness, but suppressed tenderness." But without a strong supporting cast and good writers, Brennan would not have had the opportunity to produce such a modulated performance.

It strikes me now that *The Real McCoys* appealed, among other audiences, to Americans with extended families who had made similar moves and lived with several generations in the same home or close by. My own immediate family, for example, moved in 1961 from Detroit to the suburbs, where my grandparents moved into my home to help my mother out after my father died. The series was about building a new life. Richard Crenna, who played Grandpa's grandson, told an interviewer in 1999 that he had only recently understood the program's widespread appeal:

> I was doing a show a couple of years ago and I was in a gymnasium and we were in a university situation and there were a couple of young, African-American athletes working out there. They were in their late 20s. . . . And they came over and said, "When we were growing up, we loved 'The Real McCoys.'" And I said, "Oh, really? What attracted you?" And they said, "Well, as a minority group, it was one of the few shows we could relate to. It was one of the few shows that had the same kind of problems we had in our family life, problems with money and making ends meet, and there was a strong family relationship we related to."

This was not an isolated example of Brennan's appeal to the black community. In *Brothers: Black and Poor* (1988), the story of twelve African American men in a housing project on Chicago's South Side, one of main characters, Half Man Carter, has a prized record collection that includes "Mama Sang a Song," by Walter Brennan. In the early 1960s, Brennan became a recording star, narrating brief stories like "Old Shep" and "Tribute to a Dog," and producing several popular albums, which have had an extended life on CDs and the web, where many of his songs can be downloaded. In *A World of Miracles* (1960), to the accompaniment of orchestra and choir, he recites the stories of Noah, the Ten Commandments, and the Resurrection, transforming his familiar way of speaking into a solemn, yet friendly New England accented prophetic voice.

As Grandpa McCoy, Brennan's energetic hobble personified his indomitable reaction to hardship. Fans always asked Crenna if Brennan actually limped. "No, that was acting," Crenna replied. "Off the set, Walter was like a Boston businessman. He was a very tall, erect, very proper kind of guy. But when he got into the character of Grandpa McCoy, no other actor could do that kind of character better." Before taking on the role, Brennan went through entire wardrobes, rejecting many outfits, shoes, and hats, until he found the right long underwear and overalls. "Then he WAS Grandpa McCoy," Crenna concluded. "You could say that it was his style of method acting."

Brennan grew to love the five-day-week schedule of television work; it suited an actor who was never happy during even brief lulls in his motion picture work. "By Sunday night I can hardly wait to get started on Monday morning," he confided to a journalist. Brennan would begin his workday at 7 am, driving (he liked big and powerful cars) from his home in Ventura County to the studio, where he worked a twelve-hour day. Nolan remembered him showing up like a workman, with his own black lunch box. Walter disliked the commissary sandwiches: "Too much mayonnaise," he said. Not every episode went smoothly, of course. A five-page scene could take close to three hours and as many as eleven takes to complete. Brennan would sometimes tire and stumble over lines. But the cast pressed on, fueled by one rule every show observed. "[W]hatever it is, Grampa is against it," Hy Averback explained. "He's against TV sets, against hot rodders, against Air Force jets flying over his head. He is a great 'againster.'" After his long day, Walter Brennan returned home, and now out of character, he enjoyed a very cold and dry martini.

Walter Brennan was now a star and could not go anywhere without exciting attention. "I've never seen anything like it. I've been around for years and I've never had so many fans—10-year-old kids on planes, old people in grocery stores and people in show business." On May 27, 1958, the *Charleston Daily Mail* reported that Brennan had been awarded an honorary doctor of arts degree by Morris Harvey College (now the University of Charleston). Walter was asked if West Virginians he had met were like those portrayed on *The Real McCoys*. "Not quite," Brennan said, laughing, "but I just love 'em—the dozen or so I've met since last night," the newspaper reported. "Obviously proud of receiving his first college degree this morning, the actor said he was excited, and proud, and 'I couldn't eat breakfast.'" Governor Cecil Underwood honored him as the "first Mountaineer," and he appeared with the governor at the Farmer's Day parade and picnic lunch and at another dinner hosted by Underwood. Brennan had just been named "Grandfather of the Year," the paper noted.

More public honors and celebrations followed, including a luncheon celebrating Brennan's thirty-fifth year in Hollywood on February 23, 1959, at the Roosevelt Hotel,. Comedian turned television producer Danny Thomas hosted the affair attended by Barbara Stanwyck, George Murphy, Fred MacMurray, and other stars, as well as both the mayor of Los Angeles and the state's governor. Brennan also invited the old timers, those who had stuck it out with him in his days as an extra. Brennan, near tears, "glowed." A week later, he also took his place among business tycoons at the annual installation banquet of the Panorama City Chamber of Commerce.

Walter Brennan was still wary of appearing as himself on television, although he made a guest appearance on *The Perry Como Show* in October 1959 in a segment concerning his hometown, Lynn, Massachusetts. And he enjoyed appearing as himself at public events. "Walter Brennan to Throw First Ball At Opening," the *Van Nuys (CA) News* (June 3, 1960) announced in its notice of the Western Boys Baseball Association of Northridge opening at Erickson Field. As honorary mayor of Panorama City, Brennan wielded a chrome plated shovel to break ground for the R. E. Driscoll Realty Co. and Insurance Agency, the *Van Nuys (CA) News* reported on June 12, 1960.

For its first three seasons, *The Real McCoys* was the number one television show in its time slot; even after that, it remained very high in the ratings. Kathleen Nolan explained just how deeply the series marked careers. No role that she or Crenna ever played afterwards could replace their identities as Kate and Luke. Awarded an Oscar for his appearance in *The Sand Pebbles* in 1967, all Richard Crenna could hear as he walked up the red carpet were people calling "Luke." When Nolan appeared on a radio program during which listeners were asked to call in and identify the nickname Luke called Kate in *The Real McCoys*, the switchboard immediately lit up because so many people knew it was "Sugar Babe." Imagine then the kind of impression Walter Brennan made on millions of viewers. The press asked for his views about a range of subjects that he would not have been expected to consider in his Hollywood, pre-television career. How could a man who was asked to lead civic parades and, in a sense, confer his blessing on communities not speak out? The line he had drawn between the man and his work had to be crossed. At the same time, such a man—so confident in the 1930s and 1940s that his characters reflected a national consensus, bolstered by a regime of censorship in Hollywood that ensured that crime did not pay, that God-lessness could not triumph— suddenly felt isolated in a culture in which the Hollywood production code was breaking down. Television, with its core audience sitting in their living rooms, offered him an opportunity to reinstitute the piety being eroded by popular films like *Rebel Without a Cause* and *Blackboard Jungle*.

And when he was not working, Walter Brennan stayed at home with his wife, playing tunes such as "Bedelia, I Want to Steal Ye" on the organ:

> *If you love me half as much as I love you,*
> *There is nothing in this world could ever cut our love in*
> *two.*

Part of one lyric is as practical as it is romantic: "I'll even bring your breakfast up to bed." In all likelihood, they had heard a version of the song sung by the popular vaudeville "piping Irish tenor" Edward M. Favor (1856–1936) first recorded in 1903. Walter made a point of saying how much he disliked songs like "Laura," perhaps because they expressed an obsessive passion, a darker strain in love that played no part in Walter Brennan's world.

When Walter Brennan was asked how close in character he was to Amos McCoy, he replied, "Sure, I'm a mean old so-and-so." More to the point, though, Brennan believed in Grandpa's "godliness, a reverence for his family." It was a good description of himself, although he did not discuss his faith or philosophy with his fellow actors. When I asked Kathleen Nolan if she knew that Brennan was a devout Catholic, she was startled. "We never, ever, talked about religion," she said. And yet, when interviewed Brennan always gave thanks to God: "I said to a very successful director once, 'God has been very kind to you.' He said: 'What do you mean! I did it all myself.' I said—well, you can't print what I said.'" Without God or patriotism a man was lost, in Brennan's book. "I don't care whether a man's a Catholic or Protestant or Jew or whatever if he's got the belief in God, I'm for him," he told a reporter. "And I don't care if a man's a Republican or Democrat or what he is, if he loves his country, I'm for him."

Nearing the end of *The Real McCoys*, in its fifth season, Nolan noticed that Brennan was slowing down and relying on cue cards. She left the show before the sixth season, which lasted only thirteen weeks. "The chemistry was no longer there," she explained. She remembered remaining on good terms with Brennan, although at least one report suggested that in the immediate aftermath of her departure hard feelings arose that took some time to repair. The series lasted one year longer than Brennan had projected. All along, he had figured that by the fifth year the show would reach its saturation point. And yet *The Real McCoys* started a trend that resulted in *The Andy Griffith Show*, *Petticoat Junction*, *Green Acres*, and *The Beverly Hillbillies*.

Brennan carefully nurtured the benevolent side of his grandfatherly persona. In a 1959 Warner Bros. press release, he sounded quite tolerant:

It's part of youth, and growing up to be so intense, so sure of things, so idealistic and impatient with compromise. Perhaps if some of those traits weren't kicked out of them by life, this might be a better world in many respects. Maybe what irritates us oldsters is that when we see and hear these wide-eyed, idealistic kids we see ourselves before the pressures of our civilization began to warp our sense of values.

On the *Date with Debbie* [Reynolds] television program in 1960, Charlie Ruggles, another veteran character actor used to playing grandfathers, asked Brennan in mock outrage, "How did you get to be the main grandfather?" Brennan did not answer the question, but instead told a joke about Martians who land in Hollywood: One Martian says, "First take me to Marilyn Monroe and then to your leader." He enjoyed that kind of comic misdirection. He did not care to explain the reasons for his success—although he enjoyed that success mightily. He loved parades and loved serving as grand marshal, usually decking himself out in cowboy clothing, as he did on December 2, 1961, in the Bethlehem Star Parade that marched near his Northridge home.

Walter's granddaughter Claudia recalled that the Brennan Northridge home spanned an entire city block. The land was later subdivided to accommodate two dozen homes. When Claudia visited the original Brennan house recently and spoke with the owner, he praised its solidity. "It would have been like my grandparents to use the best materials and work," Claudia said. The extensive property had a main house, two guesthouses, and a pool with a cabana. Farther out toward the back of the property, Ruth kept her animals. Claudia remembered walking through a long, covered grape arbor to see the pheasants, chickens, and turkeys. On the main lawn, there was a swing Claudia enjoyed as a child. Walking into the house from the front, one entered into the kitchen, which had a brick fireplace and a big, open picture window looking out on the lawn. After passing through the long, rectangular kitchen, one reached the formal dining room. To the right was a tiled entranceway to the living room. To the right were a bathroom, master bedroom, and a corner den where Walter kept an office.

Claudia remembered her grandmother telling her about the hard times before Claudia's grandfather was a success. "We had our depression before the Depression," Ruth liked to say. When they had no money for dinner, Ruth put a chicken's head between two nails sticking out of stump, then and chopped the head off. But after so many years of raising chickens, Ruth said, "Now I just swing them around and wring their necks." This was the kind of story all Brennans comprehended. You took care of yourself and got your own meals, and it was understood that you had to be resourceful and practical.

CHAPTER 9

The Politics of Becoming Walter Brennan

1960–73

WITH HIS NEW PUBLIC PLATFORM AS TELEVISION STAR AND AMERICA'S grandfather, Brennan began to bloviate. "Walter Brennan Flays U. S. Forced Retirement Practice," ran the headline in the January 19, 1960, edition of the *Ukiah (CA) Daily Journal*. "Nothing ages a man faster than inactivity," the actor declared. He remained jaunty, favoring bow ties made of fabric featuring fluttering butterflies. With a new television season of *The Real McCoys* ahead of him, Brennan said he felt the "old tension . . . just as it was when I was a kid."

At the same time, the Kennedy-Nixon presidential contest provoked Brennan to become active in California politics on both the state and local level. On September 15, 1960, the *Van Nuys Valley News* reported that the actor had agreed to serve as honorary chairman of Republican William Dentzel's campaign for a state assembly seat. Brennan noted, "I have never taken an active role in political affairs, but I feel this is a critical year for our state and nation whose vital issues should require all of us to stand up and be counted." Dentzel, Brennan believed, was an independent politician who declined to be "all things to all people." Brennan singled out for approval Dentzel's positions on narcotics, taxation, the water supply, and "efficiency in government." Dentzel, who urged voters to support the Republican ticket, spoke Walter Brennan's language: "The gift of self-determination is the greatest gift any of us have ever been given. This gift is under great jeopardy from abroad and from within. If we sleep, there are others, less patriotic, who will work toward other subversive ends, and some day we may wake to find our freedom has fled." "GOP Dinner at Brennan Home Slated," a piece that appeared in the *Van Nuys News* on September 18, 1960, explained that this fundraiser for Congressman Edgar Hiestand and William Dentzel, candidate for the 41st District Assembly, featured a spaghetti dinner in the Brennan garden, followed by a film of Richard Nixon's visit to Russia. The Brennans hosted similar events later that September and in October. Hiestand won his race, but Dentzel lost.

Kathleen Nolan recalled that when Brennan heard she and Richard Crenna had voted for John Kennedy in the 1960 presidential election, Brennan cried out, "How can I do this? How can I work with these Commies?" He railed against Spencer Tracy, even saying that "he could not act," Nolan said. And this was a sore point for Nolan, since Brennan knew how close she was to Tracy. She had received her first fan letter from Tracy. He also became her son's godfather. Brennan erupted after seeing a copy of the *New York Times* on the set of *The Real McCoys*. Nolan thought Brennan hoped he could make her a convert to his politics, but Nolan would change the subject, and she thought he realized she was a lost cause. Dick Crenna, more than anyone else, knew how to divert Brennan from launching into a tirade, Nolan said. Yet "as an actor," she pointed out, "all that went away and he was Grandpa."

Walter Brennan's fierce opposition to godless communism stimulated his desire to promote public events that celebrated religious faith. "Walter Brennan Named Marshal of [Bethlehem] Star Parade," announced the *Van Nuys Valley News* on November 24, 1961. The televised event included fifty floats depicting the "life and ministry of Christ" in a "spectacle" designed to "put Christ back into Christmas." Two weeks later, in the Shrine Auditorium in Long Beach, he introduced "Project Alert," a series of five anti-communist programs, the first one featuring Francis E. Walter, chairman of the House Committee on Un-American Activities.

In an oral history, cinematographer Lothrop Worth (1903–2000) recounted what it was like to encounter the political Walter Brennan in 1962, when Worth was working on *The Real McCoys*:

Walter Brennan branded me a communist because I wouldn't vote for Nixon for governor! . . . I said, "Well, if I'd done what Nixon did, I'd be in the penitentiary, accepting two hundred and fifty thousand from Howard Hughes, gave it to his brother to put up drive-ins . . ." and *oh* he was furious! I was a communist from the word go, from then on. . . . my relationship with everybody was fine, except Walter . . . he *forced* himself on you. The little restaurant on the lot wasn't very good, and we all brown-bagged it. We were there, and Walter, so *he* began brown-bagging too. We'd pick a place to eat, and here he'd come with *his*. He'd sit down and eat and he'd . . . start this thing, everybody was a communist.

I said to him one day, I said, "Walter, have you ever worked for Billy Wilder?"

He said, "No."

I said, "You should, you'd like him."

"Oh," he says, "he's a communist."

I said, "What do you *mean*? He isn't a *communist*! I know him very well."

He said, "Oh yes, he is." He brought in the list, and Billy was on a certain Democratic committee, and everybody on that committee, according to Walter, was a communist! . . . Walter asked me, and he asked Lee [Davis], my operator . . . "Who are *you* voting for?"

Lee says, "Walter, it's a private ballot. It's nobody's business but *mine*. Nobody even has the right to *ask* me." And that shut him up. But me, *I* had to tell him! (*Laughs.*)

After these confrontations, Worth said he had trouble getting work for about a year, and he suspected his difficulty resulted from Brennan putting the word out about him. Enforcers of the conservative line did operate in Hollywood—Ward Bond was one of them—but I have found no evidence that Walter Brennan was a blacklister.

Kathleen Nolan, who worked with Brennan for more than five years, doing thirty-nine shows a season, and served as president of the Screen Actors Guild, doubted that he would have had the inclination or the power to blacklist anyone. "It does not seem plausible to me," she said. Nolan noted that Brennan believed actors had to organize and was a "very solid union guy." Extras were treated little better than the horses when he started out. Brennan used to say, "They barely gave us blankets." So, Nolan concluded, "[H]e went with the [Screen Actors] Guild, which started in 1933. Anything that I brought to him, and said 'You really need to do this,' when actors' contract pay was reduced, for example, he said, 'Give me the paper,' which he would sign." He was an actor first, Nolan believed. And Brennan the actor could apparently be forgiven most anything. Nolan said that Tony Martinez, who played a Mexican farm hand in *The Real McCoys*, "just laughed," when Brennan called him "the wetback."

Andy Brennan noted that his father supported "prayer in the schools" and was called a "flag-waver" by columnist Drew Pearson. Andy quoted his father's rejoinder: "I *am* a flag waver. When the flag goes by, I stand up and take off my hat. And I kneel down in prayer every morning and night." Two Supreme Court decisions, in 1962 and 1963, that reaffirmed the constitutional principle of separation of church and state, rankled certain conservatives and traditionalists, who decried a secular society that had steadily eroded religious faith. School districts over the last fifty years have attempted to devise various ways of evading and challenging the High Court's prohibition of state sponsored prayer and Bible readings. In short, Walter Brennan was hardly alone in expressing not only his uneasiness, but also his anger over the diminution of religion's role in public life. When he said he thanked God for his life, as he did in countless interviews, he meant it. And as a person of faith, he did not—like some persons of faith—believe that the polity could survive, even thrive on strictly secular principles. The Roman Catholicism that Walter Brennan had imbibed during his New England childhood remained his bedrock, the foundation of his life and work and the calling of his country. "Why, I haven't changed to the new fasting laws before Communion. I'm used to the old way. I fast from midnight," he told an interviewer. To abandon the practice of his faith would mean to be utterly lost, and he could not imagine a world configured along strictly secular principles. And the world seemed headed in another dangerous direction. As he said, "[Y]ou hear people say the H-bomb and guided missile are so horrible and maybe their very horror will avert war. But I don't believe it. It's just wishful thinking. One of these days we'll probably all be blown to bits."

An avid collector of Old West memorabilia, Walter Brennan remained ensconced in a vision of the American frontier and the myth of bootstrap individualism. As early as 1962, he was deploring the image of America that Hollywood sent abroad with pictures such as *West Side Story*. "Why don't we make more pictures like *How the West Was Won, The Alamo, The Best Years of Our Lives*, and *The Westerner*?" he asked journalist Jean Bosquet of the *Los Angeles Herald-Examiner*. Brennan did not seem to realize that in his portrayal of Judge Roy Bean, a character whose mentality borders on a kind of homegrown fascism, he had conveyed the impression of a lawless West.

In *How the West Was Won* (February 20, 1963), Brennan, in a Benjamin Franklin hairstyle, is a gleeful villain, Colonel Jeb Hawkins, a river pirate who deprives mountain man Linus Rawlings (Jimmy Stewart) of his beaver pelts. Masquerading as a merchant with an American flag serving as a backdrop in his general store, Brennan's Hawkins a character right out of Herman Melville's *The Confidence Man*.

When Brennan began his first scene for *How the West Was Won*, he seemed to have his Amos McCoy fans in mind. "He would limp," recalled Karl Malden, who did a few scenes with Brennan. Director Henry Hathaway said, "Hey, you're doing that in your TV show, don't do it for *me*!" Malden remembered Brennan replying, "Okay, Henry, I won't do it for *you*." But it didn't matter, Malden laughed. "He was the heavy! He was stealing from people."

Hawkins gets his comeuppance when Rawlings stages a successful counterattack. In an especially satisfying scene, Rawlings smashes the smarmy miscreant across the face with a chair. But no matter how nefarious the characters become, this pious and patriotic picture, a Cinerama epic, treats evil as merely an obstacle to be overcome on the way to the promised land.

The first section of the film, however, conveys a sense that something important was lost when the bond between the mountain man and the Native Americans was broken, when trapping—an industry that left Native American land intact—was replaced with the white man's rush to settle the West. Folksy Stewart and Brennan are alike in their impact on the indigenous population. But Stewart finds his mate among the westward bound travelers, and it looks as though he will settle down amidst the civilization that Huck Finn so desperately wanted to escape. For Brennan, the western acknowledged corruption, but also contained or overcame it. But an evil Brennan in any guise was too much for some. "There were complaints from the public. People didn't want to *see* me as a bad man," Brennan said. As Kathleen Nolan commented, "Talking about Mr. Brennan is like talking about the Statue of Liberty. I mean, what can you say about an *institution*."

The world outside a western like *How the West Was Won* seemed far more insidious and subversive, as a letter to Brennan from Mrs. Helen Willy demonstrates. She had met him sometime earlier, and they had discussed the state of the country. She wrote to him as one who understood that "people are afraid to say they are patriotic." It was a dangerous business, declaring your love of country. One woman working undercover to expose communists had been beaten up and tortured. If Brennan decided to join forces with those fighting communism, he should realize the "pressure that comes with this type of thing, and that this could either ruin your career completely or make you another Paul Revere." Presumably she meant that Brennan could sound the alarm that the communists were coming. Mrs. Willy's phone was tapped, she wrote, even though she was "just a peon in this movement." If she was being watched, she implied, surveillance of her proved just how deeply communists were penetrating American society. She was telling him this "not because I think you aren't aware of them [the communists], but to let you know that we are also aware of them, and the honest facts that most people in the country find hard to believe but that are nonetheless true." She was part of a besieged group, she added, the "smear campaign against Anti-Communists has been very effective." She had a script in mind that might entertain as well as indoctrinate a public "weary of deliberate education on Communism."

Whatever Walter Brennan made of this letter (his archive includes no response from him), on August 28, 1962, the *Los Angeles Herald Examiner* reported Brennan's statement in support of Proposition 24: "Why this reluctance on the part of some of our elected representatives to take legal action against subversive elements in our state? Especially since no major anti-Communist law has been enacted in California during the past decade." With Proposition 24, Republican assemblyman Louis Francis was proposing a constitutional amendment that would have given judges, grand juries, and other public officials the right to designate certain organizations subversive. The *Daily Review* (September 10, 1962) in Hayward, California, welcomed Brennan's support as an augury of the measure's success: "Some of the strong backers of the anti-red initiative see stronger and stronger reason for passage every day with the buildup of the Communist base in Cuba, a short boat ride from our shores. The probability of attempts to infiltrate our nation with fifth-column bile increase daily, as Castro hands Cuba lock, stock and barrel to the Kremlin agents. Our nation must be armed with the legal weapons and must resolve to prevent any trespassing."

Walter Brennan did more than write letters to newspapers. He became state chairman of Californians for Proposition 24. On August 29, he was quoted in the *Daily Review*: "Fifty thousand citizens took bold action last spring to invoke the right of the initiative petition. They obtained approximately a million signatures of voters to place the strongest subversive measure on the November ballot." He also appeared on KBAK-TV, Channel 29, in a broadcast, "Combat Communism," part of the campaign for Proposition 24. An advertisement in the *Bakersfield (CA) Californian* (October 27, 1962) listed as speakers Brennan, Louis Francis (author of Proposition 24), Harry Von Zell (TV and radio personality), and Dr. John Lechner (holder a diploma mill PhD). The ad claims Proposition 24 "throws a bombshell into the Communist ranks. Learn why the Communists are frantic to defeat this measure." Lechner had been a vehement anti-communist since the 1930s. Von Zell's radio announcer voice would have been familiar to viewers then, and some would have recognized him from various appearances on television as a character actor. The proposition, which did not give accused communists the right of due process, failed to pass in the November election. The Brennans, while on the extreme right of the anti-communist movement, were still Republicans in good standing. Indeed, Ruth Brennan often hosted various Republican social events at the Brennan home. And she spoke publicly about the communist menace—at one point delivering a stirring speech at the Joseph Civic Center.

Walter Brennan's increasingly outspoken politics did no harm to his image as Grandpa. Indeed, his recording career added a sort of griot quality to his public persona. Typical is a reviewer's praise for Brennan's poignant rendition of "Old Rivers" in a newspaper that had also reported on the actor's political activities. An old man, reacting to a letter from home saying Old Rivers has died, tenderly retells a memory. "He used to plow them rows, straight and deep," Brennan intones in "Old Rivers." "And I'd come behind, bustin' up clods, with my own bare feet," Brennan's voice recalls in the refrain. "Old Rivers was a friend of mine." The story of this simple farmer, living in a one-room shack, delivered in the recognizable Grandpa McCoy voice—stripped of its querulousness—grounds the listener in banjoed country rhythms and the cadence of a consummate storyteller. The song soars as a chorus accompanies Brennan, whose voice rises slightly to describe Old Rivers standing by his plow saying:, "One of these days I'm going to climb that mountain. Walk up there among them clouds where the cotton's high and the corns agrowin' and there ain't no fields to plow." His ballad becomes as much about his own thoughts on passing away as he evokes—in a voice that trembles only on the last two words—the "sun beatin' down across the fields" where he sees "that mule, Old Rivers, and me." As one commentator on the ballad puts it, "The sun is eternal, the earth is eternal, but flesh and blood vanishes like an old man's voice on the wind. We have it but we have it not, for it passes. The narrator becomes Old Rivers, and so do you." The song was much parodied at the time. A disk jockey changed the lyrics to, "When the sun would get high, Old Rivers would, too." A UPI story carried by the *Humboldt (CA) Standard* (May 2, 1962) reported that Mitchell College students in New London, Connecticut, were going for a "record": They had played "Old Rivers" continuously 350 times and were still "going strong."

Four 45 singles recorded by Walter Brennan made the Billboard Top 100 in the early 1960s. He was sixty-six when he charted first with "Dutchman's Gold" (with orchestrator Billy Vaughn for Dot Records.) It debuted April 25, 1960, hit number 30 on the chart, and stayed on the chart for twelve weeks. Almost two years later, on April 7, 1962, Brennan's smash single, "Old Rivers" (for Liberty, like all his subsequent singles) debuted. It climbed all the way to number 5 and stayed eleven weeks. Brennan recorded long-playing albums as well, some featuring Christmas songs and other readings of short stories, including Mark Twain's "The Celebrated Jumping Frog of Calaveras County."

Many of Brennan's recordings that do not have an avowedly religious cast nevertheless have a sacerdotal quality, as though he has taken on a kind of priestly role. In "A Lesson I've Learned from Life" (*Parade*, March 3, 1963) he fervently wrote:

> The greatest lesson I've learned from almost 70 years of life is the power of prayer.
>
> During World War I, I saw a lot of combat. I felt fear, and because of that fear, I found myself cursing with one breath and praying with the next. Somewhere up there in the front lines, I suddenly realized that I was being a fool and a hypocrite. I decided to cast my lot with prayer. When the going got really tough and the bombardments heavier and heavier, I turned more and more to prayer.
>
> When it was all over, I was genuinely grateful and gave thanks. That was the lesson I learned—the power of prayer. Not the prayer that asks for something, but the prayer that gives thanks for blessings received.

At no earlier time in his career could Brennan have published such an article. Who would have listened? But the urge to gently sermonize—like Pastor Pyle in *Sergeant York*—had become irresistible.

And Walter Brennan was not alone. Stars such as John Wayne, Robert Taylor, Robert Stack, Glenn Ford, Lew Ayres, Rhonda Fleming, Lloyd Nolan, and Pat Boone were part of Project Prayer, which sponsored meetings and rallies that supported Congressman Frank Becker's constitutional amendment permitting voluntary prayers and Bible reading in schools. The group had also procured a statement from Gloria Swanson: "Under God we became the freest, strongest, wealthiest nation on earth. Should we change that?" Brennan was quoted as saying, "I'm too old not to be a religious fella . . . it appears we are losing something that a lot of people made a lot of sacrifices for." He was bearing witness not simply to what he believed, but to what he was sure the world could not do without. "I think prayer is the greatest force of mankind," he wrote in his *Parade* article. He got down on his knees every night like a child, he wrote, and gave thanks for his wonderful life. Not all lives, he realized, were wonderful when judged by certain worldly standards, but each life has its own kind of worth to be grateful for, he was certain. Prayer ought to unite everyone, he declared: "I'm a Catholic, but I know of times when I have been prayed for by ministers and rabbis alike. It is the great, irrevocable universal privilege that each of us has, no matter where we live—no matter who or what we are."

Gary Cooper had died in the spring of 1961, and Brennan narrated a one-hour NBC special, "The Tall American" (broadcast March 26, 1963) about his friend's life. Cooper was still very much on Walter Brennan's mind as he thought about his own end. "Despite all the suffering and knowledge of what was happening to him, Coop was able to say that it was the will of God," Brennan said. "He was the complete man who could still find plenty of reasons for saying thanks." Brennan was not exaggerating. Two months before Cooper died, he narrated a documentary about the American West. In extreme pain, he could work only one hour at a time. At a dinner held in his honor at the Friar's Club during his work on the documentary, Cooper spoke in words that echoed those of Lou Gehrig, the baseball star Cooper had played in *Pride of the Yankees*: "If someone asked me tonight was I the happiest guy alive, I'd say yup." This "wonderful spiritual outlook"—as Brennan called it—made the dying actor's last hours more bearable and would, in Brennan's case, do so as well. He did not speak of his own death, but of aging—and with his usual wry humor. It might take him longer to mount a horse, he admitted, but "I can get off a darn sight quicker."

Brennan hosted a television special, "The Red, White and Blue" (June 9, 1964) exploring the "apparent decline in patriotism," as one review put it. The program also featured upbeat scenes of people from nineteen different countries becoming American citizens, interviews with American heroes like John Glenn, and excerpts from a fourth grader's patriotic written remarks: "My country, everyone's country, is an orchard of freedoms, ready to be picked." By September 29, 1964, Brennan, acting as the master of ceremonies for the San Fernando Valley Business and Professional Association, was photographed with Senator Strom Thurmond as part of a fund-raising drive for Republican congressional candidates. Ronald Reagan, co-chairman of the Citizens for Goldwater-Miller, listed Brennan among "active boosters," which also included Roy Rogers, Dale Evans, Raymond Massey, Randolph Scott, Cesar Romero, Jimmy Stewart, June Allyson, John Payne, Irene Dunne, and Walt Disney.

Then Brennan turned to a new, absorbing television project, *The Tycoon*, for the 1964–65 television season. He was willing to commit himself to a five-year contract if the show proved successful. He was guaranteed $6,000 an episode for a minimum of twenty-six and a maximum of thirty-two episodes, and the pay would escalate to a high of $7,500 in the fifth year of the series. He was to be consulted about the cast and other important aspects of the production, but the producers had the last word.

The show began with business tycoon Walter Andrews dictating memos, such as one about coffee breaks. He complains that they aren't being taken at the stipulated times, and that the coffee should be two degrees cooler so employees can gulp it down quickly. Observing these rules will save the company $2,000 a week. This sort of fussy micromanaging is supposed to be funny to everyone except the board of directors. In one episode, the board meets to discuss how to get rid of Andrews. They don't know his age, and his doctor says he is healthy. When he shows up at the board meeting he is asked, "When are you going to take it easy?" He replies, "The day after I die." The corporation has just acquired a parcel of land as part of its plan to build a new plant, but the current occupant of the land, an immigrant, won't leave his house. Andrews—constantly in motion, eating only sandwiches— flies, then drives out to see the immigrant who has lost his wife and has no family. He can't pay his taxes, and Andrews's corporation has bought the property by paying them. The immigrant levels a shotgun at Andrews, but the tycoon just sits and listens to the immigrant. "What if you had gotten killed?" the immigrant asks. "Then everyone would have moved one up," Andrews answers. Andrews decides to give the land back to Nick so that he can grow his grapes. To his business associates Andrews remarks, "Think I'm cracking up giving back the land? I sure don't want to sit on a park bench like Bernard Baruch. Look at Dr. Schweitzer running around the jungle. How do you pay a man for 50 years? What is a fair price for his little piece of America? Gentlemen, I say, Nick wins." Winning means that Nick's greenhouse will be incorporated into the factory site, where he can grow his grapes and retire.

In another episode, Walter Andrews goes undercover, so to speak, to resolve a union-management bargaining impasse. He works incognito in the factory and does so well he is promoted to shop steward. Short synopses of other episodes display the tycoon's truculent but also generous and vulnerable sides: "Walter makes like Horatio Alger in a wager with Wilson [his corporate nemesis] that it's still possible to start from scratch"; "Walter lends a helping hand to get the son of an old friend started on a business career"; "Walter starts his tinkering in his own neighborhood, and soon is up to his ears in a small-repairs business"; "Walter makes some startling discoveries when, disguised as a handyman, he investigates a senior city community"; "Walter investigates a customer complaint and finds it came from an 11-year-old boy"; "Walter gets pangs of conscience when a lie detector test reminds him he may have ruined a man's life 50 years before."

ABC promoted the show this way: "A temperamental tyrant at times . . . one of the last of the rugged individualists, whose talent for engineering profitable business deals and making fortunes is exceeded only by a heart that never loses site of human values (though the intrinsic kindliness in his nature is artfully masked by a gruff exterior." In other words, the western mentality survives in the figure of the iconoclastic businessman who does battle against the "superautomated, overly efficient corporate mind," as Marian Dern wrote in *TV Guide* (April 10, 1965). But of course Andrews can do no such thing, since he is not simply dictatorial, but is also a time efficiency expert on a par with Frederick Winslow Taylor. What worked on *The Real McCoys*, a grandpa who really was a relic of the past who nevertheless had relevant things to say in the present, simply cannot be transferred onto a corporate hero. The contradictions in Andrews's character are just too glaring. This time, *Variety*'s review of the pilot episode proved prophetic: "The optimistic spirit of enterprise which has characterized America's economic growth . . . appears ridiculously exaggerated." This was "hokum" that asked for more tolerance than the audience could bear. The series lasted only one season (thirty-two episodes), although it received respectable ratings. Brennan's son Mike believes a network executive acted hastily in canceling the show.

Brennan was well aware of the irony inherent in catering to an audience who still thought of him as a hillbilly: "Some of my friends say that the Tycoon is remarkably like myself, much more so than McCoy." Almost plaintively he declared, "I do wear suits, shirts, ties, and even shoes. . . . The fact is that I actually do have business interests, and am in personal life much closer to being an executive than a farmer." Richard Crenna said as much about his *Real McCoys* co-star. In fact, Brennan owned a piece of *The Tycoon* not to mention his ranch and other properties in California and Oregon. And like Walter Andrews (his first and middle names, which as an extra he sometimes used together), he enjoyed learning other peoples' business—as when he ran the store in Joseph when its owner was late showing up. When in Joseph, he always liked to stay in room 16 in his motel, which had an adjoining room he used as an office.

Also like his character Walter Andrews, Walter Brennan engaged in cost-benefit analysis. During the making of a *Tycoon* episode, his son Andy noticed his father grimacing with pain. "What's the matter?" Andy asked. "Oh, these damn dentures are bothering me again," Walter growled. "Dad," Andy said, "why don't you go to some over-priced guy in Beverly Hills who'll give you a decent set of teeth so you won't suffer?" But his father had inquired and was told the price was $450. "So what?" Andy replied. But Walter wondered, "Do you think it's worth it for just a couple more years?"

Undoubtedly, the tycoon role appealed to Brennan as a way to break out of the typecasting that beset him after the success of *The Real McCoys*. He rarely complained about his "dirty shirt" roles, but he confessed that he wanted to play Lincoln. "I'm a great student of Lincoln's life," Brennan noted. He wanted to portray both the "admirable and not so admirable" aspects of the man. Clarence Darrow was another role he coveted. Yet there were roles he would have rejected: Hamlet, for example. "He's just too mixed up for me," Brennan explained. It was a revealing comment. Although Brennan had a wide range as an actor, virtually every role he played—even "weak" characters like Eddie in *To Have and Have Not*—were written so that the character had a strong sense of identity and a powerful set of convictions.

As usual, Brennan's television and film roles avoided politics, although he continued to be outspoken off-screen. Responding to the Watts race riots (August 11–17, 1965)—in which thirty-four people died, over a thousand were injured, and something like $40 million in property damage was reported to have occurred—Brennan said, "I'm a little disappointed in youth today. I think they could have stopped that thing in Watts [the riots] with a machine gun. I'd have *made* them observe the laws." Law breaking, in his view, constituted a deliberate and unpatriotic act. He considered congressman Adam Clayton Powell's comments supporting black power treasonous, and he thought no better of Martin Luther King Jr. "I'm sure all this trouble with . . . the Negroes is caused by just a few of them," he told Carolyn See of *TV Guide*.

Brennan's reaction to the disruptive events of the 1960s reached a crescendo in a live recording he did for Key Records of a script written by the company's founder, Vic Knight, a song composer and writer for television. The album, "He's Your Uncle! Not Your Dad," with a picture of Uncle Sam on the cover, was delivered as a stand-up routine ridiculing Lyndon Johnson's Great Society programs, especially the War on Poverty. Sounding very much like a Calvin Coolidge New Englander, Brennan tore into liberals and big government with relish—and with a well paced delivery that made him the equal of Ronald Reagan at his best. Brennan begins with a story about a woman who listens to a man say that several generations of his family have been conservatives, and he is one, too. "I suppose if they had been baboons, you would be a baboon," she says to the man. "No ma'am," he replies, "I'd be a liberal." Brennan dissects the concept:

> Liberal. What a warm and friendly word it used to be. It meant helping the other fella when he was in trouble. We didn't need welfare experts or social do-gooders or psychiatrists. It was a kind of me to you or you to me sort of thing. But somewhere along the line a smart politician saw real possibilities in it. He said, "If I can sell the tax payer on letting me handle this sort of charitable contribution, I can perpetuate my own power. It means I can be the one to control the handouts. I'm the fellow who gives away the goodies."

Although Brennan's targets are mainly political, he also speaks as a traditionalist who does not like the changes in his own church. Another of his jokes concerns a man confused by the Catholic Church's modernization program, including the alteration of nuns' habits. On an elevator the man turns to a group of women and asks them what order they belong to, and they tell him they are airline stewardesses. The eroding distinction between the religious and the secular troubles this Will Rogers of the right, who excites the audience to loud applause when he declares, "This great nation was not made by men who held out their hands but by men who stuck out their necks." Even zip codes, area codes, and interstate highway signs seem to Brennan to obliterate the individual identity of states, amalgamating the country into administrative districts under the control of the federal government.

Brennan's special bête noir is Sergeant Shriver, whose anti-poverty programs are bankrupting the country and fostering a culture of dependency. "If this fella had been running things at the Boston Tea Party, I guarantee you we'd still be a British colony," Brennan declares. Complaining about high taxes that deprive Americans of too much of their income, while funding programs that support freeloaders, he sums up the story of the welfare state: "The government sponges off half the people so that the other half of the people can sponge off the government." Brennan tells his audience that he was asked if he is going to have the program recorded in stereo. Doing so would mean having speakers on the right and the left, he explains, "and I refuse to listen to anything on the left." The audience is jubilant, in sync with his denunciation of the rising national debt, increased sums for foreign aid, and the decreasing value of the dollar.

This comprehensive condemnation of the federal government is delivered in a wry, cracker barrel philosopher's monologue that undercuts stridency with wry humor, sadness, and regret over what has come to pass. Brennan's authority, in the end, comes down to a personal story about "my great-great-great-uncle Michael Brennan . . . a real two-fisted hard drinking New Englander. When Uncle Mike came back from fighting the British at the Boston Massacre, every man in that brave little group had been shot—all except Uncle Mike. He was stoned." The audience responds with surprised laughter, as Brennan continues the story:

> But Uncle Mike took a vow. He said if we could succeed in declaring our independence and really establishing a free nation, he promised never to take another drink of hard liquor. Well time wore on, and when the Boston Tea Party came in 1773 and our boys dressed up as Indians to dump those boxes of tea into the harbor, it was my Uncle Mike who was chosen for the very important job of standing by to take an actual count of the bundles of tea—one by one—as they were pushed over and dumped into the sea. Yes sir, that's how Michael Brennan became America's first tea totaler.

The joke is a set up for a peroration about how this country is losing its liberty in a world that is already beset with "six hundred million people in slave labor camps. Heartless, godless, communism is consuming the world. And we respond by financing them and even protecting their own agents in our government. The more we pretend we have a bottomless treasury, the more we really prove that what we've really got is topless government." Walter Brennan was always careful with money and believed that its value had to be carefully managed. And he believed, as many do today, that his country was spending itself into oblivion.

Regardless of politics, the Brennan persona now occupied an immaculate, sentimental place on American television that he was eager to maintain, no matter how weak the script. Another series pilot, *Horatio Alger Jones*, filmed some time in 1965, never aired. Once again, Brennan plays a grandfather, but this time one who becomes more directly involved with the younger generation. The pilot begins with Brennan in a movie theater watching a James Bond movie. He says to his granddaughter, who admires the hero, "I used to fight that way. They just didn't photograph it." He organizes breakfast, timing what each grandchild does, down to the second. He has been retired for a week and is devoting himself to his grandchildren, who have set up a "garage à gogo" complete with a woody station wagon, a surfboard, and a Triumph convertible. Brennan watches the kids dancing, and his granddaughter tells him she is teaching them the new dance moves. He says, "I didn't know they had to be taught to do that. I thought it was some kind of nervousness." He sets the surfboards on fire accidentally. Then he steps on a guitar when he runs to get the hose. After several other mishaps he vows to leave, because he realizes he cannot be a guide to "you kids." They beg him to stay, and he says he will so that they can be a credit to him. They are nice kids, he says. A more contrived use of Brennan's talent is hard to imagine. But less than a year later, on April 24, 1966, he was among twelve prominent Americans to win the annual Horatio Alger Award.

By November 1965, Brennan was hard at work on a Disney movie, *The Gnome-Mobile* (July 19, 1967), playing, in Roger Ebert's words, "the world's most grandfatherly grandfather." Actually, Brennan appears in two parts—in fact, he plays two grandfathers: D. J. Mulroney, a timber tycoon, and Knobby, a gnome. It is a grand film with set pieces like one showing a very Irish Brennan driving a 1930 Rolls Royce and singing along with his two grandchildren, "Jaunting along in me jaunty car." Stopping to eat a picnic lunch in one of the redwood forests he owns, Brennan's granddaughter encounters a gnome who is the last of his kind (he thinks) lamenting that he will never find a mate. Indeed Knobby, his grandfather, is slowly pining away, because they have reached the end of their line. The plot progresses into pure foolishness as the granddaughter enlists the timber tycoon in a successful search for other gnomes in another forest, even as the gnome's grandfather upbraids the tycoon for his despoliation of the woodlands, which has driven the gnomes out of their natural habitat. It is fun to watch Walter Brennan scold Walter Brennan. As with *The Tycoon*, the film purports to reconcile the rapacious capitalist with the humanitarian, making of Walter Brennan yet another walking contradiction—albeit a charming and sincere one. The young gnome says he spots a shifty look in Brennan's eyes; the older gnome sees something "honorable" in those same eyes. Both are right. After all, Walter Brennan, a cattleman, did revere the wilderness and freely admitted that indigenous peoples had been deprived of their land and their dignity.

When Vernon Scott interviewed him on the set of *The Gnome-Mobile*, Brennan said, "A two or three week vacation is all right, but that's all. Retirement? Never! That's just sitting around waiting for the undertaker. . . . I'm in every scene. But I love it." He was still working twelve-hour days, beginning at 7:00 am when he was chauffeured to the studio, and returning home at 7:00 pm. He started the day with a steak and organic vegetables grown in his own garden. His wife called organic gardening "God's way of growing things."

In *Who's Minding the Mint?* (September 26, 1967), Brennan plays Pop Gillis, a printer chafing over his forced retirement at sixty-five and eager to join a gang with a plan to break into the mint and print off several million dollars. His contribution to the heist is almost sabotaged, however, when he refuses to abandon the pregnant dog he has brought along. He refuses to budge when she goes into labor, and he appropriates a box reserved for the newly printed currency in order to assist in the whelping. Although the film is a trifle, Brennan's character remains a fascinating mix of juvenescence and senescence. Somehow he belongs with younger people, even though he seems close to played out.

Walter Brennan, the on-screen grandfather, was also a grandfather on his ranch. Tammy, Mike's daughter, remembered this period during a tour of Lightning Creek we took with Mike in July 2014. "When the lights were off, the lights were off," Tammy recalled, "because of the gas generator. You had to find the bathroom in the dark." "Grampy loved it," Tammy said, "surrounded by quiet." Still standing is the cathedral sized, handmade barn Ray Pogue set up just before selling the ranch to Walter, "212 feet long, about 65 feet wide," Mike said. "I don't know if Grampy had any funny things happen to him out here," Tammy mused, perhaps wanting to help out a biographer. "No, none." Mike said. "He just came out here, sat, and left," Tammy suggested. "He'd come up and go deer hunting with us," Mike added. "I don't recall him ever shooting anything. I'd shoot something. I took the liver out of a deer. I didn't have anywhere to put it, so I just tucked it in my shirt, the whole bloody thing. He'd get a kick out of it."

Walter told stories to entertain his grandchildren. One of these stories involved the Civil War, retold with extraordinary detail. Walter could wind himself up for a good half hour, describing Lee and his grey beard, and Lincoln with a wart on his face. Mike used to wonder how his father could have absorbed so much lore—and then just as Walter was reaching some kind of denouement when he had everyone's interest, he'd say, "Oh the heck with it. Why don't you just get a book and read about it." The grandchildren remained far removed from Hollywood, and he certainly did not care whether any of them took up acting careers. "He might even have actively discouraged it," Tammy says. "It was pretty cool to live up here. I'd just take my horse and ride off, go up on top, pick a canyon to go down, and see if I came out where I thought I would." This was part of the wonder of the West.

People in Wallowa County who did not know the Brennan family seemed to think that Mike's children had it easier because Walter was their grandfather. Such suspicions arose when Tammy and her sister Patricia appeared as part of the court for Chief Joseph Days. As Tammy explained it, "Selling the most rodeo tickets was one of the contests that court members competed in to win the title of 'Queen.' Frequently, the girl who sells the most tickets is named queen." When someone suggested that Walter would buy all of the Chief Joseph Days rodeo tickets, thus making one of his Brennan granddaughters queen, a friend of the Brennans scoffed: "That will be the day! He's not going to put any money into those girls. If they're going to do it, they're going to do it on their own." Tammy adds, "No one in my family would ever have even considered doing something so underhanded."

Tammy remembered her grammy as warmhearted, loving, and possessed of a great sense of humor. Ruth was fond of quoting the words of utopian socialist Robert Owen (1771–1858): "All the world is queer save you and me, and even thou art a little queer." During a difficult time in Tammy's life, her grandmother told her, "We are not what happens to us. The measure of a person is in how we deal with what happens to us." Ruth was a very hands-on person, as Louise Kunz recalled. In her nineties Ruth watched Louise work a potato digger (harvester), and then she "climbed up and rode for an hour with us. She said, 'I always wondered what you gals did up there.'"

Walter was the same way, taking a keen interest in a logging crew planting trees. The encounter was brief, Mark Burlingame remembered, "because I felt like my crew was acting like school girls bothering him with a bunch of palavering jabber." One of the other Brennan grandchildren, Laura (Ruthie's daughter), who lived near the Brennan's Moorpark home (built in the mid-1960s), remembered just taking it for granted that her grandfather was an actor. Didn't everyone know someone who appeared on television? Laura used to go into her grandfather's Moorpark home office and watch him write his signature on small notepad. He would explain that people often asked him for his autograph. And yet, as Laura's sister Claudia said, their grandfather "never, ever acted as though he was famous." Laura didn't realize just how special Walter Brennan was until a party was held at Disneyland for *The Gnome-Mobile*. When the crowd recognized Walter Brennan, standing next to the engineer on the Disney train, they swarmed him, asking for autographs. And he was able to accommodate them by pulling out a pad of his elegant signatures and distributing pages to his fans. To Laura, then eight or nine, the episode was almost scary, and the look on her grandfather's face told her he was desperately hoping his autographed pages would appease them.

Moorpark, forty-six miles from Los Angeles was their "city home," a twelve-acre spread with a grapefruit orchard. The main residence had three bedrooms, three baths, a formal dining room, and kitchen with a breakfast area. Three fireplaces, a workshop, and a solar heated pool with brick deck were part of the layout. The Brennans also had a separate building with a projection room that included a recording studio with a four-channel microphone-phonograph mixer of Walter's own design, and a one-bedroom guesthouse with a wine cellar. A caretaker's one-bedroom house and a potting shed were also part of the property when it was priced at $1.25 million in 1980 after Ruth Brennan decided to sell the property. Sprinkler and irrigation systems took care of a 875-tree fruit orchard and 345 avocado trees. Walter had no extracurricular interests other than to take care of his land, his animals, and his family He had no hobbies "except working," he liked to say. He would get up at 6:30 am every morning and return home from the studio after dark.

One of Laura's earliest memories is of her grandfather's monkey puppet. This stuffed animal had mitten-like hands he could place his fingers in so as to manipulate the puppet while he spoke in a monkey voice. Both sisters remember a very playful grandfather. Claudia said he would make up words in funny combinations, a kind of double speak. "He was very much a grandfather," Laura said. "I don't remember him talking about movies enough to remember anything." But Claudia, three years older than her sister Laura, remembered her grandfather handing out a script, saying they could help him by reading the other parts. Most often, though, "he wanted to know how we were doing in school, and we'd walk around the property," Laura said. "It was small talk with kids. He was in his seventies, and he liked to do magic tricks for us like pulling a coin behind your ear. He'd do a one-man band, puffing out his cheeks and tapping like on a drum." Claudia remembered her grandparents had a beagle, Poochie, who would put his two front paws on Grandpa's lap as Grandpa told a story that always ended with a dog dying. Then Poochie would slink sadly away. "It was too funny," Claudia laughed.

Guests at the Moorpark home were rare, although Laura remembered a visit from Richard Crenna. It was very much a self-contained Brennan world. Laura liked to see the twinkle in her grandfather's eyes when he became excited about something, and "he could really get sympathy from you when things were not going well for him." Claudia interviewed him for her ninth grade student newspaper, and he told her a typical story about how he started his first business when a man gave him twenty-five cents for a drink of water during a baseball game in the field behind Walter's grandmother's house. Walter returned to the field with a pitcher of water and was soon collecting nickels and dimes for drinks. When he had accumulated sixty cents, he bought a twenty-four-bottle case of tonic water and sold each bottle for five cents. Soon he began doubling and quadrupling his business until heavy competition from others put an end to his profits.

Laura could tell her mother adored him. Claudia said the same, that her mother was "Daddy's girl"—almost too much so, Claudia thought. "She did not want to displease him." Claudia remembered an incident dating from when she was about twelve. From the back seat of a car, she asked her mother, "What if the communists are right?" Her mother's reaction was instantaneous, "Don't you ever say anything like that!" Claudia never saw her grandfather take advantage of Ruthie's devotion. "I didn't see any indication that he was manipulating her or trying to control her any more than a Dad would," although Claudia, a child of the sixties, remembered that her mother told her about buying two Beatles albums. "He *implored* her not to give them to me. Then she told me what he had said, 'Don't give her that. That's bad music.'" But Ruthie did not get rid of the records, and Claudia has them, still unopened.

It was a modest household, where Laura saw her grandfather practice his faith every day. She saw him on his knees every morning next to his bed. His son Andy once asked his father what he said in his morning prayers. "I'm thanking God for being so good to me," Walter replied. In Moorpark, they attended the Holy Cross Church. Both her grandparents liked to hear mass in Latin. The church changed, but not Walter Brennan. Moorpark then still had a country atmosphere with not much around it. The house had a calm and ordered sense that remains a part of Laura's memories. "My grandmother would make his lunch every day," Laura said. Ruth was happy to do so. Walter carried an ordinary lunch box to work and was happy to have it. Why buy your lunch when you did not have to? Walter had a driver, who became his friend, and they rode in Walter's own car, a Lincoln. When Walter returned from a long day at work, Ruth would be waiting. Claudia remembered that her grandfather would walk into the house, and her grandmother would go over to him, "close her eyes, and lean forward, and he would kiss her forehead. Every day."

Claudia's beloved grandma "ruled the roost. But I never saw that. She was very respectful and very much the wife." Claudia remembered her grandmother explaining that if she was out late at a political meeting, when she came home she put bacon fat and onions in a skillet, so that when Walter appeared, he would say, "Oh, smells good, what's for dinner?" Laura understood that "if Grandma wanted something some way, it was going to happen. If they had an argument, he would start getting red. In the Moorpark house there was an island in the middle of the kitchen. I can see them. He's on one side and she's on the other. It wasn't like they were fighting. But I could hear this tone. She would raise her voice a little and say, 'Now W-a-l-t-e-r.'" People used to ask Claudia if her grandfather really had a limp. Well, she said, when he was irritated and annoyed, he would just leave and fall into a limp. His shoulders would slump and his elbows would be thrust out as he marched away. Ruth was Walter's rock—that was clear to Laura from a very early age. Compared to Walter, who had his sentimental side, Ruth could be hardnosed and practical. Ruth did not seek public attention. She rarely granted interviews, explaining, "I feel people are disappointed when they meet me. They expect me to be glamorous and sophisticated. This causes me to feel that I don't live up to the expectations of others."

Laura said her grandfather's political views were plain, but she does not remember him as especially outspoken. She does recall that her grandmother was quite involved in the John Birch Society, and that there would be meetings at the Moorpark house. Her grandfather would participate, but she does not remember him taking a particularly active role in the meetings. Ruth was the driving force, even taking Claudia to some of the John Birch Society meetings. Founded in 1958 by Robert Welch in honor of a missionary who had lost his life in China to the Communists, the organization came into public view in the early 1960s, when a series of articles in the national press dispatched Birchers as right-wing fanatics headed by an ideologue with quasi-fascist views. Welch was an easy target because of his inflammatory rhetoric, including an attack on Eisenhower claiming that the president was a communist agent. Welch called for the impeachment of Chief Justice Earl Warren, and vehemently defended Joseph McCarthy and the campaign to root out what Welch regarded as widespread infiltration of communists in government— and also in every aspect of American life that led to disintegration of American individualism, the rise of big government (well underway since the New Deal), and the steady remorseless march to the nation's status as a slave state. Welch opened himself up to further suspicion by keeping Bircher membership lists secret, refusing to report how many members the society had, and ruling his following with a seemingly dictatorial hand.

As the latest historian of the John Birch Society points out, however, the successful effort to sideline Birchers as an extremist element overlooked several important facts. In the early 1960s, many Birchers were Republicans agitating to make their own party more conservative—in effect, more vehemently anti-communist and anti-big government. Birchers included Democrats as well. And Robert Welch was hardly a Hitler demanding absolute fealty. He had a board of founding members that included prominent businessmen and former government officials, some of whom disagreed with his decisions. You could be a Bircher and not necessarily have to hew to every aspect of the party line, as communists were required to do—although Welch certainly adopted a militancy that took its inspiration from his communist nemesis. But, as Bircher historian D. J. Mulloy shows, fears that Birchers had infiltrated the armed services and might attempt an American-style coup like the one French generals had contrived in Algeria were without much foundation—even if individuals like General Edwin Walker promulgated the Bircher platform. Neither anti-Semitism nor distrust of capitalism formed any part of the Birch agenda, making efforts to brand Birchers as neo-Nazis little more than wild distortions.

For purposes of this biography, the most telling point about the John Birch Society is that Ruth took her grandchild to some of the group's meetings. For Ruth, and for Walter Brennan, the John Birch Society was a community-based assembly of citizens who wanted action, not just words from their political parties. As D. J. Mulloy notes, the society "at the height of its power in the mid-1960s was taken very seriously by considerable swaths of the American population, as well as leading politicians, journalists, academic, and cultural commentators of all kinds." Walter and Ruth Brennan were, in their estimation, part of an exciting new vanguard. Like Robert Welch, this devoutly Catholic couple believed that conventional politics would not lead their country to salvation. Welch saw himself as blazing a "path of truth through the darkness of deception and immorality and cruelty and corruption, which now hovers over our whole earth" in order to reach a new "plateau of light and sanity and freedom and kindness, and honesty and peaceful labor, which other men may then behold with longing and with hope." Mulloy's succinct summary of the Birch mentality matches the Brennan mind-set: "Prosaic yet grandiose; practical but conspiracy-laden; reassuring if fearful; radical and conservative: this was the world of the John Birch Society."

The Brennans were also a part of a longstanding American tradition of viewing politics in conspiratorial terms. The belief that communists wished to reduce American to a slave state echoed Thomas Jefferson's denunciation in the Declaration of Independence of George III's "deliberate, systematical plan of reducing us to slavery." Apocalyptic language, Mulloy points out, suffused the arguments of both the Right and the Left during the Cold War period, which itself grew out of FDR's determination to resist Hitler's drive toward world domination. Like Welch's opponents on the Left, Welch was also deeply impressed with George Orwell's predictions about the modern de-individualized totalitarian state that might materialize by 1984. As Mulloy concludes, "various groups and individuals, conservative and liberal, anticommunist and antifascist, were tightly bound together in a conspiratorial dance of suspicion and fear." In 1960, John F. Kennedy concluded, "The enemy is the Communist system itself—implacable, insatiable, unceasing in its drive for world domination."

Birchers were masters at letter writing campaigns and petitions protesting Nikita Khrushchev's visit to the United States, and summit meetings between American and Soviet leaders Birchers were convinced would lead only to a weakening of America's resolve to combat the worldwide spread of communism. This dispersal, they believed, led to communist takeovers in Eastern Europe, China, and Cuba, and would lead also to the weakening of America's religious and moral fiber. Federal programs like the War on Poverty, they feared, sapped individual initiative, even as the promulgation of federal civil rights laws undermined the authority and the cultures of the states. Birchers, by and large, were not racists, Mulloy argues, even if the consequences of opposing federal enforcement of civil rights laws meant keeping segregation intact. Like many Americans, Birchers believed that relations between the races were steadily improving without the imposition of legislation from Washington. An argument common at the time held that you cannot use laws to change minds.

This history is essential to understanding that Walter and Ruth Brennan did not regard themselves as extremists or as members of a fringe group. On the contrary, they believed they were part of an organization dedicated to restoring American values that had been eroded by communist infiltration of the civil rights movement, for example. That infiltration (and there were some communists in the movement) resulted in depriving African Americans of their will to succeed on their own. The Brennans were among the twenty-seven million people who voted in 1964 for conservative Barry Goldwater, who ran on principles that would later be successfully adopted by Ronald Reagan. Andy Brennan remembered that his father campaigned for Goldwater. In an open car on the way to the Manchester Armory before the New Hampshire primary in March 1963, Goldwater was joined by Efrem Zimbalist Jr., Walter Brennan, and, via film, Ronald Reagan. Andy remembered his father telling him, "I was waving at the crowd, and Efrem was looking for rifles sticking out the windows."

Ruth was a member of the El Camino Federated Republican Women's Club. She hosted many events for Republican candidates, including a reception in 1966 for William Penn Patrick, described as a "right-wing gubernatorial candidate." On Sunday, October 16, 1966, Walter Brennan joined Andy Devine, Buddy Ebsen, and Robert Taylor at Ronald Reagan's Malibu ranch for a televised barbecue at which Reagan, now the frontrunner in the race for governor, urged his supporters to help him "get rid of that gang that's in Sacramento now." Mike Brennan remembered that at one point Reagan asked Walter if he would take over the hosting duties of Reagan's weekly television series. "You bet I would," Walter said (this did not happen).

Working on television and in film always fed Walter's anticipation of the next day. Acting remained not merely his profession, but a kind of trial that he never wanted to shirk. "Years ago," he recalled, he confessed to Lewis Stone, a friend and co-star in *Three Godfathers*, that he was nervous about starting a scene. Brennan never forgot Stone's reply: "You'd better stay a little nervous if you're going to last." By early 1967, Brennan had begun work on another television series, *The Guns of Will Sonnet* (1967–69). He was paid $5,250 an episode to play an ex-cavalry scout riding into western towns in the 1870s looking for his gunfighter son. He is accompanied by his grandson, Jeff (Dack Rambo), who wants to learn the truth about his father, Jim Sonnett. Despite this frail premise, the series lasted fifty episodes. It is fascinating to watch Brennan's scriptural persona, playing a family elder patiently teaching Jeff how to be a man and defend himself without becoming like the villains they encounter. What is irritating, though, is Jeff's naïveté—which is implausible even in a young man just starting out to prove himself. Dack Rambo is not given much in the way of a character to work with, it is true, but he also does not seem to have the skill to make his character at least a little more nuanced than his lines. But Walter Brennan seemed to want his grandson to appear innocent. The emphasis on sex in contemporary film and television was a pet peeve. "We did a saloon scene," he explained to a journalist, "in which I ask the bartender for a drink. The boy wanted one, too, but I told him he wasn't old enough. Then a saloon girl was supposed to say that the boy wasn't man enough for her, either. I thought, 'wait a minute. Hold it. There'll be none of that in my series.' They changed the girl's line."

Episode titles such as "Sins of the Father," "Stopover in a Troubled Town," and "A Town in Terror," suggest the kinds of jams Sonnett and his grandson get into and out of. The epic nature of their ride through the West is rendered more grandiose by the poetry Brennan recites at the beginning of each episode:

> We searched for a man named Jim Sonnett.
> And the legends folks tell may be true.
> Most call him gunman and killer.
> He's my son
> Who I hardly knew.
> I raised Jim's boy from the cradle
> Till the day he said to me
> I have to go find my father
> And I reckoned that's how it should be.
> So we ride
> Jim's boy and me.

The success of Brennan's recordings undoubtedly inspired this versifying Western, which does have its finer moments—especially when Brennan's character deflects the need for violence and finds other ways to triumph over his foes.

Walter Brennan said the role of Will Sonnett fit him like an old hat: "And the hat I wear as Will is the one I've used for every 'good guy' role I've played in the last 35 years." Brennan defined what it was about these roles that made such an indelible impression. The cowboy was the complete man, standing for a generous yet economical way of life that the actor absorbed: "He could sew on a button, brand a dogie . . . rustle up his own grub. He never locked the door of his cabin, and anyone could use it. Those that took advantage of this hospitality always cleaned up before leaving." As Brennan saw it, the cowboy led an uncomplicated life and was as good as his word. The cowboy was, in short, his own man, and Brennan believed the country could still look to the western as a moral exemplum. "It's very lightweight," he said referring to *The Guns of Will Sonnett*. "It isn't much, maybe, but . . . it teaches young people." For Brennan, such programs were the best way of reaching the public. When a *TV Guide* reporter asked him if he was interested in going into politics, he replied, "No! I'm interested in what's *right* for this country and that's something politicians will never know anything about."

Brennan lived by the same stoic cowboy code. During a scene on a western street, he explained to an interviewer, "[M]y horse moved too close to the steps on a building, stumbled and fell. He rolled me all over the ground. When the doctor X-rayed me he found I had three broken ribs. Right now I'm taped so tight I can hardly breathe." Brennan had a sleepless night, but he was on the set at 7:30 the next morning, ready for work. Of course, age had caught up with him. Like John Wayne, he let others handle the horses: "I'll get on and get off but they can get someone else to do the riding."

Brennan had become such a fixture on-screen that he came riding in on his own atmosphere, so to speak. "Forty-six years ago I was what they called an atmosphere player," Brennan told columnist Vernon Scott. "We were used to fill up space." In a way, this was still true, although now the space was configured around him even as he had become the voice of the West, soberly narrating *The End of the Trail* (March 16, 1967), a devastating history of the onslaught against Native Americans by the United States Army and white settlers. He would provide another narrative voice for the first episode of *The American Experience* series (October 20, 1972) as the "storyteller of the Old West sequences."

Playing Grampa Bower, a Grover Cleveland Democrat, in *The One and Only, Genuine, Original, Family Band* (April 25, 1969), did nothing to change Walter Brennan's politics. "I told him [Walt Disney] I'd play it—under duress," he told an interviewer. Bower has composed a campaign song with the refrain "Let's put it over with Grover. / Don't rock the boat, / Give him your vote." He rejects his granddaughter's Republican suitor, Joe Carter (John Davidson), saying "He don't look like he'd have enough sense to pound sand in a rathole." But when Grandpa really gets heated up, he says Carter is guilty of treason for advocating splitting the Dakota Territory into two states against the express wishes of the president and Congress. It is a surprisingly solemn and portentous moment in a Disney musical when Walter Brennan has an opportunity to play a man of political conviction—even if his character is a Democrat. Buddy Ebsen (1908—2003), in reality an actor who shared Walter's politics, plays Grandpa Bower's Republican son, Calvin, who takes the recalcitrant Bower, quite literally, to the woodshed, where he insists his father say nothing more about politics to Carter. Anything less would mean Bower would be obligated to leave his family—a familiar plot development in so many of Walter Brennan's grandpa movies and television shows, in which he puts himself in the wrong, only to do what is right in the end. Just when Bower's granddaughter Alice (Lesley Ann Warren) seems about to lose her teaching job because he has made a political speech to her students, Bower shows up at school board meeting and says, "If I'd a took time to thought about it, I'd have realized I was doin' wrong." He confesses to an impulsiveness that has always been a problem. If the board will rehire Alice and keep the school open, he will not say another word about politics. When Calvin asks his father to return home, a smile—not much more than a twitch—appears on Walter Brennan's face. It is a microsecond of acting as good as any moment in his films.

Sometimes screen images, as purveyed in the Disney films, sanitized Brennan to such an extent that his occasional off-screen lapses are surprising. Janet Blair, who plays Katie Bower, Grandpa's daughter-in-law, remembered, "I'd give him [Brennan] a good morning kiss on the cheek, and he'd give me a kiss on the cheek, and then when I wasn't looking he'd give me a friendly good morning pat on my bustle. [*Raucous laughter.*] He's still young and full of beans." Marjorie Stapp, who appeared in *The Far Country* with Brennan, remembered an even earthier side: "At four in the afternoon, a pretty, young boy, who was a grip, was standing there. Walter grabbed him by the crotch and laughed, 'I couldn't help it—it comes over me this time of the day.' So, I avoided Walter Brennan each afternoon around 4, that's for sure!"

To Carolyn See, writing a profile for *TV Guide* ("An Old Actor Stands Fast in a Changing World," March 3, 1968), Brennan described the communist plot to take over the country by infiltrating "many creeds and colors." To her, this vision was one with the black-and-white world of melodramatic B movies. "Don't you know what's going on in this country?" Brennan asked her. "It's a wonder I have a job at all." And then he revealed how deeply disaffected he had become from mainstream politics: "'A lot of my friends think Reagan is a liberal,' he says judiciously, 'but I say give the man a *chance*.'" When he cited his favorite right-wing publications, See responded she had never heard of them. An incredulous Brennan said, "Don't you *read*? You ought to keep up with what's going on." See had no reply but wondered later if Brennan had heard of the *New York Review of Books*. She reported that the Brennans were known to some neighbors as reactionary agitators who had campaigned to shut down a San Fernando Valley FM educational station's "Renaissance Pleasure Faire" because, in Mrs. Brennan's words, it was a "hotbed of dope addicts, beatniks, and unsavory types not suitable to the Southern California landscape." Walter Brennan did not want to talk about the episode, and See let it pass, except to comment, "I think of the unflattering posters of Mrs. Walter Brennan for sale in local psychedelic shops. She's probably a very nice lady."

Brennan reminisced about his struggling days as an extra, telling See a story about a "Hebe" who used to accept Brennan's ten dollar gold piece (a gift from his parents) in exchange for a loan, until the "Hebe" realized the old piece was worth $1,500 and sold it before Brennan could redeem it. The actor got into trouble for what one commentator called a "religious slur." Aaron Spelling, the producer of *The Guns of Will Sonnett*, said Brennan's language was in "bad taste," but Spelling explained that "unfortunate expression" was just Brennan's habitual way of speaking, without any intention of offending Jews. Producer Irving Pincus told publicist Michael Druxman that Brennan was the "world's biggest anti-Semite" who was "very verbal about his feelings . . . I was his favorite Jew because I signed his checks."

On April 4, 1968, Walter Brennan was working on *The Guns of Will Sonnett*, when he was told Martin Luther King Jr. had been assassinated. At this point, Walter was as firmly convinced as ever that the civil rights movement was a front for communist subversion, and he is said to have danced a jig at the news. This story is part of his IMDb biography, and it is attributed to crewmembers on the show. "I was there," said Andy Brennan, who shares his father's politics. "He didn't dance a jig. He said something like, 'It's good enough.' You got the idea he was not sorry about it. Martin Luther King was a communist."

Brennan's politics did not prevent John Forsythe, a staunch liberal, from insisting on Brennan as his co-star in *To Rome with Love* (1969–71), a television series struggling into its second season. As one reviewer put it, "Walter Brennan is one of those insurance policies who bailed many a movie out of trouble and is now coming to the aid of a faltering television series." Brennan, who had never met Forsythe, agreed to watch the show and decided the role designed for him fit well in a series that had "style and class." But in fact Brennan's character seems simply a slightly improved version of his role in the failed pilot for *Horatio Alger Jones*. Forsythe plays Michael Endicott, a widower who has taken his family to Rome, where he has accepted a teaching position, and Brennan is Andy Pruitt, Forsythe's father-in-law and a retired Iowa farmer. "Grandpa in Charge" is a typical episode. Pruitt calls off a date his granddaughter has with Giovanni, and then he falls asleep trying to read a story to his youngest granddaughter, while she remains awake. He asks the children to forgive him. Then Grandpa is arrested for planting corn in a historic Roman spot while trying to teach his granddaughter about farming. Unfortunately, he has planted his crop in a national shrine. "I've overstayed my welcome," Grandpa announces. "I ought to just plumb get out of here." But then he looks at his grandchildren and decides he can't go and instead says they are going for a drive. *Variety*'s verdict (October 1, 1969) on the first episode can stand for the whole series: "A cast of supporting characters was introduced in as artless a script as one is likely to see with every clichéd role handled by a performer far superior to his material."

Hollywood producer John G. Stephens, involved in the production of *To Rome with Love*, remembered visiting Brennan at his Moorpark home. Stephens was amazed to hear Walter call John Wayne a communist. Brennan showed Stephens his bunker, complete with firearms and a two-year supply of food. Brennan assured Stephens that the Russians were going to invade the United States. While directing John Forsyth and Brennan during the making of *To Rome with Love* (1969), Stephens called the actors, who were feuding, into his office. Feeling like a grammar school principal, he told them, "Guys, I'm sick and tired of you tacking up signs on stage doors, and giving political speeches. This has to stop." Brennan thought nothing of asking someone he had just met about his or her National Rifle Association membership. If the individual was not a member, then Walter would say, "You better join. Otherwise they'll take away your guns."

Just how opposed Brennan was to the Great Society agenda became apparent on May 9, 1969, when Walter and Ruth were greeted by nine hundred cheering fans in Marion, Alabama, where John and Evelyn Ames had founded the Perry Christian School, an institution determined to avoid government ordered integration. The spirit of the visit is captured in a letter Laura Dunlap sent to Mr. and Mrs. Ames. Dunlap extolled an America that once allowed people to live according to the dictates of their hearts and minds. "So the first log cabin school room came into existence," she reminisced. "Then came the Civil War and we were reduced to 'nil' (except our spirit) and had to start from scratch. We were making progress for both races—now the buildings remain but the principles involved are gone. They are truly not our schools any more." But because of the Ameses, Dunlap thought it was "the time of beginning again. . . . As long as there are people like you, some of the youths of our country are in good hands." Ruth Brennan had befriended Evelyn Ames, an activist in Republican Party politics, and was now paying her respects along with Walter, who was treated with a degree of reverence and awe that might have done a founding father proud. Students and teachers had put together a scrapbook (now part of the Brennan archive at the National Cowboy & Western Heritage Center) commemorating the Brennan visit. "Come again some day to our lovely gentle South," read a typical message.

In 1970, Brennan was still aboard the Ronald Reagan express, supporting the governor's re-election bid at a fund-raising dinner attended by Buddy Ebsen, Robert Stack, Robert Cummings and some two hundred other supporters. In 1972, Brennan joined Congressman John Schmitz's campaign for president of the United States as national finance chairman of the American Independent Party. Ruth Brennan, the Schmitz headquarters coordinator, was "in the office daily to answer questions and furnish information on 'how the AIP's philosophy differs from the two major parties.'" Brennan called Schmitz "one candidate who is not committed to the big money establishment that dominates both the old political parties." Schmitz criticized Nixon for reneging on his anti-communist platform, especially regarding the Eastern European nations in the Soviet orbit. Brennan's archive includes Schmitz campaign literature alleging the Nixon administration had covered up the drug trade directed by communist China, which had massively increased its opium production and made billions of dollars in the American narcotics market. A

Schmitz pamphlet includes a photograph of Nixon toasting Chou En-Lai with a caption that reads, "Richard Nixon hunts drug traffickers with a smile and a wine glass."

On August 23, 1972, the *Hollywood Reporter* published an item headlined "Fear of Blacklist Keeps Actors From Politicking," which reads in part:

> Walter Brennan, honorary national chairman of the American Party campaign, headed by presidential candidate John Schmitz, a member of the John Birch Society, has an explanation for the failure thus far of other show business personalities to come out in support of the ticket.
>
> He thinks they are fearful of being blacklisted.
>
> "I haven't heard anybody commit themselves," Brennan said yesterday. "I imagine a lot of them feel that way, but they don't say anything. They might not get a job. But I don't give a shit, you know."

Only rarely, however, did Brennan expose the depth of his apocalyptic pessimism. His Roman Catholic faith prevented him from becoming an end of days fundamentalist, and yet he took part in an evangelistic crusade in Hawaii in 1973, reciting "Old Rivers." In December 1973, Brennan went to hear evangelist Bob Harrington at the First Baptist Church in Ventura, not far from Brennan's Moorpark home. Harrington, celebrated for his emotional grip on audiences—provoking both laughter and tears—impressed Brennan, who attended one of Harrington's services. "He's dynamite," Brennan said. "He could be a great actor."

CHAPTER 10

The Legacy Years

1969–74

ON APRIL 27, 1970, WALTER BRENNAN WAS INDUCTED INTO THE HALL of Great Western Actors at the Cowboy Hall of Fame's annual awards ceremony in Oklahoma City. After listening to several speakers lavish praise on him, he stood up and said, "Other than that, I'm a dirty old man." He often liked to undercut a compliment with a self-directed jibe. But as his son Andy said, his father was thrilled with the honor. Later Brennan donated his papers to what is now the National Cowboy & Western Heritage Museum.

A more studied Brennan surfaced during interviews for a television documentary about him that appeared on May 24, 1970, and featured admiring comments from Buddy Ebsen, Andy Devine, James Garner, and others. As usual, the personal side of Brennan's life received little attention from him. He acknowledged a reference to his brother but would say no more. The program did not bring up the subject of politics.

On December 12, 1970, organizers of the Camarillo Christmas Parade honored Walter Brennan, who had served as grand marshal every year since 1962. Floats with themes chosen from his movies and television series were part of "Walter Brennan Day." Camarillo mayor Stanley Daily presented Brennan with a plaque that included his photograph and a large satin banner that in hand sown letters proclaimed, "Camarillo Salutes Walter Brennan." The actor, close to tears, said the presentation had been "an emotional experience that will remain long with him." In the fall of 1971, Brennan's status as a national icon received more reinforcement when he visited Norman Rockwell at his Stockbridge, Massachusetts, home to pose for a portrait. The Cowboy Hall of Fame had commissioned the artist, and Brennan was deeply moved by the honor. As he told one of his Moorpark, California neighbors, "I would crawl back there to have that man paint my picture." For the sitting Brennan took a parachute bag of shirts and hats, since he would be painted in his western gear. His final choice was a fifty-year-old Stetson, well-worn and sweat stained after many appearances in countless films. When Ruth saw the finished portrait, she said, "That expression on his face is just exactly—you can tell he's listening to somebody and he's got a joke, and the corner of his mouth is turned up like he's waiting to tell his story."

In the right mood, Brennan could seem downright indulgent. "What's all the fuss about kids and long hair?" he asked a reporter. What mattered was what a boy had in his head, not on it, Brennan quipped. Humor and nostalgia seemed to settle into Brennan's roles, which became self-reflexive, a part of the man himself. He relished appearances on *The Red Skelton Show*, where he spoofed the western. In an October 12, 1970, program, Skelton, as Deadeye, the town marshal, walks into a saloon and has trouble disentangling his spurs. Then his deputy (Doc), a bent over Brennan, wearing glasses, looks in the wrong direction as he announces a jailbreak. "Look, I'm over here, Hawkeye," Skelton tells him. The Mooney brothers are after the marshal and his deputy, who says they can do one of two things: face the outlaws or run like hell. Skelton and Brennan elect to do the latter. But the outlaws enter the saloon and quickly spot the room next to the bar where the lawmen are hiding. The outlaws, with guns drawn, demand that Deadeye and Doc come out. The two emerge in dancehall girl costumes, with Brennan holding up his hands with a delicately poised finger pointed upward. The outlaws are—improbably—taken in by the disguises, and one of them makes a pass at Brennan, who slaps him. Brennan draws back grinning, joining Skelton in his typical habit of breaking character and letting the audience know that he knows how ridiculous the scene is. The ruse suddenly is exposed when the enthusiastic Skelton tosses his head, knocking his wig off and jostling Brennan, who also loses his. The skit ends with the outlaws shooting each other in the stupid supposition that they are shooting at bulletproof medallions that Skelton has hung around their necks. The skit is lame, but also an index of how popular Brennan remained.

Walter did some of his best television work on three episodes of *Alias Smith and Jones*. Centered around two bank robbers, Hannibal Heyes (Smith) and Kid Curry (Jones), the series probably appealed to Brennan because the two criminals never shoot anyone and usually end up doing good—sometimes in spite of themselves. On September 16, 1971, Brennan appeared in "The Day They Hung Kid Curry" as Silky O'Sullivan, an irascible retired ex-con who does one more job posing as Kid Curry's grandmother for his ex-outlaw buddies. It was a difficult but intriguing role, said Walter, who had to wear twenty pounds of dress, wig, veil, shawl, and all the other paraphernalia of a widow's ensemble. The hot weather that prevailed during the eleven-day shooting schedule exacerbated Walter's emphysema, but on-screen in his first scene—before he dons his widow's weeds—he looks as vital as ever. He is turned out well in a good suit, chewing out a cab driver who asks him how such an ornery man got a name like Silky. "On account of my lyrical voice, you young squirt. Now get on before I call the police. Git! Git! Git!" Silky shouts in anything but a velvety voice, shooing away the horse drawn carriage. The bravura part of Brennan's performance is withheld until the moment when the wrong man, pretending to the glory of being Kid Curry, is about to be hung for a murder he did not commit. His grandmother's arrival, a ruse engineered by Smith and Jones, causes a delay in the execution, so that the putative Curry's aged relative can pay a last visit to her grandson. Walter, in his womanly disguise, enters the jail—even flirting with the sheriff, turning his head and simpering while his accomplices accomplish the jailbreak. In the end, the real murderer confesses, and the judge decides not to prosecute the jail breakers because they have saved an innocent man from the gallows. An angry Silky, sorry to have been part of the plot, tells Smith and Jones he has paid any debt he owes them. They dismiss his threats to turn them in to the law for a reward and say he hasn't been the same since he became a woman. "Never turn a good friend into a lady," Jones quips. "Never turn a lady into a good friend," Smith ripostes. The plot is ridiculous, but the characters are amusing, the writing is mildly clever, and the acting is good.

A second episode (January 6, 1972) was a tribute, of sorts, to Brennan, who plays Gantry, a toothless, whiskery, and crusty trail cook who relishes watching a good fight between trail hands and is ready to do his own shooting if provoked. "Get it while it's hot," Gantry shouts, as he bangs on a tin plate. "We ain't got all night!" Then, at a pivotal point, he accuses Terrence Tynan (Pernell Roberts), the cattleman whose herd he is driving, of murdering Ralph, one of the drovers, who is rumored to be having an affair with Tynan's wife. When Gantry realizes that it is the trail boss (Steve Forrest) who is the murderer, he maneuvers the trail boss into a showdown that Gantry resolves by shooting him in a scene reminiscent of *Rio Bravo*.

In a third episode (February 17, 1972), "Don't Get Mad, Get Even," Brennan reappears in a brief but effective performance as a well tailored

Silky O'Sullivan, who is threatening to kill Smith and Jones. They have borrowed a $50,000 pearl necklace as part of a scheme to swindle a swindler who has cheated them in a poker game and then organized a holdup to steal the necklace. Naturally, the duo gets out of this jam. Unfortunately, no more is seen of Silky. As in so many of Walter Brennan's cameo appearances, he is there to add interest to otherwise lackluster material.

Brennan seemed less reluctant to appear as himself on *The Dean Martin Comedy Hour* (October 23, 1969), *The Joey Bishop Show* (December 23, 1969), *The Tim Conway Comedy Hour* (December 13, 1970), and other television programs. On *The Glen Campbell Goodtime Hour* (May 10, 1970), Brennan once again performed "Old Rivers."

Brennan's movie appearances in *The Over the Hill Gang* (October 7, 1969) and *The Over the Hill Gang Rides Again* (November 17, 1970) are fairly routine, except for raspy exchanges with Andy Devine that make for a tangy duet between two consummate character actors who had known each other since their days as extras in 1926. In both films, Brennan heads out with a team of ex-Texas Rangers, brought out of retirement, to restore justice, once again, to the Old West. Old age is played for laughs, but also for vulnerability. Watching veteran character actors like Edgar Buchanan, Chill Wills, and Jack Elam is more than enjoyable. Walter complained about Buchanan, a staunch liberal, but Walter got along well with Fred Astaire, a lifelong conservative and member of the Republican Party. Astaire seemed to enjoy being in a western, working with Walter so many years after *The Story of Vernon and Irene Castle*. Like the other veterans in the cast, Walter balked at the idea of a television series based on the movies. "Too much work," the cast agreed.

In *Support Your Local Sheriff!* (March 26, 1969), Brennan benefitted from a much better script. He appears as Pa Danby, a knockoff of Old Man Clanton and Pop Courteen—wearing, it seems, the same outfit in all three roles. But he spoofs himself, portraying a character who takes himself too seriously, thinking he can outgun the new sheriff, Jason McCullough, played with customary charming nonchalance by James Garner, who flusters the aging ruffian by simply placing his finger in Danby's gun when Danby points the weapon at him. For James Garner, this scene, was a dream come true, since *The Westerner* was a favorite of his, and now he had the opportunity to perfect his own droll style opposite Brennan, just as Cooper had done three decades earlier.

In the obligatory O. K. Corral-like showdown at the end of the film, Danby turns to one of his sons, asking him to hold on to his pouch containing his "eatin' teeth" so that they are not damaged in the shoot-out—thus closing another circle in Brennan's movie career. With Jack Elam playing an inspired comic version of the ne'er-do-well deputy, and Harry Morgan as the officious mayor, Brennan joined an incomparable cast of character actors thoroughly reveling in this sendup of the traditional western. The flavor of the film is best captured in a line of Morgan's referring to his "dear departed wife." Garner asks, "Dead?" The deadpan Morgan answers, "No, just departed."

James Garner told an interviewer that Brennan was "the consummate professional who respects everyone in the production. He does his thing, and you know what to expect. You don't have to worry about him doing things behind your back." When I asked Garner for a comment on Walter Brennan, he replied, "He was old before he actually was & he was an unbelievably talented actor. He was a very nice guy." Brennan's memories of the picture were pleasant. He enjoyed working with director Burt Kennedy, also "a nice guy," and seemed pleased to be playing a "dirty old man." Garner remembered that Brennan was the first actor he had ever seen use cards: "He knew the dialogue and never flubbed a line, but I guess he just needed to know that his words were there as backup. He put a card up here and another down there and just kind of glanced at them to make sure. You couldn't tell, though." Brennan also had a great deal of respect for the lines as written. Even in old age, he refrained from indulging an actorly desire to "improve a script." The major exception, of course, had been his work with Howard Hawks, who treated screenplays as a template designed to be modified.

By the late 1960s, Brennan's breathing had become more troubled. Special steps were constructed so that he could mount horses in the television and movie Westerns he still appeared in. His granddaughter Laura watched him as he leaned over and put his hands above his knees, as if to steady and calm himself. In late November 1972, he had surgery for a bleeding colon. But he did not dwell on his ailments or his age. He liked to joke, "I get up in the morning and look in the mirror. If I'm there, I shave and go to work." In other versions, he said he checked the obituaries for his name, and if it wasn't there, he went to work—where access to oxygen tanks kept him going.

In *Home for the Holidays* (November 28, 1972), Brennan plays a dying man, Benjamin Morgan. His four daughters, Frederica (Jessica Walter), Joanna (Jill Haworth), Alex (Eleanor Parker), and Christine (Sally Field) visit him. Alex has summoned them because their father suspects their stepmother, Elizabeth (Julie Harris), is slowly poisoning him. The setting for this television horror/thriller is a dark and stormy night. When Morgan's daughters enter the room, the point of view switches to Morgan, lying on his deathbed, as a low angle shot pans across their wary faces and a cantankerous Morgan barks, "Shut the door. That woman [Harris] has ears that can hear sunshine." He runs down the lineup of his daughters as though assembling a charge sheet for drug abuse, drinking, and promiscuity. Only Alex escapes his Lear-like ferocity. When he is pressed to say why he has requested their presence after nearly a decade of separation, he explains that Elizabeth killed her first husband and now she will do the same to him. When he is asked what he expects them to do about it, he shouts, "Kill her." Does he mean it? And how can they trust a man who abused their mother and carried on an affair with Elizabeth? Elizabeth tells the youngest daughter, Christine, that it is hard for families to accept suicide, an allusion to the sisters' suspicions that their mother was murdered.

Then Joanna is stabbed in the back with a pitchfork as she tries to leave the house (the assailant is shown from the rear in a yellow slicker that Elizabeth wears in an earlier scene), and the phone goes dead. Morgan rises from his deathbed at strategic intervals to peer apprehensively through doors left slightly ajar. Then a drunken Frederica is drowned in the tub, her legs pulled by a pair of hands wearing Elizabeth's kitchen gloves, so that the corpse's head is submerged. An agitated Morgan comes out into the foyer and is told that drunken Frederica has either committed suicide or has accidently taken too many pills. Suspicion of Elizabeth mounts, as the rain continues to come down, and the river rises and washes out the roads. When Christine cannot find Alex, she suspects the worst and flees from Elizabeth, who follows her in that yellow rain slicker. When Christine is able to flag down a car, she finds Alex inside, and the truth emerges. Not only has Alex killed her sisters, she has done in her father as well. "I want to be free of you all," she tells Christine, her last victim. But Christine survives to expose Alex. What began as a promising Gothic thriller that should have used much more of Brennan fizzles out into the pathetic story of a demented sororicide and patricide.

On March 13, 1974, Walter Brennan made his first and only appearance on a talk show. Merv Griffin rightly made a big deal about snagging Brennan as a guest. Walter had always said actors made a mistake appearing on such shows, which took a special kind of talent they did not necessarily possess. You had to be quick witted and agile with your answers if you wanted to compete with the better talk show hosts. Of

course some actors, like Oscar Levant and Henry Morgan, were racon-
teurs who could hold their own with a master talk showman like Jack
Paar. But most actors—most guests—were well advised not to compete
with the host. This was true with Griffin, who would often skewer a
guest with a combination of mock reverence and faux naïveté that led
the overconfident into a Griffin set up. A deft host developed a certain
rhythm of engagement and looked for openings to display his quips.

But in less than ten minutes it was clear Griffin had met his match.
Discarding his garrulous grandfather persona, Walter played it cool to begin with, laconically answering Griffin's query about Brennan impersonators, whom Walter said had paid him a compliment. He liked Rich Little
and "that colored fella." "George Kirby," Griffin broke in, paying no attention to Walter's superannuated usage. Walter relaxed and mentioned
an older fellow in an airport who inquired about his rheumatism, con-
fusing the actor with Amos McCoy. No, Walter never wanted to be a star,
he replied to another Griffin question. As a character man Walter never
got blamed for a bad picture. These replies were nothing new—just part
of the Brennan repertoire built up over decades—but Walter delivered
his lines crisply and with a spontaneity that delighted the audience and
intrigued Griffin—adding that his sidekick, the English character actor
Arthur Treacher, said the same: He wanted to be a supporter. "A sup-
portah," said Walter, to the audience's delight assuming an impeccable
Arthur Treacher accent.

Now Walter turned the interview his way, "I'm a square," he an-
nounced, voicing his thankfulness to the picture business and to God.
Was this the best time of Walter's life? Griffin wanted to know. "It has
always been the best time of my life," Walter said. Did Griffin know that
Walter was playing with Griffin as much as Griffin was with Walter?
Griffin was not prepared when Walter suddenly interjected—apropos of
saying he had been advised to behave himself in the interview—"Like
General Lee said to General Grant, 'Watch your step, boy.'" Whatever
Walter may have meant by that crack, it made Griffin retreat to a seemingly innocuous question: Did Walter start acting as a young man? "I
was always an old man," Walter replied, provoking more laughter. As a
young man, he continued, he saw rich comic possibilities in playing old
men, but now that he was old he saw nothing funny about it. Almost
every line now evoked laughs.

He amused the audience when he said he postponed meals in his
hardest days but never really did without. He knew that understatement

was the best way of turning a joke. He had reached that stage when a performer can get an audience to laugh at anything—as he did when he said he was grateful to Goldwyn, who had him under contract for ten years, during which he did eight pictures for the producer and thirty-two for others. It was a fact, but it became fun just to hear him recite the record. He said Goldwyn looked out for him and protected him—although what Walter said next revealed the actor's place in a benign dictatorship. Imitating Goldwyn, Walter repeated what the studio head said when he saw Walter in his Judge Roy Bean getup: "It's not doity enough." Brennan assured Goldwyn it would be when filming began. "I never let you down, Sam," Walter assured him. "No, you never did," Sam agreed. Then he added, "But I got to see it." In a few deft phrases, Walter repeated stories about Norman Rockwell, who called Walter nothing but a kid because he was born in July 1894, six months after Rockwell; about the days with Gary Cooper when they were extras; and about his service in World War I, when he was gassed once and frightened five hundred times. Griffin mentioned Walter's cattle business and asked if he know much about it. "No," Walter replied. After the laughter subsided, he added, "Nobody does." Griffin touched on politics very delicately, getting Walter to reminisce about seeing Teddy Roosevelt when he came to Lynn in 1906. Was Walter upset about what was going on now? Walter sure was, mentioning the sheriff in Lynn (Ruth's kin) who complained that judges were letting go of criminals that the sheriff had arrested. Walter even got in his complaint against his father for not making money on those patents. "You couldn't tell Pa nothing," he said. For Walter, making good on your talent, your genius, was paramount—as he emphasized by telling the story of how Glen Campbell, then a star, came up to Walter and reminded him that he had played as a backup musician on Walter's recording of "Old Rivers." Walter said, "There is nothing to stop you here." He could have added, "unless you stop yourself," but that was his point in mentioning his father.

Going on to seemingly safer subjects, Griffin asked, "Do you enjoy your grandchildren?" Walter replied, "Nah," to much startled laughter. By now it was evident that Walter, unwilling to provide the accustomed answers, had completely taken over. Even when the segment segued to the appearance of Eva Gabor, Griffin could not count on a conventional response. Griffin was startled, and Gabor was amused, when Griffin asked for Walter's impression of Gabor. "She's much prettier than I thought she would be," Walter said, bringing the house down. This

Walter Brennan was the same performer who would make brief appearances after Lux Radio Theatre programs, engaging in brief and dryly witty exchanges with interviewers.

At eighty, Walter Brennan was the same unpretentious, casually dressed man he had always been—although he was dying from emphysema when biographer Carol Easton interviewed him in 1974 for a biography of Samuel Goldwyn. When Easton spoke with him, Brennan was sitting in what he called "my room," a space full of paintings of him sent by artists grateful for his performances. He was embarrassed by this display, but also proud of the portraits, including the one by Norman Rockwell (now on display at the National Cowboy & Western Heritage Museum in Oklahoma City). In retrospect, Brennan spoke well of Goldwyn, who gave him good pictures and protected him. Working for Goldwyn was like belonging to the "country club of the motion picture industry," he told Easton. "Sam didn't think chicken . . . . He was class."

In his last days Walter Brennan presented himself as the national institution he had become, rarely stepping out of his role as senior statesman. Faithful to his wife for fifty-three years and a self-described loner who had nothing to do with the follies of Hollywood, he did not want to do anything to degrade the dignity of his office. He remembered Gary Cooper as "Coop," who "wore like an old boot." Of himself, Brennan said, "I'm the last of the moccasins around here." Brennan had promised the biographer only thirty minutes but went on for ninety, bidding her farewell in a warm fashion that belied his fragile condition. He maintained the deceptively ruddy glow of a man in his prime.

Walter Brennan kept on working—right to the end—on another Walt Disney film, even when doing so meant hooking up to an oxygen tank between scenes to ease his emphysema. The disease, he said, resulted from being gassed during the war, but it was clearly exacerbated by a heavy smoking habit. He had stopped smoking in the early 1950s when he began to have trouble breathing. Mike remembered the day on the ranch when his father quit, saying, "'That's a dirty deal.' And he threw his cigarette on the ground and said, 'I'm not going to do that anymore.' He took out his pack of cigarettes and put it in another guy's pocket."

One of Walter's granddaughters remembered one of his spells, which occurred when he was resting on his bed. He said to her, "Laura, I want to tell you something, Honey, and I want you to remember this for the rest of your life." An excited Laura awaited his momentous words: "Honey, you need to talk slower. Otherwise people won't understand you." On another occasion, Laura walked into the room and heard her grandfather say, "The reason I don't want to die, Ruth, is I don't want to leave you." Ruth did not stop washing the dishes, but she answered, "Oh, Walter, you can't be talking that way." Laura thought this exchange so typical of the two of them. "He was so broken up when I walked in, but she didn't cede it. She was the strong one."

Walter Brennan was hospitalized for respiratory problems and tests in March of 1974, then again shortly after his eightieth birthday on July 25. As the ambulance took Walter Brennan to St. John's Hospital in Oxnard, near his Moorpark home, he tried to console his son Andy. "It's okay," he said, looking up at his son. "I made it to eighty." He struggled through the summer with the assistance of a pulmonary machine, as local newspapers provided bulletins on his condition. In early August, he seemed "slightly improved" and "resting comfortably." On August 10, he was moved out of intensive care. On August 20, St. John's Hospital reported he was making "steady progress," but was not expected "to be going home very soon." He was able to read and watch some television. In early September his condition worsened and was listed as "poor." Walter Brennan was watching *The Westerner* when he died at 4:30 pm on September 21, 1974.

SOURCES

The Dickinson Research Center of the National Cowboy & Western Heritage Museum in Oklahoma City houses the Walter Brennan papers, an extensive collection of over thirty boxes (20.2 cubic feet) of material that includes scripts, photographs, contracts, other business records, scrapbooks, and miscellaneous items. That storehouse of Brennan lore offers a biographer extraordinary bounty—not to mention the biographical and production files for his pictures housed at the Academy of Motion Picture Arts and Sciences, in clipping files, in Fox and Warner Bros. records at the Cinema Arts Library of the University of South California, and other collections. I am also fortunate to have had access to Walter Brennan's memoirs, recorded in 1971 for Columbia University's Center for Oral History.

Unless otherwise noted, quotations from members of Walter Brennan's family are from my interviews with them. Complete citations of works I have consulted appear in the bibliography. Here citations are by author, or by author and title, if I have relied on more than one work by the same author.

For frequently cited sources, I have used the abbreviations listed below.

AB: Andy Brennan, "My Father."
ACAD: Academy of Motion Picture Arts and Sciences, Margaret Herrick Library.
COH: Reminiscences of Walter Brennan, August 11, 1971, Oral History Collection, Columbia University.
HH: Hedda Hopper radio interview with Walter Brennan, May 17, 1960, ACAD.
HHB: Hedda Hopper, "Walter Brennan Picks Unorthodox 'Ten Best,'" *Baltimore Sun*, March 7, 1943, USC.
JH: Joe Hyams narrated a television documentary about WB, a copy of which I viewed at NCWHM.
LPL: Lynn Public Library.
MB: Mike Brennan.
MD: Marian Dern, "Foxy Grampa in a Business Suit," *TV Guide*, April 10, 1965, USC.
NA: newspaperarchive.com.
NCWHM: National Cowboy & Western Heritage Museum, Walter Brennan Papers.
TVG: Dwight Whitney, "A Man in His Right Mind," *TV Guide*, March 7–13, 1959, 18, USC.
USC: University of Southern California Cinema Arts Library.
WB: Walter Brennan.

INTRODUCTION

Howard Hawks expressed many tributes to WB. See Breivold, McBride, and Kobal.

"The real parts": Dana Andrews in Lillian Ross, *The Player*.

For comments on character actors by Arnheim and Thomson, see Wojcik, 205, 208.

"You can't do that": Breivold, 83.

McCrea and Stanwyck to WB: Wilson, 547.

WB's sets of false teeth and old shoes: Heffernan, Soanes.

Marsha Hunt: McClelland, 93.

CHAPTER 1: THE BEGINNING (1894–1927)

Epigraph: Lines from a poem by Josiah Gilbert Holland, quoted by Calvin Coolidge in February 1916 during a victory party for his election as lieutenant governor of Massachusetts. See Shlaes, 140.

"Is he going to walk or fly?": *Framingham-Natick (MA) News*, June 4, 1968, clipping file, NCWHM.

Church of the Sacred Heart: WB's attending mass at the Church of the Sacred Heart is mentioned only briefly in the *This Is Your Life* television program about him, but in interviews he often mentioned the vital role faith played in his life. The church was built in stages and completed in 1909, according to the privately printed history of the parish I obtained at a school connected to the church.

"I wish they'd have them again": "Young Fans Nearly 'Mob' Walter Brennan in Lynn," *Lynn (MA) Item*, July 7, 1960.

Shoemaking in Lynn: Words like shank, a supportive structure for the insole and outsole; skiver, which can be a term for soft leather or a tool that cuts leather; stiffenings, molded leather for shoes; and rands, a layer of rubber above the sole, were terms of art easily recognizable in a leather bound age.

"voice tone": TVG.

Early schooling: I was not able obtain records of Brennan's academic progress.

"But I don't want to be Abraham Lincoln": Sarah Hills recalling Brennan's childhood on *This Is Your Life*.

Driving an express wagon: *Good Old Days Magazine* (1971), ACAD biography clipping file.

"I never cost them a penny": See clipping file, USC.

"What do you mean upbringing": Roberts, NCWHM clipping file.

29 Franklin: I am grateful to Mrs. Dorothy Gregory, the third owner of 29 Franklin, for giving me a tour of the home. She was able to verify which parts of the home remained unchanged from when the Brennans lived in it. Mrs. Gregory discovered the pipes in the walls for the gaslights when she had the home rewired.

Jobs while in high school: "Actor Visits North Shore," October 16, 1970 and untitled article in *Lynn (MA) Item*, May 24, 1940, LPL clipping file.

Football playing and swimming: "The Town's Favorite 'Grandpa' Is Dead," *Swampscott (MA) Reporter*, September 26, 1974, 4. I have not been able to find in the *Lynn (MA) Item* an account of Brennan's swim to Egg Rock, which is now the site of a bird sanctuary.

"As a boy": "Walter Brennan's Still Going Strong," *Greenville (TX) Herald Banner*, June 18, 1972, B4.

April 1914: Jack Butterworth, "Walter Brennan's School Days," *Lynn (MA) Item*, August 23, 1990.

Rindge: http://www.cambridgehistory.org/rindgetechschool; "Actor Walter Brennan Dies at 80," clipping file, USC.

Returning to Rindge: An article about Brennan's return appears in the December 18, 1959, issue of *Rindge Register* (Cambridge, MA).

After Rindge: Shaffer.

"chorus line of youth": The somewhat blurred photograph appears on the Swampscott annual report for 1994, courtesy of local historian Louis Gallo.

Arthur McNamara's letter: NCWHM.

Oldsters on stage: Mayme Ober Peak, "Brennan's Missing Teeth Won For Him a Star Role," *Boston Globe*, September 15, 1935, NCWHM clipping file.

"I was never really stage-struck": "Walter Brennan Gets First College Degree," *Lynn (MA) Item*, May 29, 1958, LPL clipping file; "Biography of Walter Brennan," Warner Bros. Studio, USC; "Walter Brennan: From Lynn to Hollywood Fame," *Lynn (MA) Item*, September 23, 1947, LPL clipping file.

"it was a good chance to get away": JH.

"half-holiday": "Off to War Half Century Ago," July 27, 1967, *Lynn (MA) Item*.

"I learned to run": Clipping file, NCWHM.

Imitating the sound of artillery shells: Harry Brand, Fox studio biography of WB, October 3, 1936, USC.

Gassed with high explosive projectiles: "Americans Heavily Gassed," *New York Times*, April 4, 1918.

Relatively few casualties: Fitzgerald.

Loss of his lower front teeth: Swampscott Town Report 1994.

"I probably knew Tony's father": "Material is Actor's Best Friend, Says Walter Brennan, in Reviewing Career on KABC—Radio's 'Personal Portrait,'" September 24, 1964, USC.

Osgood Perkins: http://en.wikipedia.org/wiki/Osgood_Perkins.

"They defied you to be good": *Current Biography 1941*, 99.

"Just goes to show": Scott.

Writing letters to her: Kirk.

"she'd get it": Edith Lindeman, "Film Actor Pays Visit to Richmond," October 4, 40, biography clipping file, ACAD.

Simmons College: I am grateful to Justin Snow, archives assistant at Simmons College, for providing me with a list of courses in secretarial studies.

"No, thank God": Brennan, "My Father."

"decided to take Greeley's advice": JH.

"My wife is a convert": WB's granddaughter Laura said Ruth never did have a good word to say about her mother-in-law; see also Erskine Johnson, *Kenosha (WI) Evening News*, March 8, 1958 (clipping with no title), NCWHM.

Walter washing the floor: E-mail from WB's granddaughter Laura Schaffell, August 4, 2014.

Becoming an actor: Kirk.

Ironing Walter's one shirt: Interview with WB's granddaughter, Laura.

"I was glad to get the dough": Joseph; JH.

Universal: Schatz.

"What's your name": COH.

Shared their meager earnings: Warner Bros. Biography of WB, n.d., USC.

"Those were the days": Walter Brennan, "I Think I Know Why I'm Still Around," *Guideposts* July 72, clipping NCWHM.

Interview with Hopper: HH.

Actors Equity dispute: "Third Week of Fight, Equity Makes Three Strong Points Against Producers; Gets Support from American Federation of Labor," *Hollywood Filmograph*, June 22, 1929, USC, courtesy of Ned Comstock.

His best week: Joseph, 95.

"I never missed any meals": "Material is Actor's Best Friend, Says Walter Brennan," *KABC Radio News*, USC.

CHAPTER 2: THE RACKET (1928–35)

"I had to be doing": COR.

Bad back: Keavy.

"My wife Ruth": Walter Brennan, "I Think I Know Why I'm Still Around," *Guideposts*, July 72, NCWHM.

Silent films that seem lost: IMDb has very little information for these films—not even plot summaries.

1929: *Hollywood Filmograph*, February 15, 1930, reports that WB will be part of the cast for Hoot Gibson's *Trigger Tricks*, but IMDb does not list him in the cast, USC, courtesy of Ned Comstock.

"nothing they have had since": *Baltimore Sun*, October 6, 1940, clipping in WB biography file, ACAD.

"There we were": AB.

"they looked like the West": COR. The transcript of an interview records WB saying he grabs hold of an "apple," but this is clearly a mistake.

Jerry Blake: See his account of *Phantom of the Air* on IMDb.

The stuttering animal imitator: Joseph, 95.

Gossiping townsman: Universal Pictures Corporation production estimate, November 21, 1934, USC.

"damn and hell": Joseph Breen to Samuel Goldwyn, December 26, 1934, ACAD.

It was Bellamy: Interview with Andy Brennan.

He was paid $300: Universal Pictures production estimate, USC. I found only a few records at USC specifying Brennan's pay rate for his bit work. For *Half a Sinner* he was paid fifty dollars for a day's work on March 12, 1934, as a radio announcer; for *Uncertain Lady* he earned fifty dollars for one day's work (n.d.) as a gas station attendant.

CHAPTER 3: ACCLAIM AND AWARDS: SAMUEL GOLDWYN, HOWARD HAWKS, FRITZ LANG, AND HOW WALTER BRENNAN BECAME A REAL CHARACTER (1934–39)

Little Accident: Joseph, 95.

"There never has been a time": James Wingate to Maurice McKenzie, June 26, 1934, ACAD. All correspondence concerning *Barbary Coast* is in ACAD.

Deflated actor: Carpenter tells this story to her collaborator in her memoir, *A Loving Gentleman*, which focuses on her long affair with William Faulkner. The Brennan story was cut from the book, but it is part of a recording in her collection at the University of Mississippi. And WB's reaction to Hawks's put down is cut from the typescript of the memoir that is also part of her collection.

Parts that Gary Cooper rejected: An early production still shows Cooper and WB together in a scene from *Barbary Coast*. But Cooper was evidently re-assigned to another picture.

"Valter": Whitney, "Walter Brennan," 18.

"Darryl": Rick Du Brow, "Walter Brennan Adds to the Goldwyn Lore," *Hartford (MA) Courant*, July 19, 1959, USC.

Dyer: McBride, *Focus on Howard Hawks*, p. 84.

"emotional mechanics": Wakeman, 39.

"that man's death": The clipping in the USC collection has no title, but it is an article by Cecil Smith that appeared in *Los Angeles Times*, February 22, 1959.

"I have made 80 pictures": Chester Morris to Pat McDermott, February 15, 1959, NCWHM.

"we were very happy": John Stanley, "Brennan: God, Prayers and Honest—That's No Brag," October 22, 1967, *San Francisco Sunday Examiner & Chronicle*, NCWHM, clipping file.

"further development of Walter Brennan": Unidentified clipping, ACAD.

Brennan became ill: Unidentified articles, clipping file, ACAD.

Fritz Lang: Grant, 110.

Frances Farmer: Wood Soanes, "Star Light Star Bright," *Oakland (CA) Tribune*, January 3, 1937, NA.

First Academy Award: Goldwyn replaced Hawks with William Wyler after Goldwyn and Hawks argued over Hawks's rewriting of the screenplay. As a result, both directors were given screen credit. The change in directors does not seem to have affected Brennan's performance.

"I stepped up": Twentieth Century-Fox studio biography, c. 1946, USC.

"I'll see you at the preview": JH.

The exchange between the Breen office and Fox regarding *Banjo on My Knee*: ACAD.

"Turn out the lights": Jim McLam, "Mrs. Walter Brennan," *Ventura County (CA) Star Free Press*, July 16, 1978, USC.

"Well, I'm thinking": HH.

Walter liked to sit around: Bob Thomas, "Life in Hollywood," *San Mateo (CA) Times*, May 28, 1947, NA.

Return trip to Swampscott: May 24, 1940 article in *Lynn (MA) Item*, LPL clipping file.

"old man with a heart of gold": COR.

She's Dangerous: Weekly production report, USC.

His salary: Universal Pictures production estimate, December 22, 1936, USC. Why the total is not $2,400 I can't say.

When Love Is Young: Weekly production report, USC.

The neat editing: Davis, 12.

"Oh, he will swear at you": COR.

Pay rates for *The Buccaneer* and *The Texans*: Paramount contracts, ACAD.

The Texans: Excerpts from the reviews can be found in *Motion Picture Review Digest*, v. 3, No. 39, 76–77, USC.

"To Walter": COR.

"synthetic affair": For a summary of the reviews, see *Motion Picture Review Digest*, March 27, 1939, v.4, no. 13, 48–49.

Louella Parsons: "'Kentucky' Big Triumph for Technicolor," January 5, 1939, USC clipping file.

Second Academy Award: Clipping from *Boston Globe*, April 3, 1939, ACAD.

"It was the picture business": AB.

"The Brennans are": Edith Lindeman, "Film Actor Pays Visit to Richmond," October 4, 40, ACAD clipping file.

Bill Steele: A veteran of John Ford pictures, Steele would appear with Brennan in *The Westerner* and *The Showdown*.

"a city of $100 millionaires": Harry T. Brundidge, "Expert Actor of Films is Former Real Estate Man Who Became an Obscure Extra After Losing $2000-a-Month Business," *St. Louis Star Times*, April 14, 1937, NCWHM clipping file.

"I remember Andy": Walter Brennan as told to Joseph N. Bell, "My Kids Don't Owe Me a Thing," *Today's Health*, December 1962, NCWHM clipping file.

"My wife": AB.

"I know all the words": HH.

"You can fire me": Rex Polier, "Brennan Stays in Character as Years and Show Roll on," *Philadelphia Bulletin*, February 2, 1969, clipping, NCWHM.

Philip Dunne: oral history, ACAD.

Both Academy Award winners: Curtis, 366.

"Might be entertaining": Curtis, 370.

Shooting *Northwest Passage*: Behlmer, 45.

And you had a pack: COR.

Bodily harm: Curtis, 599.

"Don't get yourself heated up": *San Mateo (CA) Times*, April 6, 1939, NA.

Brennan's character and his fluctuating fortunes: Fox studio memo, USC.

"tired out": *San Mateo (CA) Times*, NA.

"punchdrunk": "Walter Brennan Punchdrunk," *Atlanta Constitution*, March 24, 1940, USC.

CHAPTER 4: THE APOTHEOSIS OF WALTER BRENNAN (1940)

Unpublished autobiography: ACAD.

"My part is such that": "Hollywood Today," April 24, 1940, USC.

"He must always be himself": Elizabeth Copland, untitled clipping from *Richmond (VA) News-Leader*, October 4, 1940, ACAD.

"I always say": COR.

"Of course, we're all little boys": COR.

"everything an actor can ask for": Walter Brennan, "The Role I Liked Best," *Saturday Evening Post*, January 22, 1949, USC.

CHAPTER 5: PRIMAL BRENNAN: GARY COOPER, HUMPHREY BOGART, FRANK CAPRA, JEAN RENOIR, HOWARD HAWKS (1940–44)

Brennan's pet hobby: Twentieth Century-Fox studio biography, ACAD.

He bought a 12,000-acre ranch: WB to Ray Pogue, May 18, 1941, courtesy of MB.

Ruth liked to tell the story: Interview with MB.

"We woke up the next morning": Interview with Caroline Ward.

Vivian Strickland: Interview.

Ray also complimented Walter: Ray Pogue to WB, May 7 and 26, 1941, courtesy of MB.

"Dad purchased": AB.

Early July: Interview with Tammy Crawford.

"If you're not the star": AB.

Lewis Stone: Sara Hamilton, "Round Up of Pace Setters," *Photoplay*, May 1941, USC.

Meet John Doe: Production details are in the Warner Bros. collection at USC.

"Why don't you keep Cooper": COR. Brennan does not actually identify the production that kept Cooper working late at night, but the details fit *Meet John Doe* better than any other picture the two actors worked on together.

Years later: Stephens.

"My weakness: Mayme Ober Peak, "Brennan's Missing Teeth Won Him a Star Role," *Boston Globe*, September 15, 1935, NCWHM.

"When human beings": Laura Kaiser, UCLA film archive April 7, 1995.

"Are you interested in": Lockhart's reminiscence is part of *Sergeant York: Of God and Country*, a documentary that is part of the DVD release of the film.

"I was scared": Warner Bros. pressbook, ACAD.

"Now would you turn": Leslie's reminiscence is part of *Sergeant York: Of God and Country*, a documentary that is part of the DVD release of the film.

"never hurried": COR.

"40,000 Italians": All the details of the *Sergeant York* production are taken from the Warner Bros. legal and production files at USC.

"huge pair": "Hedda Hopper's Hollywood," *Berkeley (CA) Gazette*, December 4 1943, NA.

This Woman Is Mine: This film is so obscure IMDb does not even supply a plot summary. There is only one user review, which acknowledges WB's magnificent performance.

"The greatest bugaboo": Fox publicity release, n.d, ACAD.

"finish him off": "Hedda Hopper's Hollywood," *Berkeley (CA) Daily Gazette*, December 15, 1941, NA.

"letter-perfect": Harry Brand, Fox publicity release, ACAD.

After the production wrapped: "Hedda Hopper's Hollywood," *Berkeley (CA) Daily Gazette*, December 15, 1941; "Hedda Hopper's Hollywood," *Berkeley (CA) Daily Gazette*, September 21, 1941, NA.

Swamp Water: During the making of the film WB told Harold Heffernan ("Hollywood Highlights," *Hartford (MA) Courant*, September 11, 1941, USC) that he had filmed the scene with the snake and had "cheated" by stretching out a couple of inches farther from the snake than he had rehearsed. Supposedly screenwriter Dudley Nichols later said he put the scene in the script as a joke, never dreaming it would actually be filmed. Mike Brennan said that a pane of glass was put between the snake and Walter in the scene where the cottonmouth bites Keefer.

"wonderful": COR.

"How was that Gene": Twentieth Century-Fox press release from Harry Brand, November 3, 1941, ACAD.

"The swamp is": Dudley Nichols memo to Darryl Zanuck, October 16, 1940, USC.

Specially built projection room: HHB.

"I rate Gene": HHB. Lockhart also appears with Brennan in *Meet John Doe*.

John Wexley: Wexley is not credited, but "Bert Brecht" is.

"she's truly a great dramatic actress": HHB.

"He amused and amazed us": Edith Lindeman, "Film Actor Pays Visit to Richmond," October 4, 1940, clipping file ACAD.

"feel right in those dress-up parts": Bob Thomas, "Lid Taken Off Baseball Movie Yarns," *Oakland (CA) Tribune*, March 25, 1948, NA.

"Hang on!": WB to Ray and Bessie Pogue, January 9, 1944, courtesy of MB.

"everyday occurrences": Ray Pogue to WB, January 19, 1944, courtesy of MB.

February 1944: WB to Ray and Bessie Pogue, February 26, 1944, courtesy of MB.

He would never work with: Patricia Brennan e-mail to CR.

"He's so good": HHB.

"dazzling blonde": Archer Winston review, *New York Post*, June 22, 1944, USC.

"good mechanic": COR. The October 2, 1944 Lux Radio Theatre production of *Home in Indiana* tones down Brennan's violence considerably and shortens the scene in which he loses control of himself—in all probability because it would have been difficult to present such disturbing material in a one-hour adaptation listened to by families gathered around the radio.

"warm, modern yarn": John T. McManus review, *PM*, June 22, 1944, USC.

"Camden Boy": Fox press release, c. 1944, USC.

"The general unacceptability of this story": Joseph Breen to Jack Warner, February 18, 1944, USC.

"all right": COR.

CHAPTER 6: WESTERN BRENNAN: BOB HOPE, HENRY FONDA, JOHN WAYNE, JOHN FORD, HOWARD HAWKS, ROBERT MITCHUM (1944–48)

Cub: I'm indebted to Cub's daughter, Judy Lamy, for telling me about her father's experiences with WB.

"Walter Brennan almost collapsed": Bill Rice, Warner Bros. press release, USC.

"I've had very few people": COR.

Butler and Brennan: Unidentified clipping, ACAD. I can give an approximate date for the article about "The Old Character" because it mentions the recent release of *Nobody Lives Forever* (1946).

"curiously disturbing": February 10, 1945, *New York Motion Picture Critics' Reviews 1945*, USC.

"being talked up": *San Mateo (CA) Times*, November 29, 1944, NA.

Vera Ralston: My praise of Ralston is perhaps the only time she has received a good notice. Critics seem to go out of the way to deplore her acting.

"You know Ned": "Walter Brennan," TVG.

"protected me": HH.

"This character": Fox publicity release, c. 1946, USC.

"But do you know how?": Fox publicity release, c. 1946, USC.

"To hear people talk": Fox studio press release, c. 1946, USC.

"Don't whip me": Harry Brand, Fox production notes, n.d., ACAD.

John Ireland: oral history, ACAD.

Red River: Both versions of the film are now available on DVD.

"When I see a good Western": COR.

"Monty is one of the finest young actors": Fox production notes, n.d., ACAD.

CHAPTER 7: WESTERN BRENNAN REDUX: ROBERT MITCHUM, JAMES STEWART,
SPENCER TRACY, JOHN WAYNE—*THE FAR COUNTRY, BAD DAY AT BLACK ROCK,
RIO BRAVO* (1948–58)

"sitting down to lunch": AB.

Routine roles: Lambert, fifty-two, calls *Driftwood* and *Scudda Hoo! Scudda Hay!* "two negligible movies."

"doing any job well": HH. Tobias has an important role in *Sergeant York.*

"Ruth, trained since childhood": Patricia Clary, "Brennan Boasts Too Soon," *Long Beach (CA) Press Telegram,* July 17, 1948, NA. The article exaggerates Brennan's concern over his daughter's stunt when an Indian rider had refused to do the scene.

"as already reported": Warner Bros. files, USC.

Could be someone else: Apparently Brennan did dress for the role, according to "Walter Brennan Plays First 'Female' Role," *Hartford (MA) Courant,* March 27, 1949, USC. "I can't say I like the role," Brennan is reported to have said. "I was hurrying across the lot to my dressing room to get out of this costume the other day when a studio copy yelled at me, 'watch yourself, grandma, this is a dangerous street.'"

A new business: The description of the theater is taken from the opening night brochure, courtesy of Darlene Turner.

"cry room": Today the theater is a Baptist church, and the cry room remains intact and in the same location.

"Walter, I don't think": Harold E. Swisher, *Movieland,* n.d., USC.

"Walter Brennan's Indian Lodge Motel": brochure, NCWHM.

"It takes about a day": Frank Neill, "In Hollywood," *Long Beach (CA) Independent,* December 6, 1949, NA.

"Well, the only thing wrong": Interview with MB.

"TV is the thing": TVG.

A gala opening: Warner Bros. press release, USC.

"I wouldn't hurt a fly": Warner Bros. Press release, USC.

"It's 90 percent material": Brennan is quoted in an otherwise unidentified *PM* article, USC.

Caught in an unexpected flood: "Stars Caught in Mt. Flood," *Berkeley (CA) Daily Gazette,* August 12, 1950, NA.

"He was not a warring Indian": COR.

"it was a trick shot": COR.

A case of poison oak: *Berkeley (CA) Daily Gazette,* December 22, 1951, NA.

Brennan and Cooper: Universal press release, USC.

Drums Across the River: All production details are from the Universal daily minutes, USC.

"Jimmy's a great actor": Erskine Johnson, "Hollywood Today," *Humboldt (CA) Standard,* May 7, 1954, NA.

"good judgment": Lovell, 103.

It made you think: COR.

"Good enough": Scott Eyman, "At 91, Ernie Borgnine Still Loves His Work," *Palm Beach (FL) Post,* March 30, 2008.

"When he came out": COR.

Reviews of WB's television work: *Variety,* November 16, 1953; January 29, 1954; April 12, 1955; November 25, 1955; July 16, 1956; November 20, 1956; December 4, 1956; December 24, 1956; November 4, 1957.

"Mr. Tutt": According to IMDb, an episode entitled "Mr. Tutt" was broadcast on *Colgate Theatre* in 1958.

"There's no big mystery": Erskine Johnson, "Hollywood Today," *Humboldt (CA) Standard,* May 20, 1954, NA.

"Tennessee's Partner": "[A] story of a prospector who stands by a no-good friend though he knows he's being exploited," *Oakland (CA) Tribune,* September 22, 1954, NA.

"A Kind of Treasure": Bob Foster, *TV-Radio,* January 21, 1953, NA.

"They tell me": "Walter Brennan Enjoys Being Aged Amos McCoy," *Hartford (MA) Courant,* December 28, 1958, USC.

Greg Ford: "Mostly on Rio Lobo," *Focus on Howard Hawks.* Prentice Hall, 1972, 157.

"being Stumpy": Angie Dickinson e-mail via Alan Rode to Carl Rollyson, June 7, 2013.

"He amazed me": Joseph McBride, ed., *Hawks on Hawks.* University of California Press, 1982, 109.

CHAPTER 8: *THE REAL MCCOYS:* AMERICA'S GRANDPA (1957–63)

My discussion of *The Real McCoys* draws on my interviews with Kathleen Nolan, Mike Brennan, Andy Brennan, and the Lothrop Worth oral history at ACAD, as well as the following *TV Guide* articles supplied to me by Ned Comstock at USC: "Walter Brennan Bids Goodbye to Make-Up," February 15, 1958, 28–39; "Walter Brennan Knows His Mind," March 7, 1959, 17–19; "*The Real McCoys* Admiration Society," January 23, 1960, 5–7.

The number of viewers had tripled: Erskine Johnson, *Redlands (CA) Daily Facts,* March 15, 1958, NA.

"pure and simple competition": MD.

"You're doing it": Hal Humphrey, "Brennan is Finally Acting His Age," *Los Angeles Mirror News,* July 21, 1958, USC.

"It's a tricky business": Steven H. Scheuer, "Walter Brennan Enjoys Being Aged Amos McCoy," *Hartford (MA) Courant,* December 28, 1959, USC.

"I should know you": Interview with MB.

"Why do you waste your time": Interview with MB.

"An episode like": TV talk, IMDb.

"I was doing a show": David Martindale, "Rural Comedy with a Hitch," *Houston Chronicle,* August 8, 1999.

"I've never seen anything like it": Erskine Johnson, "Walter Brennan 'Corny'? Not So Says Veteran," *Redlands (CA) Daily Facts,* March 15, 1958, NA.

receiving his first college degree: Brennan kept clippings of this event, which are now in NCWHM.

"glowed": *San Mateo (CA) Times,* February 26, 1959, NA.

among business tycoons: Photograph in *Van Nuys (CA) News,* March 1, 1959, NA.

"Laura": Larry Wolters, "TV Beats Brennan's 3 Oscars," *Chicago Daily Tribune,* November 7, 1958, NCWHM.

"I said to a very successful director": Brennan is quoted in the *Los Angeles Times, TV Times, Weekly Magazine,* June 13, 1964, clipping file, NCWHM.

Hard feelings: MD.

The land was subdivided: Kevin Roderick, "Home Town Memories: Once a Nice Quiet Place, Northridge Is Thrust Out of Its Obscurity," *Los Angeles Times,* January 24, 1994, http://articles.latimes.com/1994-01-24/local/me-14895_1_nice-quiet-place.

Edgar Hiestand: Hiestand served in Congress for a decade. He was a fervent anti-communist and a member of the John Birch Society.

"I have never taken": "'Let's All Register, Vote' Campaign Begun in Valley," *Van Nuys (CA)
News*, August 25, 1960, NA.

The Brennans hosted similar events: "North Valley Fete Honors Republicans," *Van Nuys
(CA) News*, September 29, 1960; "Brennans Host Candidate Dentzel," *Van Nuys (CA)
News*, October 13, 1960; "Public Invited to Attend Hiestand-Dentzel Brunch," *Van
Nuys (CA) News*, October 10, 1960, NA.

Lothrop Worth: Oral history, ACAD.

Ward Bond: On his activities as a blacklister, see Nollen.

"prayer in the schools": AB.

"I *am* a flag waver": AB.

"You hear people say": "The Queen's Work," April 1958 interview by Kerwin Tanguay,
NCWHM.

How the West Was Won: As several critics point out, the Civil War section, directed by John
Ford, transcends the platitudinous quality of the rest of the film.

"There were complaints": MD.

"He would limp": Karl Malden oral history interview, ACAD.

"people are afraid to say": Mrs. Helen Willy to WB, May 28 1962, NCWHM.

A stirring speech: Interview with Judy Lamy.

In a newspaper: "Record Review," *Redlands (CA) Daily Facts*, June 13, 1962, NA.

"When the sun would get high": http://trackofthecat.blogspot.com/2013/01/an-analy
sis-old-rivers-by-walter.html.

Walter Brennan record sales: Joel Whitburn, *Top Pop Singles 1955–1990* (Menomonee
Falls, WI, 1991), p. 65. I am indebted to my friend and fellow biographer, Chip Bishop, for this account of Brennan's recording career.

Brennan's long-playing albums: YouTube and other websites provide selections from
these albums.

Janet Blair: JH.

Marjorie Stapp: http://www.westernclippings.com/interview/marjoriestapp_interview
.shtml.

"I'm too old": Drew Pearson, "Flood of Letters on Prayer Ban Attributed to the Radical
Right," *Oxnard (CA) Press-Courier*, May 14, 1964. "Project Prayer Will Hold Meeting,
Hear Talk," *Van Nuys(CA) News*, December 19, 1963; *Long Beach (CA) Press Telegram*,
April 10, 1964, NA.

"If someone asked me": Allan Gill, "TV Probes the Life of Gary Cooper—A Real 'Mr.
Deeds,'" *Oakland (CA) Tribune*, March 24, 1963, NA.

"My country": *Long Beach (CA) Press Telegram*, June 9, 1964 NA.

photographed with Strom Thurmond: *Long Beach (CA) Press Telegram*, June 9, 1964 NA.

"active boosters": "Film Stars Divided Over LBJ, Barry," *Long Beach (CA) Press Telegram*,
September 16, 1964, NA.

The Tycoon: Brennan's contract is at NCWHM.

"What's the matter?": AB.

"dirty shirt": Pat Nogler, "Brennan Fears He's 'Victim' of Type-Casting," *Pasadena (CA)
Independent*, July 24, 1958, NA.

"I'm a little disappointed": See.

Key Records: Key Records, founded by Knight in 1956, recorded founder of the John Birch Society, Robert Welch, and Ronald Reagan. Brennan's album is available at these two websites http://blog.wfmu.org/freeform/2012/11/hes-your-uncle-not -your-dad-by-walter-brennan.html; http://blog.wfmu.org/freeform/2012/12/walter -brennans-hes-your-uncle-not-your-dad-part-two-and-vick-knight-and-the-key -records-story.html.

Careful with money: Maurine Myers Remenih, "Everybody's Favorite Grandpa," *Chicago's American TV Pictorial*, November 20, 1960, NCHM: "The only critical thing anyone can say about the man, it would appear, is that 'he is very careful with a dollar.'"

Horatio Alger Jones: The pilot is available for viewing at the UCLA film and television archive.

But less than a year later: "12 Named to Receive Annual Alger Awards," *Los Angeles Times*, April 24, 1966, USC.

"God's way": Walter Brennan, "Don't Crack the Shell," *Harrisonburg (VA) Daily News Record*, March 10, 1973, 12.

"We are not what happens to us": Tammy Crawford e-mail to CR, June 14, 2014.

"because I felt like my crew": Mark Burlingame e-mail to Caroline Ward (Walter's granddaughter), July 17, 2014, courtesy of Caroline Ward.

Pulling out a pad: Tammy Crawford showed me one of those pads and tore off a page with Walter Brennan's beautiful signature on it.

The Moorpark home: Bob Foster, "A Brief Look at the New Television Season," *San Mateo (CA) Times*, September 30, 1974; "Former Walter Brennan estate listed," *Los Angeles Times*, December 12, 1980, USC.

"I feel": "Old-Fashioned Marriage and a Quiet Family," *Oxnard (CA) Press Courier*, October 29, 1967.

John Birch Society: I am deeply indebted to D. J. Mulloy. All quotations and summaries of the John Birch Society are derived from his impressive study. In response to my query, Mary F. Hare, member services, the John Birch Society, wrote that it was the society's policy not to disclose its membership. Mike remembered his father's picture appearing on the cover of the John Birch Society magazine: "That rubbed people pretty hard the wrong way."

William Penn Patrick: "Former County CRA Chief Deplores Snub to Kuchel," *Ventura County (CA) Advisor*, April 6, 1967, NA.

"get rid of": "Brown Tries to Catch Reagan by 'Harry Truman' Comeback," *Long Beach (CA) Press Telegram*, October 17, 1966, NA.

anticipation of the next day: "Walter Brennan Loves His Work," *Oxnard (CA) Press Courier*, November 18, 1965, NA.

"You'd better stay": "Walter Brennan: Straight Talk on Acting," *San Mateo (CA) Times*, September 9, 1967, NA.

The Guns of Will Sonnett: Contract is in NCWHM.

"We did a saloon scene": Glenn Hawkins, "Brennan: 'Good Story,' and No Laugh Track, No Sex," *Los Angeles Herald-Examiner*, August 27, 1967, USC.

"And the hat": Walter Brennan, "Walter Brennan Feels Cowboy Unsung Hero of the Movies," *Mansfield (OH) News Journal*, August 3, 1968, 12.

"It's very lightweight": See.

"my horse moved": Tom McIntyre, "Stalking Big Game on a Hollywood Set," *Gastonia (NC) Gazette*, September 3, 1967, NCWHM.

"I'll get on": Bob Pool, "Grampa McCoy'll Be on Hand for CVD Parade," *Thousand Oaks (CA) News Chronicle*, May 12, 72, NCWHM.

"Forty-six years ago": "Walter Brennan Likes to Work," *Redlands (CA) Daily Facts*, April 19, 1967, NA.

"storyteller of the old West": "Television Highlights," *Ukiah (CA) Daily Journal*, October 20, 1972, NA.

"I told him": Army Archerd, *Variety*, May 18, 1967.

"bad taste": Barney Glazer, "The TV Scene," *Oxnard (CA) Press Courier*, April 21, 1968, NA.

"Walter Brennan is": "Brennan: Weak Show Saver," *Hayward (CA) Daily Review*, June 4, 1970, NA.

The Forsyth-Brennan feud: Stephens.

Fundraising dinner: Gayle Montgomery, "S. F. Reagan Dinner Brings in $350,000," *Oakland (CA) Tribune*, March 13, 1970, NA.

Finance chairman: A photograph of Brennan in Schmitz's office appears in the *Van Nuys (CA) Valley News*, October 19, 1972, NA.

"in the office": "Votes to AIP's County Opening," *Oxnard (CA) Press Courier*, September 13, 1972, NA.

"one candidate": "Actor Heads American Party Drive," *Bakersfield (CA) Californian*, August 9, 1972, NA.

"He's dynamite": "Famed Evangelist to Conduct Services," *Oxnard (CA) Press Courier*, December 1 1973, NA.

CHAPTER 10: THE LEGACY YEARS (1969–74)

"Other than that": "Brennan Quips at West Honor," *Bakersfield (CA) Californian*, April 27, 1970, NA.

"an emotional experience": Dave White, "Tribute Moves Veteran Actor," *Oxnard (CA) Press Courier*, December 17, 1970, NA.

visited Norman Rockwell: A photograph of Rockwell painting Brennan's portrait appears in the *Pasadena (CA) Star News*, November 30, 1971, NA.

"I would crawl": Donna Di Paolo, "Walter Brennan: The Old West Personified," *News Chronicle*, September 4, 1980, ACAD.

His final choice: Bob Pool, "Grampa McCoy'll Be on Hand for CVD Parade," *Thousand Oaks (CA) News Chronicle*, May 12, 1972, NCWHM.

"That expression on his face": interview with Mike Brennan.

"What's all the fuss": "Walter Brennan's Going Strong," *Greenville (TX) Herald Banner*, June 18, 1972, B4.

Twenty pounds of dress: "Grandma Curry Comes to Town . . . Oops, It's Walter Brennan," *TV Guide*, September 4, 1971, USC.

"got along well with Astaire": Interview with Mike Brennan.

"too much work": Interview with Mike Brennan.

"He was old": I am indebted to James Garner's daughter for relaying her father's message to me via Twitter. I also draw upon James Garner and Jon Winokur, *The Garner Files*, Simon and Schuster, 2011, 187–88 and Garner's comments in JH.

"a nice guy": COR.

In late November 1972: Marilyn Beck, "Hollywood Hotline," *Pasadena (CA) Star News*, November 29, 1972, NA.

"I get up in the morning": AB.

Heavy smoking habit: Jim Morse, "Grateful Grandpa," *Milwaukee Journal*, January 17, 1960, NCWHM.

Walter Brennan was hospitalized: "Brennan released," *Pasadena (CA) Star News*, March 25, 1974.

"It's okay": AB.

"slightly improved": "Walter Brennan 'Improved,'" *Fremont (CA) Argus*, August 7, 1974; "Walter Brennan Still in Hospital," *Fremont (CA) Argus*, August 5, 1974, NA.

On August 10: "Brennan Leaves Intensive Care," *Oxnard (CA) Press Courier*, August 10, 1974, NA.

"steady progress": "Walter Brennan Held Making Steady Progress," *Van Nuys (CA) Valley News*, August 20, 1974, NA.

He was able to read: "Walter Brennan Still Recuperating," *Fremont (CA) Argus*, August 23, 1974.

Walter Brennan was watching: "Colleagues Praise Walter Brennan," *Hartford (MA) Courant*, September 23, 1974, USC.

BIBLIOGRAPHY

Behlmer, Rudy. "To the Wilderness for *Northwest Passage*," *American Cinematographer*, November 1987.

Breivold, Scott, ed. *Howard Hawks: Interviews*. University Press of Mississippi, 2006.

Brennan, Walter (Andy). "My Father . . . The Real McCoy," *Persimmon Hill Magazine*, Fall 1981, 44–55.

Butler, David. *David Butler* (interview). Scarecrow Press, 1993.

Curtis, James. *Spencer Tracy: A Biography*. Knopf, 2011.

Davis, Ronald L. *The Glamour Factory: Inside Hollywood's Big Studio System*. Southern Methodist University Press, 1993.

Dewey, Donald. *James Stewart: A Biography*. Turner Publishing, 1997.

Dixon, Wheeler Winston. *American Cinema of the 1940s: Themes and Variations*. Rutgers University Press, 2005.

Druxman, Michael B. *My Forty-Five Years in Hollywood And How I Escaped Alive*. BearManor Media, 2010.

Easton, Carol. *The Search for Sam Goldwyn*. University Press of Mississippi, 2014.

Eyman, Scott. *John Wayne: The Life and Legend*. Simon and Schuster, 2014.

———. *Print the Legend: The Life and Times of John Ford*. Simon and Schuster, 1999.

Fitzgerald, Gerald J. "Chemical Warfare and Medical Response During World War I." *American Journal of Public Health*, April 98 (4): 811–25. http://www.ncbi.nlm.nih.gov/pmc/articles/PMC2376985/#!po=21.2500.

Fujiwara, Chris. *The World and Its Double: The Life and Work of Otto Preminger*. Faber and Faber, 2008.

Garner, James. *The Garner Files*. Simon and Schuster, 2011.

Graham, Alison. *Framing the South: Hollywood, Television, and Race During the Civil Rights Struggle*. Johns Hopkins University Press, 2001.

Granger, Farley. *Include Me Out: My Life from Goldwyn to Broadway*. St. Martin's Press, 2007.

Grant, Barry Keith, ed., *Fritz Lang Interviews*. University Press of Mississippi, 2003.

Heffernan, Harold. "Physical Misfortunes Have Helped Filmites," *Hartford (MA) Courant*, May 25, 1941. USC clipping file.

Joseph, Robert. "Up From the Bottom," *Motion Picture*, August 1937, 94.

Keavy, Howard, "Hollywood Screen Life," *Poughkeepsie (NY) Daily Eagle*, October 21, 1935.

Kirk, Lynn. "Ruth Brennan Remembers a Long, Happy Love Story," *Camarillo (CA) Sunday Daily News*, November 26, 1989.

Kobal, John, ed. *People Will Talk*. Knopf, 1996.

Lambert, Gavin. *Natalie Wood: A Life*. Knopf, 2004.

Lovell, Glenn. *Escape Artist: The Life and Films of John Sturges*. University of Wisconsin Press, 2008.

McBride, Joseph, ed. *Focus on Howard Hawks*. Prentice Hall, 1972.

———, ed. *Hawks on Hawks*. University of California Press, 1982.

McClelland, Doug, ed. *Forties Film Talk: Oral Histories of Hollywood*. McFarland, 1992.

Marill, Alvin. *Samuel Goldwyn Presents*. Gazell Books Services, 1977.

Mast, Gerald. *Howard Hawks, Storyteller*. Oxford University Press, 1982.

Meyers, Jeffrey. *Gary Cooper: An American Hero*. William Morrow, 1998.

Monroe, Sylvester, Peter Goldman, and Vern Smith. *Brothers: Black and Poor*. William Morrow, 1988.

Mulloy, D. J. *The World of the John Birch Society: Conspiracy, Conservatism, and the Cold War*. Vanderbilt University Press, 2014.

Nollen, Scott Allen. *Three Bad Men: John Wayne, John Ford, Ward Bond*. McFarland, 2013.

Pacheco, Manny. *Forgotten Hollywood Forgotten History*. Book Publishers Network, 2009.

Parish, James Robert. *Hollywood Character Actors*. Arlington House, 1978.

Quirk, Lawrence. *James Stewart: Behind the Scenes of a Wonderful Life*. Applause Books, 2000.

Reynolds, Debbie. *Unsinkable: A Memoir*. William Morrow, 2013.

Roberts, Eleanor. "Work Is My Hobby: How Walter Brennan Stays Young," *Boston Herald Traveler*, August 12, 1968.

Rollyson, Carl. *Hollywood Enigma: Dana Andrews*. University Press of Mississippi, 2012.

Ross, Lillian. *The Player: A Profile of an Art*. Limelight Editions, 1984.

Schatz, Thomas. *The Genius of the System: Hollywood Filmmaking in the Studio Era*. Henry Holt, 1988.

Scott, Vernon. "Real-Life Walter Brennan Is No 'Grandpa McCoy,'" UPI, March 3, 1963.

See, Carolyn. "An Old Actor Stands Fast in a Changing World," *TV Guide*, March 30, 1968.

Server, Lee. *Robert Mitchum: "Baby I Don't Care."* St. Martin's Press, 2001.

Shaffer, Rosalind. "Minor Actor Steals Show in New Film," *Chicago Daily Tribune*, October 27, 1935, E16.

Shlaes, Amity. *Coolidge*. HarperCollins, 2013.

Slide, Anthony. *Hollywood Unknowns: A History of Extras, Bit Players, and Stand-Ins*. University Press of Mississippi, 2012.

Soanes, Ward, "Star Light Star Bright," *Oakland (CA) Tribune*, January 24, 1937, newspaperarchive.com.

Stephens, John G. *From My Three Sons to Major Dad: My Life as a Hollywood Producer*. Scarecrow Press, 2005.

Swindell, Larry. *Gary Cooper: The Last Hero*. Doubleday, 1980.

Thomson, David. *The New Biographical Dictionary of Film*. Knopf, 2014.

Twomey, Alfred. *The Versatiles: A Study of Supporting Character Actors and Actresses in the American Motion Picture, 1930–1955*. A. S. Barnes, 1969.

Wakeman, John, ed. *World Film Directors, Volume One, 1890–1945*. H. W. Wilson, 1987.

Whitney, Dwight. "A Man in His Right Mind," *TV Guide*, March 7–13, 1959.

Wilson, Victoria. *A Life of Barbara Stanwyck: Steel True*. Simon and Schuster, 2013.

Wojcik, Pamela Robertson, ed. *Movie Acting: The Film Reader*. Routledge, 2004.

Zolotow, Maurice. *Shooting Star: A Biography of John Wayne*. Simon and Schuster, 1974.

FILMOGRAPHY AND
TELEVISION APPEARANCES

1. *Webs of Steel* (1925) Extra (uncredited)
2. *Lorraine of the Lions* (1925) Extra (uncredited)
3. *Watch Your Wife* (1926) (uncredited)
4. *The Ice Flood* (1926) Lumberjack (uncredited)
5. *Spangles* (1926) Lunch counterman (uncredited)
6. *The Collegians* (1926) Various roles (uncredited)*
7. *Flashing Oars* (1927) Hula Hula Hut customer (uncredited)*
8. *Sensation Seekers* (1927) Below deck yacht crewman (uncredited)
9. *Tearin' into Trouble* (1927) Billy Martin*
10. *Alias the Deacon* (1927) Cashier at Cunningham's Rink (uncredited)
11. *Blake of Scotland Yard* (1927) Henchman (uncredited)*
12. *The Last Performance* (1927) Clown (uncredited)
13. *The Ridin' Rowdy* (1927) (uncredited)
14. *The Michigan Kid* (1928) (uncredited)
15. *Hot Heels* (1928) Pool hall habitant (uncredited)
16. *The Racket* (1928) Man on street in front of barbershop (uncredited)
17. *The Ballyhoo Buster* (1928) (uncredited)
18. *Silks and Saddles* (1929) (uncredited)
19. *The Cohens and Kellys in Atlantic City* (1929) Man at police station (uncredited)
20. *Flight* (1929) Marine pilot
21. *Flying High* (1929) Kidnapper (uncredited)
22. *One Hysterical Night* (1929) Paul Revere
23. *The Lariat Kid* (1929) Pat O'Shea
24. *The Shannons of Broadway* (1929) Hez
25. *The Long, Long Trail* (1929) "Skinny" Rawlins
26. *Smilin' Guns* (1929) Ranch foreman
27. *King of Jazz* (1930) Desk sergeant, soldier, quartet member
28. *Dames Ahoy* (1930) Side show barker (uncredited)
29. *Captain of the Guard* (1930) Peasant (uncredited)
30. *The Little Accident* (1930) Milkman
31. *See American Thirst* (1930) Spumoni bodyguard (uncredited)
32. *Parlez Vous* (1930) (uncredited)
33. *Ooh La-La* (1930) Bit part (uncredited)*
34. *Hello Russia* (1931) Bit part (uncredited)*

35. *Many a Slip* (1931) (uncredited) *
36. *Heroes of the Flames* (1931) Bit part (uncredited)
37. *Honeymoon Lane* (1931) Driver (uncredited)
38. *Grief Street* (1931) Walt (as Arthur Brennan)
39. *Dancing Dynamite* (1931) Henchman*
40. *A House Divided* (1931) Musician (uncredited)
41. *Scratch-as-Catch-Can* (1931) (uncredited)*
42. *Neck and Neck* (1931) Hector*
43. *Is There Justice?* (1931) Rollins*
44. *The Impatient Maiden* (1932) Cigar stand proprietor
45. *Fighting for Justice* (1932) Cowhand Fletcher (uncredited)
46. *Speed Madness* (1932) Joe
47. *Two-Fisted Law* (1932) Deputy Sheriff Bendix
48. *Law and Order* (1932) Lanky Smith
49. *Texas Cyclone* (1932) Sheriff Lew Collins (uncredited)
50. *The All-American* (1932) Bit part (uncredited)
51. *Scandal for Sale* (1932) Newspaperman (uncredited)
52. *The Air Mail Mystery* (1932) Holly
53. *Miss Pinkerton* (1932) Police dispatcher (uncredited)
54. *The Iceman's Ball* (1932) Officer Dugan
55. *Cornered* (1932) Court bailiff (uncredited)
56. *The Fourth Horseman* (1932) Toothless town drunk (uncredited)
57. *Once in a Lifetime* (1932) Lighting technician (uncredited)
58. *Strange Justice* (1932) Eddie, mechanic (uncredited)
59. *Women Won't Tell* (1932) Dump workman (uncredited)
60. *Manhattan Tower* (1932) Mechanic (uncredited)
61. *Merry-Go-Round* (1932) Protester sign carrier (uncredited)
62. *Hello Trouble* (1932) A Texas Ranger (uncredited)
63. *Sing Sinner Sing* (1933) Henchman Riordan
64. *Parachute Jumper* (1933) Counterman at Jewel Diner (uncredited)
65. *Sensation Hunters* (1933) Stuttering waiter
66. *Man of Action* (1933) Cashier Summers
67. *Girl Missing* (1933) Joe, garage attendant (uncredited)
68. *Goldie Gets Along* (1933) Stuttering waiter (uncredited)
69. *The Cohens and Kellys in Trouble* (1933) Bit part (uncredited)
70. *Rustler's Roundup* (1933) Walt (uncredited)
71. *Golden Harvest* (1933) Farmhand at wedding (uncredited)
72. *Silent Men* (1933) as "Coyote" Cotter
73. *Saturday's Millions* (1933) Reporter (uncredited)
74. *Sailors Beware* (1933) Stuttering thief
75. *Lily Turner* (1933, scenes deleted)
76. *The Big Cage* (1933) Ticket taker (uncredited)
77. *Baby Face* (1933, scenes deleted)
78. *Curtain at Eight* (1933) Silent detective (uncredited)
79. *My Woman* (1933) Stuttering animal imitator (uncredited)
80. *King for a Night* (1933) Soda jerk (uncredited)
81. *The Invisible Man* (1933) Bicycle owner (uncredited)

82. *Strange People* (1933) Radio repairman
83. *The Phantom of the Air* (1933) Skid
84. *One Year Later* (1933) Yokel (uncredited)
85. *My Woman* (1933) Animal imitator
86. *Death on the Diamond* (1934) Hot dog vendor (uncredited)
87. *Good Dame* (1934) Elmer Spicer
88. *Cross Country Cruise* (1934) Niagara Falls Boatman (uncredited)
89. *Beloved* (1934) Stuttering boarder
90. *I'll Tell the World* (1934) Otto, bicycle repairman (uncredited)
91. *You Can't Buy Everything* (1934) Train vendor
92. *Paradise Valley* (1934) Farmer Hiram
93. *Riptide* (1934) Chauffeur
94. *Fugitive Lovers* (1934) Bus company employee
95. *Radio Dough* (1934) (uncredited)
96. *Half a Sinner* (1934) Radio announcer
97. *The Poor Rich* (1934) Dr. Johnson, the coroner (uncredited)
98. *Whom the Gods Destroy* (1934) Clifford (uncredited)
99. *The Crosby Case* (1934) Ship's Officer (uncredited)
100. *George White's Scandals* (1934) Hick (uncredited)
101. *Uncertain Lady* (1934) Gas station attendant (uncredited)
102. *The Life of Vergie Winters* (1934) Roscoe, a gossip (uncredited)
103. *Sing It and Like It* (1934) Ticket broker (uncredited)
104. *Cheating Cheaters* (1934) Ship's steward (uncredited)
105. *Fishing for Trouble* (1934) *
106. *A Wicked Woman* (1934) Slot machine man
107. *Woman Haters* (1934) Train conductor (uncredited)
108. *Great Expectations* (1934) Prisoner on ship (uncredited)
109. *There's Always Tomorrow* (1934) Mechanic (uncredited)
110. *Tailspin Tommy* (1934) Hospital orderly slugged by Skeeter(uncredited)
111. *Gridiron Flash* (1934) Diner proprietor (uncredited)
112. *The Prescott Kid* (1934) Zeke, stage driver
113. *Murder in the Private Car* (1934) Switchman (uncredited)
114. *The Painted Veil* (1934, scenes deleted)
115. *Barbary Coast* (1935) Old Atrocity
116. *Biography of a Bachelor Girl* (1935) Reporter on ship (uncredited)
117. *Lady Tubbs* (1935) Joseph (uncredited)
118. *Helldorado* (1935) Pete, waiter (uncredited)
119. *Northern Frontier* (1935) Stuttering cook
120. *Brick-a-Brac* (1935) Lem*
121. *Party Wire* (1935) Paul, railroad telegrapher (uncredited)
122. *Spring Tonic* (1935) Bum (uncredited)
123. *Gold Diggers of 1935* (1935) Bellboy/Porter (uncredited)
124. *West Point of the Air* (1935) Soldier at Kelly's Wreckage (uncredited)
125. *We're in the Money* (1935) Wedding witness (uncredited)
126. *Law beyond the Range* (1935) Abner
127. *The Perfect Tribute* (1935) Stonecutter (uncredited)
128. *Seven Keys to Baldpate* (1935) Station agent

129. *Hunger Pains* (1935) Secretary to Sylvester J. Sutton Sr.
130. *The Man on the Flying Trapeze* (1935) "Legs" Garnett
131. *The Wedding Night* (1935) Bill Jenkins
132. *Restless Knights* (1935) Father (uncredited)
133. *The Mystery of Edwin Drood* (1935) First gossip (uncredited)
134. *The Bride of Frankenstein* (1935) Neighbor (uncredited)
135. *Public Hero No. 1* (1935) Farmer
136. *Welcome Home* (1935) Walter (uncredited)
137. *Alice Adams* (1935, scenes deleted)
138. *Metropolitan* (1935) Grandpa
139. *These Three* (1936) Taxi driver
140. *Three Godfathers* (1936) Sam Bartow, also known as Gus
141. *Come and Get It* (1936) Swan Bostrom
142. *The Moon's Our Home* (1936) Lem
143. *Banjo on My Knee* (1936) Newt Holley
144. *Fury* (1936) as "Bugs" Meyers
145. *Paradise Valley* (1936) Farmer Hiram
146. *She's Dangerous* (1937) Ote O'Leary
147. *Wild and Woolly* (1937) Gramp "Hercules" Flynn
148. *Affairs of Cappy Ricks* (1937) Cappy Ricks
149. *When Love Is Young* (1937) Uncle Hugo
150. *Kentucky* (1938) Peter Goodwin
151. *The Buccaneer* (1938) Ezra Peavey
152. *The Texans* (1938) Chuckawalla
153. *Mother Carey's Chickens* (1938) Mr. Ossian Popham
154. *The Cowboy and the Lady* (1938) Sugar
155. *The Adventures of Tom Sawyer* (1938) Muff Potter
156. *Stanley and Livingston* (1939) Jeff Slocum
157. *The Story of Vernon and Irene Castle* (1939) Walter
158. *They Shall Have Music* (1939) Professor Lawson
159. *Joe and Ethel Turp Call on the President* (1939) Jim Martin, mailman
160. *The Westerner* (1940) Judge Roy Bean
161. *Maryland* (1940) William Stewart
162. *Northwest Passage (Book I: Rogers' Rangers)* (1940) "Hunk" Marriner
163. *Sergeant York* (1941) Pastor Rossier Pile
164. *Swamp Water* (1941) Tom Keefer
165. *This Woman Is Mine* (1941) Captain Jonathan Thorn
166. *Nice Girl?* (1941) Hector Titus
167. *Meet John Doe* (1941) The "Colonel"
168. *Rise and Shine* (1941) Grandpa
169. *Stand by for Action* (1943) Chief Yeoman Henry Johnson
170. *The Pride of the Yankees* (1943) Sam Blake
171. *The North Star* (1943) Karp
172. *The Last Will and Testament of Tom Smith* (1943) George, mailman
173. *Slightly Dangerous* (1943) Cornelius Burden
174. *Hangmen Also Die!* (1943) Professor Stephen Novotny
175. *The Princess and the Pirate* (1944) Featherhead

176. *To Have and Have Not* (1944) Eddie
177. *Home in Indiana* (1944) J. T. "Thunder" Bolt
178. *Dakota* (1945) Captain Bounce
179. *My Darling Clementine* (1946) Old Man Clanton
180. *A Stolen Life* (1946) Eben Folger
181. *Nobody Lives Forever* (1946) Pop Gruber
182. *Centennial Summer* (1946) Jesse Rogers
183. *Driftwood* (1947) Murph
184. *Scudda Hoo! Scudda Hay!* (1948) Tony Maule
185. *Red River* (1948) Groot Nadine
186. *Blood on the Moon* (1948) Kris Barden
187. *Task Force* (1949) Pete Richard
188. *Brimstone* (1949) Brimstone "Pop" Courteen
189. *The Green Promise* (1949) Mr. Matthews
190. *A Ticket to Tomahawk* (1950) Terence Sweeny
191. *Curtain Call at Cactus Creek* (1950) Rimrock Thomas
192. *Surrender* (1950) William Howard
193. *Singing Guns* (1950) Dr. Jonathan Mark
194. *The Showdown* (1950) Capt. MacKellar
195. *Along the Great Divide* (1951) "Pop" Keith
196. *The Wild Blue Yonder* (1951) Maj. Gen. Wolfe
197. *Best of the Badmen* (1951) "Doc" Butcher
198. *Return of the Texan* (1952) Grandpa Firth Crockett
199. *Lure of the Wilderness* (1952) Jim Harper
200. *The Far Country* (1954) Ben Tatum
201. *Drums Across the River* (1954) Sam Brannon
202. *Sea of Lost Ships* (1954) "Chief" O'Malley
203. *Four Guns to the Border* (1954) Simon Bhumer
204. *Man on a Bus* (1955)
205. *At Gunpoint* (1955) Doc Lacy
206. *Screen Directors Playhouse* (TV series, 1 episode, 1955) Grandpa Atkins
207. *Lux Video Theatre* (TV series, 1 episode, 1955) Intermission guest
208. *Bad Day at Black Rock* (1955) Doc Velle
209. *Glory* (1956) Ned Otis
210. *Good-Bye, My Lady* (1956) Uncle Jesse Jackson
211. *Come Next Spring* (1956) Jeff Storys
212. *The Proud Ones* (1956) Jake
213. *Schlitz Playhouse* (TV series, Ezra Jenkins/Mr. Ears, 3 episodes, 1956)
214. *Ethel Barrymore Theater* (TV series, 1 episode, 1956)
215. *Cavalcade of America* (TV series, Link Morley 1956, 1 episode)
216. *The Ford Television Theatre* (TV series, Duffy, 1 episode, 1956)
217. *The Way to the Gold* (1957) Uncle George Williams
218. *Tammy and the Bachelor* (1957) Grandpa John Dinwitty
219. *The Real McCoys* (TV series, Grandpa Amos McCoy, 223 episodes, 1957–63)
220. *Zane Grey Theater* (TV series, Joe/Sheriff John Larson, 2 episodes, 1956–57)
221. *God Is My Partner* (1957) Dr. Charles Grayson
222. *Colgate Theatre* (TV series, Mr. Tutt, one episode, 1958)

223. *Rio Bravo* (1959) Stumpy

224. *How the West Was Won* (1962) Colonel Hawkins

225. *Shoot Out at Big Sag* (1962) Preacher Hawker

226. *The Tycoon* (TV series, Walter Andrews, 32 episodes, 1964–65)

227. *Those Calloways* (1965) Alf Simes

228. *The Shooting of Dan McCrew* (1965) Narrator

229. *The Oscar* (1966) Orrin C. Quentin

230. *The Guns of Will Sonnett* (TV series, Will Sonnett, 50 episodes, 1967–69)

231. *Who's Minding the Mint?* (1967) Pop Gillis

232. *The Gnome-Mobile* (1967) D. J. Mulrooney/Knobby

233. *The One and Only, Genuine, Original Family Band* (1968) Grandpa Bower

234. *The Red Skelton Hour* (TV series, Deputy "Doc" Hawkeye/Sheriff Walter/Walter Briarcliff, Sr., 3 episodes,1969–70)

235. *The Over the Hill Gang* (1969) Nash Crawford

236. *Support Your Local Sheriff!* (1969) Pa Danby

237. *The Tim Conway Comedy Hour* (TV series, 1 episode, 1970)

238. *To Rome with Love* (TV series, Andy Pruitt, 17 episodes,1970–71)

239. *The Young Country* (1970) Sheriff Matt Fenley

240. *The Over the Hill Gang Rides Again* (1970) Nash Crawford

241. *Alias Smith and Jones* (TV series, Silky O'Sullivan/Gantry, 3 episodes, 1971–72)

242. *Two for the Money* (1972) Cody Guilford

243. *Home for the Holidays* (1972) Benjamin Morgan

244. *Smoke in the Wind* (1975) H. P. Kingman

*Films that are presumably lost and have no reviews on IMDb. In some cases, IMDb does give a brief description of the film.

RADIO PERFORMANCES

Note: only some of these appearances seem to be available online, while others are available from distributors of old radio programs.

Come and Get It. *Lux Radio Theatre*. November 15, 1937. Edward Arnold and Walter Brennan reprise their film roles. The zany side of the young Swan is missing from this script.

The Westerner. *Lux Radio Theatre*. September 23, 1940. Gary Cooper and Walter Brennan reprise their film roles. Cooper gets more laughs than Brennan.

Destry Rides Again. *Gulf Screen Guild*. February 2, 1941. Brennan plays Wash Dimsdale, the town drunk, in this heavily abbreviated adaptation of the movie. Wash drinks and dreams of dead Tom Destry, his hero, while the corrupt mayor appoints Wash sheriff, and then Wash sends for Destry's son (Henry Fonda) to clean up the town—which he does, although poor Wash is killed in the outcome.

We Hold These Truths. December 15, 1941. Brennan was part of an outstanding cast, including Orson Welles, Jimmy Stewart, Walter Huston, Edward Arnold, Edward G Robinson, and President Roosevelt. Broadcast just a week after the attack on Pearl Harbor, the Norman Corwin script was a performance of the Bill of Rights and the history behind its inception and implementation. In Welles's words, the program is the "story of liberty." In a conversation with Walter Huston (playing a blacksmith), Brennan is heard reading the Third and Fourth Amendments and discussing their significance with Huston. Brennan is later heard as an Okie touting his right to go anywhere in the country to look for work.

The Charlie McCarthy Show. June 29, 1942. Brennan appears as himself in a gag in which he is asked to repeat his performances in *Meet John Doe* and *Sergeant York*, but in each scene he merely says he walked up to Doe and York and said, "Pleased to meet you." Walter says that in *Swamp Water*, he said, "Come in, the water's fine." Brennan also plays a grandfather in a horse doctor skit in which his granddaughter is visited by the "lecherous, treacherous" Squire [Edgar] Bergan. Brennan advises her, "Now remember, Dear, when he proposes on the horsehair sofa, don't say nay."

Happy Land. Lux Radio Theatre. April 10, 1944. Adaptation of the screen version of a novel by MacKinlay Kantor. A World War II drama set in Hartfield, Iowa. Grandpa Marsh, dead twenty years, appears to his grandson, Lou, to console him over the loss of his son, Rusty, in the war. Grandpa recalls the parade that ended World War I, and takes Lou through a sequence of scenes that shows the lives of families in peacetime and the values worth preserving through fighting the war.

Home in Indiana. Lux Radio Theatre. October 2, 1944. Brennan reprises his film performance in a script that somewhat dilutes his character's harder edges.

Kentucky. Lux Radio Theatre. May 28, 1945. One of the better, more stirring adaptations of a film. Brennan expertly delivers his lines for laughs, and afterwards jokes with the audience about his inability to pick winning horses. As the horse he picked passed the stands, Brennan yells, "Hey, they went that way!"

"The Law West of the Pecos." *Cavalcade of America.* June 11, 1945. Another radio adaptation of *The Westerner.*

"Ten in Texas." December 31, 1945. Brennan as Old Len Struthers, telling his tales of the Old West.

"Amazing Mrs. Holliday." *Lux Radio Theatre.* March 4, 1946. With Gene Tierney and Edmond O'Brien. Adaptation of the screen version. Gene Tierney plays Mrs. Holliday, assisted by a stalwart Irishman, Timothy Blake (Brennan), in rescuing a dozen children, refugees from China, who have survived the sinking of their ship during the war.

"Her First Beau." *Screen Guild Theater.* April 15, 1946. In this slight drama, Chuck (Lon McCallister) is hiding a glider with the help of hanger owner Elmer Tuttle (Brennan). Penny (Elizabeth Taylor), yearning for her first beau, eventually wins Chuck's love, while his solo flight impresses his father, who had vowed to destroy the plane.

"No Night Too Dark." *Family Theater.* February 20, 1947. Brennan is Jonathan Carter, who convinces Will Calder that life is still worth living, even though he has been blinded in the war. With Jonathan's urging, Will begins to experience the world with all his other senses, and he reunites with Peg, the girl to whom he was engaged before the war.

Red River. Lux Radio Theatre. March 7, 1949. John Wayne and Walter Brennan reprise their film roles.

"A Star for Helen." *Family Theater.* January 24, 1951. Mr. Brannigan (Brennan), a man of devout faith, provides comfort and counsel to a young girl, Helen Jackson, coping with her mother's alcoholism.

"The Luck of Roaring Camp." *Family Theater.* May 16, 1951. Adaptation of a Bret Harte story.

"The Land of Sunshine." *Family Theater*. March 5, 1952.

"Mail Order Missus." Family Theater. October 8, 1952.

"The Easy Chair." July 12, 1953. Brennan appears as a guest star.

"The Legend of High Chin Bob." *Family Theater*. December 9, 1953. Brennan plays a cowhand, Old Maverick, who tells the story of High Chin Bob and his quest to catch a mountain lion, the "killer cat." As he tells the story to a young boy, Old Maverick conveys the value of persistence and overcoming obstacles.

"Tennessee's Partner." *Family Theater*. September 22, 1954. Adaptation of a Bret Harte story.

"Torkelson's Flying Circus." *Family Theater*. March 2, 1955. Brennan portrays a World War I pilot down on his luck, a self-described bum who makes the most of an unforeseen opportunity to turn himself into a successful businessman. What is striking about the program is Walter's even-tempered voice, the virtuous expression of a soul who has weathered all manner of vicissitudes.

"Cow Town." *Family Theater*. July 25, 1956.

"West of the Pecos." *Family Theater*. January 9, 1957.

Interview with Hedda Hopper. May 17, 1960. The transcript is in the Margaret Herrick Library at the Academy of Motion Picture Arts and Sciences.

DISCOGRAPHY

The Stories of Mark Twain. Caedmon Records, 1956.
"The Celebrated Jumping Frog of Calaveras County"
"Blue Jay Yarn" (From *Tramps Abroad*)
From *Huckleberry Finn* (read by Brandon De Wilde)

A World of Miracles. Everest, 1960.
"A World of Miracles"
"Noah's Ark"
"The Ten Commandments"
"A Star in The East"
"Thirty-Three Years"
"The Resurrection"
"The Ascension"
"The Miracle of Love"

The President: A Musical Biography of Our Chief Executives. Everest, 1960.
"The President"
"Bunker Hill to Yorktown"
"The Father of Our Country"
"All Men"
"The People's Choice"
"The War Of 1812"
"New Frontiers"
"Andy Jackson"
"Tippecanoe and Tyler Too"
"Remember the Alamo"
"Honest Abe"
"Brother against Brother"
"The Saga of the Presidents"
"U. S. Grant"
"The Rough Riders"
"Through the Storm"
"It's Only Or-ee-vwor"
"Back to Normal"
"All Men"

"We Have Nothing to Fear"
"Go Get 'Em, Harry"
"A Free People"
"Dwight D. Eisenhower"
"The President"

Walter Brennan: By the Fireside. Record Producers Corporation, 1960.
"Sweet Little Lark"
"Deep Water"
"Twilight Rhapsody"
"The Searchers"
"The Old Church Square"
"Cottonwood Tree"
"Amor Vera"
"The Soul o' Big Jack Dunn"
"Knight in Bright Armor"
"Little Son"
"The Lilies Grow High"
"Peace Within"

Old Rivers. Liberty, 1962.
"Old Rivers"
"The Old Kelly Place"
"Conversations with a Mule"
"The Farmer and the Lord"
"Happy Birthday, Old Folk"
"It Takes a Heap of Living"
"Boll Weevil"
"Steal Away"
"Pickin' Time"
"Old Rivers' Trunk"

Mama Sang a Song. Liberty, 1962
"Mama Sang a Song"
"The Ole Blacksmith Shop"
"Family Reunion"
"Red Checkered Tablecloth"
"Two Rockin' Chairs"
"The Green, Green Valley"
"Houdini"
"Angels in the Sky"
"Who Will Take Gramma?"
"Last Will and Testament of Sam Burke"
"Touch of the Master's Hand"

'Twas the Night Before Christmas . . . Back Home. Liberty, 1962
"White Christmas"
"Just Three Letters for Christmas"

"A Farmer's Christmas Prayer"
"Henry Had a Merry Christmas"
"Old Time Christmas Prayer"
"(There's No Place Like) Home for the Holidays"
"Silent Night"
"Christmas Together"
"Let the Bells Ring Out"
"A Good Year for Santa Claus"
"O Come All Ye Faithful"

Talkin' from the Heart. Liberty, 1963.
"Detroit City"
"Scarlet Ribbons (for Her Hair)"
"Abilene"
"Waiting for a Train"
"Old Courthouse"
"Keep a Movin', Old Man"
"Moon Wanderer"
"Tennessee Stud"
"Cotton-Eyed Joe"
"Don't Go Near the Indians"
"The Sound of Silence"

Gunfight at the O. K. Corral. Liberty, 1963.
"Riders in the Sky"
"Conversation with a Gun"
"Nineteen Men"
"Sod Buster"
"Streets of Laredo"
"Run Apache"
"Cool Water"
"Rope on a Tree"
"Droop Ears"
"Gunfight at the O. K. Corral"
"High Noon (Do Not Forsake Me)"

Dutchman's Gold. Hamilton, 1965.
"Dutchman's Gold"
"Life Gets Tee-Jus, Don't It?"
"The Shifting Whispering Sands, Part 1"
"The Shifting Whispering Sands, Part 2"
"Six Feet Away"
"I Believe"
"Back to the Farm"
"Tribute to a Dog"
"Old Shep"
"Suppertime"

The Country Heart of Walter Brennan. Sunset Records, 1966.
"Keep a Movin', Old Man"
"Cotton-Eyed Joe"
"Old Courthouse"
"Detroit City"
"Waiting for a Train"
"Moon Wanderer"
"Don't Go Near the Indians"
"Scarlet Ribbons"
"The Sound of Silence"
"Tennessee Stud"

INDEX